Texts of Desire:
Essays on Fiction, Femininity and Schooling

K

To l

Series Editor: Allan Luke
James Cook University of North Queensland
Australia

Literacy remains a contentious and polarized educational, media and political issue. What has emerged from the continuing debate is a recognition by many critical researchers and theorists that literacy in education is allied closely with matters of language and culture, ideology and discourse, knowledge and power.

This new series of monographs and anthologies draws together critical, cross-disciplinary work on language and literacy in a format accessible to researchers and students of education. Its aim is to provide competing discourses and alternative practices to the extant technical literature which offers 'state of the art' insights and 'how to' formulae for the achievement of literacy narrowly conceived as individual, psychological skills. Drawing perspectives variously from critical social theory and cultural studies, post-structuralism and feminisms, sociolinguistics and the ethnography of communication, social history and comparative education, the contributors to this series began a critical interrogation of taken-for-granted assumptions which have guided educational policy, research and practice.

Social Linguistics and Literacies:
Ideology in Discourses
James Paul Gee, *University of Southern California, USA*

With Literacy and Justice for All:
Rethinking the Social in Language and Education
Carole Edelsky. *Arizona State University, USA*

A Critical Theory of Public Life:
Knowledge, Discourse and Politics in an Age of Decline
Ben Agger, *State University of New York, Buffalo, USA*

Knowledge, Culture and Power:
International Perspectives on Literacy as Policy and Practice
Edited by Anthony R. Welch and Peter Freebody, *The University of New England, Australia*

Word Perfect:
Prospects for Literacy in the Computer Age
Myron Tuman, *The University of Alabama, USA*

The Insistence of the Letter:
Literacy Studies and Curriculum Theorizing
Edited by Bill Green, *Deakin University, Australia*

Forthcoming Titles

Discourse, Gender and School Literacy:
Studies in the Social Organization of Classroom Knowledge
Carolyn Baker, *The University of New England, Australia*

Writing Science: Literacy and Discursive Power
MAK Halliday and JR Martin, *University of Sydney, Australia*

Children Talking Television
David Buckingham, *University of London, UK*

Texts of Desire:
Essays on Fiction, Femininity and Schooling

Edited by

Linda K. Christian-Smith

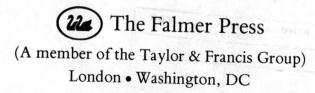

The Falmer Press

(A member of the Taylor & Francis Group)
London • Washington, DC

UK The Falmer Press, 4 John Street, London WC1N 2ET

USA The Falmer Press, Taylor & Francis Inc., 1900 Frost Road, Suite 101, Bristol, PA 19007

First published 1993

A catalogue record for this book is available from the British Library

ISBN 0 75070 003 3
ISBN 0 75070 004 1 (pbk)

Library of Congress Cataloging-in-Publication Data are available on request

Typeset in 9.5/11 Bembo by
Graphicraft Typesetters Ltd, Hong Kong

Printed in Great Britain by Burgess Science Press, Basingstoke on paper which has a specified pH value on final paper manufacture of not less than 7.5 and is therefore 'acid free'.

Contents

Contents

Series Editor's Introduction

There has been an explosion of knowledge and theory about reading and writing, texts and textuality, led by work in the overlapping fields of feminisms and gender studies, cultural and literary studies, and social theory. While educational researchers have relentlessly pursued psychological and, more recently, psycholinguistic explanations of reading in an attempt to 'fix' the problems of modern pedagogy — feminist and poststructuralist work points the way to an understanding of how reading and writing are gendered social practices, positioning and constituting communities of readers. Yet the application of these approaches to the study of 'reading' in education — much less the articulation of a reading pedagogy which would put 'woman' explicitly and powerfully into the discourses of schooling — has lagged far behind.

How 'reading' is framed in educational sites can be traced in metaphors from teacher education courses and lectures, textbooks and professional literature, staffroom, clinical, and, of course, classroom talk. There we find it described variously as gender-neutral 'natural growth', 'developmental readiness' and 'cognitive process', as 'information retrieval', 'complex behaviour', and 'personal response'. As a continuing legacy of twentieth-century applied psychology and literary Romanticism, reading is conceived of alternatively as information-gathering, mental 'process' and as affective, personal 'experience'. Despite their apparent dissimilarity, these approaches have a similar force (and myopia) in classroom practice. 'Reading in schools' typically is constructed as a private and socially unsituated act, as a matter of individual difference and proclivity, one divorced from the gendered politics of identity and social relations in contemporary cultures.

Reading is an epistemic and political practice. It entails learned and sanctioned ways of knowing and ways of doing things with written language which are tied up with power, status and position in text-based economies and societies. Literate practice and competence thus are significant forms of cultural capital, taken as markers of social class, indicators of one's capacity for textual work, and signs of participation in gendered culture and identity. There is an extensive and compelling literature on the educational stratification of literate competence according to social class and ethnicity. Ethnographic and sociological studies further document the significance of literacy in the very construction and regulation of subcultural and class identity and power, whether ruling-class or marginal, mainstream or subcultural. But considerably less attention has been paid by educational researchers and teacher educators to the significance of reading pedagogy in the construction of gendered identities and interpretive communities.

Beyond its overtly instrumental uses, reading is a means for the constructing and negotiating of identity, for the playing out of desire and pleasure. In part because of the relatively recent invention and continued educational emphasis on silent reading, reading is seen by many educators (and readers) to have personal, private value. Within Romantic literary ideology — which figures so prominently in English language and literature education (Willinsky, 1990) — reading is posited as an autodidactic, solipsistic act, a means for engaging imaginary possible worlds in psychic privacy and intimacy. Because reading is not 'natural', but rather entails the learning of the mastery of culture and subculture-specific social practices with written text, one learns how and where these practices — and their affiliated pleasures and desires — can and should be played out. In this sense the teaching of literacy, reading and literature in schools is a normative, political practice, not simply the neutral transmission of 'skills', or the cultivation of 'growth' and 'development', but a practice entailing strategic decisions about who should read, what they should read, how they should read, where they should read, and to what ends and consequences.

In the last 500 years of Western history, schooling has become the constitutive institution in the selection, shaping and certification of a reading public. Central to this apparently quite successful system of regulation has been the delegation of differing reading practices, genres, canons, and, relatedly, differing kinds of knowledge, pleasure and desire as appropriate for male and female, public and private use. Prior to the advent of mass schooling for literacy, some medieval European women belonged to religious orders where reading of sacred Latin texts was allowed (Graff, 1987). There are documented, rare cases of women writing in such institutions, usually devotional texts for other nuns. In the midst of a patriarchal, elite literate culture, a women's culture of literacy developed — delimited, isolated from lay culture and populace, and gatekept by male clerics. While some groups of women had access to the archive, that access was quite literally 'cloistered' and, in terms of their influence over the very cultural institutions which ruled their lives and bodies, profoundly passive and marginal.

This is a prototype of reading as a technology of domestication; it is silent and invisible to all but the reader(s), it is done away from public scrutiny in a self-regulating community, it is ritualized and rule-bound, and its stress is on the confessional monitoring and improvement of the self, the remaking of the reader herself (cf. Foucault, 1986; Luke, in press/1992). While this class of 'initiated' (and thereby monitored and regulated) women might have been encouraged to read for purposes of moral confession and spiritual edification, those powerful 'public' literacies remained exclusively male domains: copying, storage and exegetic recitation of sacred texts of antiquity by monastic orders; the scribing and public reading of court decrees, laws and demographic records by civil servants; the recording and storing of crop and trade records by merchants.

Yet even the lay literacy among emergent middle and mercantile classes tended to concentrate power in the hands of male intellectuals, merchants and workers. The public vocations of professing and interpreting, scribing and dictating, recording and invoicing were, from their very inception in Greek culture through their deployment in the early modern West, male domains. The technology of writing developed within the formidable institutional triad of government, religion and trade. Literacy enabled the gradual transitions from religions of the Word to religions of the Book (Goody, 1987), from governments whose authority was reliant on oral histories and aristocracy to those predicated on written laws and 'social contracts' (cf. Pateman, 1988), from cultural and economic exchange based on barter systems and face-to-face exchanges of material goods, to those based on the symbolic exchange and flow of imaginary (textual) capital. For patriarchal power to be maintained in these modern societal and economic configurations the dominant 'modes of information' (Poster, 1990) — the very media and practices, registers and genres of the textual archive — had to be tied up with masculinist epistemologies and technologies, sanctioned techniques for knowing and doing.

To this day in Western and Eastern cultures, specialized textual cants disbar women from sociocultural information, power and control over their own destinies and bodies. Islamic women are excluded from Quranic literacy. In many tribal cultures, women are not taught vernacular literacies. Across developing countries, illiteracy rates among women consistently exceed those of men. In late capitalist economies, girls and young women continue to lag far behind in the command of specialized registers of science and the 'new' technologies. In these very direct ways, the use of illiteracy as a tool against women continues worldwide.

The relationship of women to literacy is not solely and simply a matter of equitable access, however. Colonization and domestication can be achieved as readily by shaping a morally regulatory literacy, as by enforcing illiteracy — an insight that has not escaped educators and governments since the Reformation. In light of these and other historical and contemporary cases, we can revisit Luce Irigaray's (1985) controversial theses about entry into language as entry into a system of masculine representation in terms of how contemporary Western schools construct children's 'entry into literacy'. If, as Irigaray and others insist, language itself is always already written gendered practice, embodying patriarchal discourse and relations (cf. Jardine, 1985) — then learning literacy for girls would seem to amount to a 'double displacement' (cf. Luke, 1991), an initiation into both linguistic codes and into gendered public and private domains of literate practice. Just as the conventional rules of face-to-face speech genres entail gendered 'work' and patriarchal power, so too do the rules of literacy events. In homes and schools, girls learn gender-specific ways of reading, talking and making sense of texts, as work by Gilbert, Taylor, Davies, and Christian-Smith demonstrates. Furthermore, as the case studies by Cherland and Edelsky and Christian-Smith here indicate, girls construct distinct kinds of shared identities and interpretive communities bounded by the experiences, fantasies and desires of texts of popular culture.

The ritual introduction of the child into a culture of literacy, then, entails not only a partriarchal canon of laws, literature and records but, as importantly, initiation into particular gendered genres and practices. Reading pedagogy which does not explicitly address issues of language, reading and gender, thereby runs the risk of naturalizing these practices, or systematically constructing gendered literacies and then construing these as the effects of personal choice of biology. As several of the studies here suggest, by the time they have reached secondary school, many young women have internalized taught and learned reading habits, 'tastes' and practices as personal but common-sense, as 'natural' and essentially female.

The fundamental premise which runs across *Texts of Desire* is as provocative in its educational implications as it is empirically interesting; multiple institutions of popular, community and educational culture together constitute a 'grid' for that initiation of girls and boys into gendered literate practices, and with them, gendered subjectivities and social relations, gendered power and culture. As Christian-Smith suggests in her introductory chapter, the educational and ulti-mately political consequences of romance reading in particular, and of immersion in the texts of popular culture in general, remain empirically and theoretical-ly 'double-edged'. In the fields of cultural studies and social theory alike, the decade-long debate about the relative power of social structure and repre-sentation, and the possibilities for individual and group agency continues unresolved (e.g., Morley, 1991).

What case studies in this volume underline is that this new 'cloistered liter-acy' is configured similarly across English-speaking countries. Popular romance reading is a cross-cultural phenomenon, part of what appear to be patterns of gendered literacy extending globally with the reach of multinational mass culture. As a sign of what Cooper here describes as a transnational market for romance, Harlequin Romances and other examples of the genre are profitably translated and sold in many other countries. Most recently, they have been released in Russia and other Eastern European states; commodified versions of romance are a central aspect of mass consumer culture and can be connected intertextually to the sales of other commodities from cosmetics and jeans to automobiles and political parties. Variations on the genre are popular among women in other national contexts, including *fotonovelas* (quite literally, drawn or photographed soap operas in comic book frame format) in Central and South American countries, and romance comic books in Asian countries. Taken together, these 'texts of desire' provide women readers with scripts for rehearsing gender relations, marriage, sexuality and work. Significantly, their popularity in many developing countries is not confined to middle-class women, but extends across social classes and ethnic groups, in some settings acting as an inexpensive, portable surrogate for television soap operas.

There are ample historical precedents for women's 'private' reading of romance narrative. The emergence of compulsory state schooling for girls in the Reformation, the development of printing technology, and the business of bookmaking and sales all marked out the possibilities for private reading — read-ing ostensibly freed up from the authoritative translations and hermeneutics of the clergy. With expanded access to vernacular texts came the possibility for 'deinstitutionalized' reading, that is, for taking reading out of clerical control, for moving it from the church to the relative privacy of the sitting room or bedroom. The emergence of the printing press led to the mass production and marketing of secular books, including 'how to' manuals on everything from child rearing to agriculture (Luke, 1989). Home reading proliferated among women, such that French church authorities were worried by the proliferation of uncontrolled women's scripture study groups (Davis, 1987). The rise and popularity of the novel in the eighteenth century, then, was enabled by the mass educational provision of a reading public, a significant segment of which was upper and middle-class women with leisure for 'private reading'. By the nineteenth century, as Huyssen (1986, p. 62) observes, the romance novel signalled a crucial moment in modernity: 'the gendering of mass culture as feminine and inferior'. That moment, according to Huyssen, is epitomized in the *simulacrum* of Flaubert's *Madame Bovary*, a romance novel about the domestic and psychic consequences of women privately reading romance novels.

Emma Bovary's embrace of romance novels was viewed as a character defect among local parishioners and friends, her husband and, ultimately, her physician; private reading was considered a form of feminized leisure, of dalliance and fantasy, of illusion and decay. In the twentieth century, the educational status of leisure reading and of the texts of popular culture was to undergo a significant transformation. Early and mid-twentieth-century American and Canadian reading and literature curriculum named 'reading for leisure' (as against 'work-type reading') as a central curricular goal (Luke, 1988). In this way, the 'art' of private reading of popular fiction — anathema to the nineteenth-century school teacher or cleric — was incorporated into school literacy training. Reading privately, in a mental and physical 'space' of one's own, was thus reconstructed as a teachable aspect of progressive citizenship, even a legitimate focus of psychological research. The introduction of popular fiction into the classroom — whether the bookclub selections described by Cooper or the romance 'hi (interest)-low (difficulty)' reading materials for working-class girls described by Christian-Smith — is thus an historical extension of mid-century efforts to bring popular literature into the canon. While it might be condemned as the movement of *kitsch* into the curriculum by E.D. Hirsch (1988) and other 'cultural literacy' advocates, it also marks an educational colonization of the popular, a 'reinstitutionalization' of private reading, and the extension of the English, language arts and reading curriculum to include sanctions and regulations over how one is to read the popular alone, outside of schooling.

Texts of Desire illustrates how romance novels, woven into the fabric of everyday private lives and domestic work, become sites for the practice of cultural narratives of fantasy and desire. In her study of contemporary soap opera viewing, Modleski (1982) points out that a key feature of the soap opera is that 'the narrative, by placing ever more complex obstacles between desire and fulfilment, makes anticipation an end in itself' (p. 88). As a result, she argues that soap operas thematize and represent what she calls 'pleasure in the central condition of a woman's life: waiting', quite literally for the touch of Man. Romance novels typically are 'closed' texts that conclude with problems of women's identity, economic destinies resolved through male intervention and agency. Nonetheless, they share with video texts described by Modleski the effect of lodging feminine identity in narratives where identity is contingent, resolution is suspended and dependent on the mechanisms (and *deus ex machina*) of phallocentric sexuality and social relations. They are also, Christian-Smith, Cherland and Edelsky here point out, actual means for rationalizing, constructing and anticipating one's life destiny: romance, marriage, children . . . and now, as Gilbert's analysis of the 1990s' revisionist romance indicates, balanced with power dressing, independent income, and the sensitive New Man.

These studies depict girls and young women reading popular fiction in schools and in their private time and space. It is worthwhile to contrast these descriptions of literacy in girls' and womens' lives with the dominant claims about the universal cognitive, cultural and social benefits of 'literacy' and 'reading'. Consider, for instance, educational claims of the 'bias' of literacy towards the 'autonomous text', abstract, decontextualized and aligned with a scientific will to truth (cf. Brandt, 1990). This account of the consequences of literacy, developed in the work of Goody, Ong, Olson and others, defines literacy as an agent and vehicle of objectivity, analysis, logic, as the key technological implement in the 'metanarrative' of Western science. As Sandra Harding (1986, 1991) has so eloquently argued, the very stories, discourses and practices of Western science are exclusionary, hegemonic expressions of the patriarchal domination of nature. Educational and scientific taxonomies of literacy invariably affiliate 'male' genres, registers and texts with cognitive and economic power. The gendered construction and distribution of literacy in schools is Cartesian in design, extending the binary opposition which Huyssen noted is so central to modernity and patriarchy: assigning bodily, romantic, affective, private genres to women and cognate, disciplinary, intellectual texts to men.

This educational version of women's reading dovetails effectively with Romantic ideologies of personal growth and expression forwarded in much English education curriculum (Gilbert, 1989), in part accounting for many girls' relative successes at English and literature study. The ideological function of romance reading shapes it as something other than what it is. What appears to its participants as a private sanctum — autonomous and uncontaminated by the public and political — operates as a textual enculturation into gendered identity, sexuality and labor. Yet in instances girls are able to build interpretive communities where 'fans', 'viewers' and 'readers' are encouraged to generate divergent interpretation apart from regulatory institutions like churches, corporations and schools (Grossberg, 1990).

What is unresolved in contemporary feminisms, social theory, and many of the studies here is the question of the consequences of textual representation on subjectivity. The pedagogical and political problem is described by Teresa deLauretis (1987, p. 9):

> To assert that the social representation of gender affects its subjective construction and that, vice versa, the subjective representation of gender — or self-representation — affects its social construction, leaves open a possibility of agency and self-determination at the subjective and even individual level of micropolitical and everyday practices.

This dialectic of representation and identity is at the heart of the tension in *Texts of Desire* — between the role of social structure, ideology and, ultimately, text (i.e., 'social representation') in constructing gender, and the possibility of agency and self-determination at the 'micropolitical' level of 'everyday practices'.

Each of the studies here frames the question of textual effects differently, arguing for, variously, the significance of romance novels in fixing identity, in maintaining both corporate and face-to-face sexism, and alternatively, reading and writing as means to construct multiple identities and life possibilities differently. As the studies by Gilbert and Cooper argue, there is the need for more complex understanding of how texts construct 'reading positions' and 'formation'. But, to play against the dangers of the 'reading off' of ideological effects, the case studies of Canadian and American readers (Cherland and

Edelsky, Christian-Smith, Willinsky and Hunniford) here stress the need to consider 'readings' as social practices done within and in relation to the institutions of home, family, school, peer subculture. As Moss's description of Angelique's writing graphically illustrates, regardless of their semiotic power, romance novels are always read and rewritten 'intertextually', via other discourses of sexuality and gender, race and ethnicity, class and work.

Moss, Taylor and Davies here show that the possibilities for 'agency and self-determination' can be explored in those everyday pedagogic events where structure and subjectivity meet, where the very 'uptake' of social representation by readers occurs. There — whether in Angelique's writings, in Australian pre-school girls' and boys' multiple interpretations of the *Paper Bag Princess*, or in the 'feminist classroom practice' outlined by Taylor — the very work of cultural representation and self-representation, enculturation and contestation is done through writing and talk. There, Taylor and Davies maintain, feminist alternatives can be articulated, explored and 'done'.

The case studies here are tales of *gendered* literate culture. Taken together they show how girls' and young women's identity, social and economic relations are constructed and reconstructed via the social practices of reading and writing. After reading *Texts of Desire*, there should be no going back to gender-neutral psychological assumptions which continue to dominate reading and literature teaching in schools. Reading is *not* a universal skill, which can be inculcated with the value-free precision of educational science. Reading is *not* an individual cognate and affective achievement, which one takes out into a social marketplace to use according to gender-neutral psychological agency and free will. Reading as it has been constructed in Western literate traditions is a gendered practice assigned, 'done' and renegotiated in various local communities and sites, enabling and precluding differing kinds of identity and power.

Given the place of the school in the division of literate labour into public and private domains, there is a pressing need for educators to reassess the political and economic efficacy of literacy for girls and women. We can begin from this recognition that its teaching, learning and use bears necessary connection to the gendered politics of everyday life. This may enable us to reshape, to reconstruct 'reading in schools' not only as a means for access to extant economic and cultural power, but as a means for reconstructing authority, agency and identity. As the contributors to *Texts of Desire* reiterate, that reconstruction depends on a recognition of the possibilities for alternative and multiple interpretations, rewritings, and subjectivities.

Allan Luke
Townsville, Australia
February, 1992

References

BRANDT, D. (1990) 'Literacy and knowledge', in A.A. LUNSFORD, H. MOGLEN and J. SLEVIN (Eds) *The Right to Literacy*, New York, Modern Language Association of America, pp. 189–96.

DAVIS, N.Z. (1987) *Society and Culture in Early Modern France*, Cambridge, Polity.

DeLAURETIS, T. (1987) *Technologies of Gender: Essays on Theory, Film, and Fiction*, Bloomington, Indiana University Press.

FOUCAULT, M. (1986) 'Technologies of the self', in L.H. MARTIN, H. GUTMAN and P.H. HUTTON (Eds) *Technologies of the Self: A Seminar with Michel Foucault*, Amherst, University of Massachusetts Press, pp. 16–49.

GILBERT, P. (1989) *Writing, Schooling and Deconstruction*, London, Routledge and Kegan Paul.

GOODY, J. (1986) *The Logic of Writing and the Organization of Society*, Cambridge, Cambridge University Press.

GOODY, J. (1987) *The Interface Between the Written and the Oral*, Cambridge, Cambridge University Press.

GRAFF, H.J. (1987) *The Legacies of Literacy*, Bloomington, Indiana University Press.

GROSSBERG, L. (1990) 'It's a sin: Politics, postmodernity and the popular', in L. GROSSBERG, T. FRY, A. CURTHOYS and P. PATTON, *It's a Sin: Postmodernism, Politics and Culture*, Sydney, Power Publications, pp. 6–71.

HARDING, S. (1986) *The Science Question in Feminism*, Milton Keynes, Open University Press.

HARDING, S. (1991) *Whose Science? Whose Knowledge?* Ithaca, NY, Cornell University Press.

HIRSCH, E.D., JR. (1988) *Cultural Literacy: What Every American Needs to Know*, New York, Vintage Books.

HUYSSEN, A. (1986) *After the Great Divide: Modernism, Mass Culture, Postmodernism*, Bloomington, Indiana University Press.

IRIGARAY, L. (1985) *This Sex Which Is Not One*, trans. C. PORTER with C. BURKE, Ithaca, NY, Cornell University Press.

JARDINE, A.A. (1985) *Gynesis: Configurations of Woman and Modernity*, Ithaca, NY, Cornell University Press.

LUKE, A. (1988) *Literacy, Textbooks and Ideology*, London, Falmer Press.

LUKE, A. (in press/1992) 'The body literate: Discourse and inscription in early childhood education', *Linguistics in Education*.

LUKE, C. (1989) *Pedagogy, Printing and Protestantism: The Discourse on Childhood*, Albany, State University of New York Press.

LUKE, C. (1991) 'On reading the child: A feminist poststructuralist perspective', *Australian Journal of Reading*, **14**(2) pp. 109–16.

MODLESKI, T. (1982) *Loving with a Vengeance*, New York, Methuen.

MORLEY, D. (1991) 'Where the global meets the local: Notes from the sitting room', *Screen*, **32**(1) pp. 1–15.

PATEMAN, C. (1988) *The Sexual Contract*, Cambridge, Polity Press.

POSTER, M. (1990) *The Mode of Information*, Cambridge, Polity Press.

WILLINSKY, J. (1990) *The New Literacy*, New York, Routledge.

Acknowledgments

This book represents the collective visions and energies of many people. I express my appreciation to the contributors, series editor Allan Luke, the support staff at the University of Wisconsin — Oshkosh and Kenneth L. Smith.

Permissions

The editor thanks the following for permission to reproduce illustrations and an article: Annick Press Ltd, Canada for the illustrations from *The Paper Bag Princess*, copyright 1980 written by Robert N. Munsch and illustrated by Michael Martchenko; *Reading-Canada-Lecture* (Now *Reflections on Canadian Literacy*) for permission to reprint 'Reading the Romance Younger: The Mirrors and Fears of a Preparatory Literature' written by John Willinsky and R. Mark Hunniford, appearing in Volume 4, Number 1, Spring 1986; Virago Press for kind permission to reprint from *Un/Popular Fictions*; and The Ghana Education Service for permission to reprint and reproduce an illustration from An English Course for Ghanian Schools 4.

Chapter 1

Constituting and Reconstituting Desire: Fiction, Fantasy and Femininity

Linda K. Christian-Smith

At this moment, an adolescent girl is immersed in a novel which may take her on a magic carpet ride to the land of romance or, perhaps, into the murky world of the horror story. There she can escape the realities of home and school, fulfill her secret desires and fantasies, ponder the relationships between the sexes, and powerfully negotiate her place in the world. Is she reading a Janet Dailey romance secretly borrowed from her mother or a horror novel well-thumbed by her classmates? While she may be reading the occasional adult horror story, she is most likely reading a romance novel written and marketed especially for young women, perhaps the *Dolly Fiction* or *Sweet Valley High* or *Baby-Sitters Club* series. Chances are that a teenage girl of your acquaintance is among the millions of avid readers who have made these teen series international best sellers in only twelve years. Behind this fiction's current readership and popularity are several stories which form the substance of *Texts of Desire: Fiction, Femininity and Schooling*.

These stories are told through eight chapters that analyze how popular cultural genres such as teen series novels are influential in how young women think about themselves and their futures. *Texts of Desire* tells stories in which desire, fantasy, politics and economics are intertwined with literacy, femininity and schooling. Running across these chapters is a feminist cultural studies perspective which views popular fiction as potentially a point both for ideological closure and for utopian possibility. The chapters are written by eight writers, who as women and men, teachers and researchers are differently situated within the economic, political, and historical conditions of the late twentieth century. The stories they tell are powerful, disturbing, and potentially transforming in their implications for the schooling of young women.

Two broad themes here tie together literacy, femininity, and schooling. The first theme concerns the 'non-neutrality of literacy' (Luke, 1988). Reading and writing embody social, economic and political relations that shape readers' interpretations of books and the texts writers produce. Viewed in this manner, literacy represents an array of social practices learned within the home, school and community that involve the construction of identity and consciousness. Through

1

literacy, young women construct and reconstruct their desires and gender subjectivities, as well as their awarenesses of social differences and power relations. They do so on the basis of readings situated in local contexts. There readers and writers confront texts from the positions they occupy within the discourses of gender, class, race, ethnicity and age.

The second theme poses series novel reading as a means for young women's incorporation into a patriarchal and profit-driven social structure, and as a potential means of resisting women's traditional places in this structure. Gramsci (1980) singles out popular culture as a key element in the struggle for power and control in society. Popular culture can represent the 'good sense' of groups and can represent their visions for a better life. It is also the site where subordinate groups can resist ruling groups' desires to win their consent to dominant patterns of control. Popular culture today at once represents the hopes and resistances of subordinate social groups and the power of the corporate sector. Adolescent series novels are prime examples of this double-edged quality of popular culture. But it is precisely because of their contradictory nature that these texts can be parts of feminist classroom practices aimed at rethinking women's places in the world.

Packaging Texts of Desire

Books continue to serve significant social, political and economic functions in industrialized societies. Books, especially popular fiction, are commodity forms of capitalism, merchandise designed to make money for the corporate sector and a handful of writers. This aptly describes the phenomenon of recent adolescent series novels. Consider the following sales figures. Scholastic's *Wildfire* romance novels sold 2.25 million books in its first year (Lanes, 1981). There are over twenty-six million *Sweet Valley High* romances in print since their release by Bantam in 1983 (Crossen, 1988). Another Bantam series, the *Baby-Sitters Club*, has twenty million books in print (Huntwork, 1990). These series boast a loyal following among millions of preteen and adolescent girls in Canada, Australia, New Zealand and other countries, as well as the US. How do the publishers cultivate this impressive readership and what does this mean for young women readers?

Dianne Cooper here documents how the American-owned Ashton Scholastic Corporation operating in Australia goes well beyond the usual business practices associated with achieving high volume sales. Her analysis of Ashton Scholastic bookclub fliers advertising teen romance novels and *The Baby-Sitters Club* series demonstrates how one publisher is turning primary classrooms into marketplaces. However, in these instances more than books are sold; the slick bookclub fliers and the books they advertise retail gender as well. *The Baby-Sitters Club* is a case in point. While young women read about the Baby-Sitters Club — a group of teenage girls from Stoneybrook, Connecticut, who operate a baby-sitting business — their gender subjectivities and awarenesses of sexual differences are being textually constructed. With every turn of the flier or book page, young women readers are positioned as consumers, future homemakers and mothers, and not incidentally, heterosexual lovers. Cooper's chapter introduces the idea that literacy, desire and fantasy are constructed at multiple sites, especially at home and in schools.

Desire and fantasy have a number of dimensions: psychological, discursive and material. Henriques *et al.* (1984) offer instructive insights into the psychological underpinnings of desire. They argue that 'wishes and desires are based on needs that have once known satisfaction, to which, as it were, they hark back' (p. 213). Real and imaginary events from one's life history provide the reference points for desires throughout one's life. Mitchell (1975, p. 396) defines desire in relational terms as

> the desire of the other. Desire can be recognized but never satisfied, for, as the desire for what the other desires, it necessitates the wish to be the other one, or not to be different from the other one.

For women, this otherness has a double dimension, socially constructed and organized through language, popular culture and structures such as families and schools. Through these structures and practices men have become women's significant other. Women themselves are positioned as other, as the objects of desire of others, namely men.

Fantasy regulates and organizes the otherwise formlessness of desire, providing a setting for desire (La Planche and Pontalis, 1973). For Walderdine (1984, p. 167), fantasy is a process featuring 'active engagement and construction' of a wish and its fulfillment, which are linked to unconscious desires and scenes. La Planche and Pontalis (1986, p. 6) envision fantasy as the imaginary world and its contents. In this context fantasy provides a means of dealing with emotions, working out conflicts and life solutions to difficult problems. Through fantasy, one can imagine other worlds where secret hopes and dreams come true.

Yet the objects, means and stories of desire and fantasy are not intrinsic or determined aspects of existence, but are constituted in part through the discourses of romance fiction and the discursive practices of reading and writing. Longhurst (1989, p. 4) notes that discourse refers to

> all of the processes of signification, to the production and framing of meanings around social experience and their circulation throughout a range of institutional power structures. Thus a text is constituted around a discourse or even multiple discourses and readers make sense of it in relation to the discourses (of age, race, gender, class, region and so on) through which their consciousness makes sense of social reality and through which they are constituted as subjectivities.

Power permeates discourse and the texts constructed around discourses. According to Foucault (1980a, p. 108): 'Power is not an institution and not a structure; neither is it a certain strength we are endowed with; it is the name that one attributes to a complex strategical situation in a particular society.' Foucault (1980b, p. 39) further argues that power 'reaches into the very grain of individuals, touches their bodies and inserts itself into their actions and attitudes, their discourse, learning processes and everyday lives.' This is especially the case of the gender discourses of teen romance texts which speak to the unconscious and conscious desires of young women readers while using those desires to secure their consent to larger dominant patterns of power and control.

3

Young women's desires and fantasies are linked to the social, economic and political institutions of gender relations through popular culture, especially teen romance texts where they assume material form. Popular teen romance fiction is a literary fantasy which channels young women's desires towards consumption and positions them as 'material girls' in a material world. This world of teen romance fiction is built upon 'commercial femininity', consumer goods such as clothes and cosmetics which are presented as the keys to realizing one's romantic desires (see Christian-Smith, Gilbert, this volume). Romance novels themselves are the literary equivalent of the 'business deal', desire packaged between slick covers.

Constituting the Discourses of Desire

Meredith Rogers Cherland and Carole Edelsky's analysis of young women readers in a suburban area of a large Canadian city exemplifies how fantasies in texts play upon wishes and desires already present in young women's lives. The gender relations of popular fiction are foregrounded in the social positions young women occupy in their everyday lives. The 'New Town' readers discover in the world of fiction continuities and discontinuities with their lives as white middle class young women. The affluent world they encounter in *Sweet Valley High* and the *Baby-Sitters Club* is continuous with suburban life. While reading the *Baby-Sitters Club* fiction, readers envisioned a world in which they were well-liked, confident and clever, a set of circumstances different from their own lives. The novels also sharpened these readers' resentments over their dependency on adults and their minimal voice and influence over even the most mundane matters in their lives. Furthermore, these readers' literacy practices were constructed in opposition to the established patterns of school literacy which featured uninteresting reading materials. Following Lankshear and Lawler's notion of 'improper literacy'. Cherland and Edelskey argue that 'improper texts' like horror and series novels became the symbol of these readers' lack of control over one aspect of their schooling as well as a means of achieving some control. Hence, series fiction reading allowed the New Town readers to enact their desires for 'agentic femininity', for power and control over their words, power and control to resist such agency in the form of violence against women. Cherland and Edelskey conclude that the fantasies and the traditional aggressor/victim discourses that permeate this fiction *both* empower *and* disempower readers.

The social and cultural context of adolescent romance fiction reading plays a vital role in constructing desire and positioning readers in multiple gender discourses. In Chapter 4, I analyze the school literacy practices of twenty-nine young women ages 12 through 15 from various class, racial, and ethnic backgrounds residing in and surrounding the North American midwestern city of 'Lakeview'. This chapter demonstrates the political dimensions of literacy, fantasy and desire. Literacy is a significant component of the US New Right's bid to win consent to its conservative views on women and dominant economic policies. I argue that the struggle for consent is carried on in the social site of the school room, as well as in the recesses of young women's minds where fantasy and desire dwell. The study of Lakeview readers reveals teen romance novel reading as a source of opposition to a meaningless education and as a way to reflect on gender relations. Young women read teen romance fiction for a variety of reasons: primarily to escape their status as 'reluctant students', to learn about dating, to imagine themselves as affluent, smart, resourceful, and popular, and to negotiate their relationships with boys. At the same time, these readers are presented with and take up discursive positions and practices which channel them towards future marriage, parenting, and work in low paid service sector jobs. I conclude in this chapter that young women readers do not really escape when reading romance novels. In substituting romance novels for their textbooks, these readers — like their counterparts in Cherland and Edelsky's New Town study — reinforced their marginal academic status. Rather than escaping reality, teen romance reading reconciled these readers to subordinate places in the world.

In the foregoing chapters femininity and desire appear as fluid yet anchored in the traditional discourses of romance. Pam Gilbert takes this analysis of textural difference and similarity one step further in her analysis of a new teen romance series which appeared in Australia in 1988. The development of *Dolly Fiction* demonstrates one publisher's negotiation of the changing parameters of femininity and desire. Like Cooper, Gilbert argues that audiences for teen romance fiction are always already positioned within 'reading formations'. In this instance the positioning occurs through the popular teen magazine, *Dolly*, roughly comparable to the American magazine *Seventeen*. *Dolly Fiction* readers are also *Dolly* magazine readers. Like the Ashton Scholastic texts Cooper analyzes, *Dolly* situates readers within available discourses of femininity characterized by interest in boys and marked disinterest in schooling, feminisms, and politics. Gilbert argues that gender relations in *Dolly Fiction* are the outcome of publishers' accommodation to and reshaping of changes in gender relations. Her analysis of series' novels published during the first two years of the series provides a compelling glimpse of the dynamic quality of teen romance fiction. Topics such as ecology, teenage sexual intercourse, adult women in the workforce, male violence, and less than happy endings, represent the publisher's incorporation in books published in 1988 of available contemporary discourses and issues. The female characters in the 1990 novels are more assertive and independent, representing a slight reframing of subjectivity. However, these changes coexist with traditional gender discourses in which boys remain the centre of young women's lives and their objects of desire. Gilbert concludes that current *Dolly Fiction* represents a 'superficial accommodation to temporary social shifts' in femininity. Gilbert attributes this to the generic nature of the texts which limit rather than expand the representation of femininity. That this generic quality can also be a source of creativity is also apparent in Gemma Moss's chapter on the place of romance in young women's writing.

One striking aspect of teen romance novel reading is the tension between the escapist and primer qualities of this fiction. As primers, these novels provide a guide for treading the thorny path of romantic relations, as Christian-Smith and Gilbert here insist. Yet at the same time the reading of current series novels represents a new set of literacy practices. John Willinsky and R. Mark Hunniford examine this 'self-directed literacy' through their Canadian study of forty-two seventh grade readers from lower middle-class neighbourhoods and focused interviews of eight young women readers. This study paralleled Janice Radway's (1984) groundbreaking analysis of adult romance fiction readers. Using Lacan's notion of mirror stage, Willinsky and Hunniford argue that just as a child's reflected image serves as the basis for the developing identity, books provide mirrors for teenagers. However, these mirrors àre of differentially gendered possible worlds: careers for young men, romance for young women. As mirror and lamp, teen romance thus prepares young women for entry into heterosexuality. The interviews with young women here provide glimpses of the ways books position them within meaning and 'regimes of truth': boys shape young women's subjectivities and validate their worth. For readers, the pleasures of living the exciting life of the romance heroine and being able to safely peer into the future pale before these ponderous truths. Willinsky and Hunniford conclude that despite the rich interpretations by readers, teen romance fiction is 'troubling'.

Romance as genre can be the basis of writing which reflects on the 'trouble' surrounding femininity. According to Butler (1990) this dissonance can symbolize the conflicts between young women, their parents, and boys over gender-appropriate behaviour. It also can mark out the perceptions of women of color that there is something deeply disturbing about their positions within White patriarchal society. Gemma Moss's chapter focuses on the ways that Angelique, a 15-year-old Black student, uses the formulas of romance fiction to think about gender and race relations. Moss's analysis of a story Angelique wrote for a school assignment and her subsequent interviews reveal a young woman who has thought a great deal about what it means to be Black and female. In 'Again!' Angelique draws on her knowledge of romance from reading novels with White characters. She describes the problems of romance through the eyes of the character Angela who finally rejects her boyfriend when confronted with his disloyalty. Here Moss demonstrates that reading and writing are reflective practices mediated by young women's life circumstances and their previous literacy experiences. Writers, like readers, draw on various cultural literary, and linguistic resources which are transformed in use. Although Angelique uses many of the stock devices of romance fiction, these are changed through her awareness of how context shapes text. In the school story 'Again!' Angelique used 'standard' English and White characters, positioning herself as a White. However, writing at home featured patois and Black characters. Angelique's literacy reflects her divided world. At school she must be careful and constrained, while at home she can recreate the world of her former inner London neighbourhood left behind in the move to the White suburbs. Angelique, like other young women described in these chapters, uses literacy to establish spaces where they can pose and explore questions of subjectivity, emotion and power. These subjectivities of gender, class, and race are not unitary and coherent, but plural and fragmentary.

Reconstituting Desire

The foregoing chapters suggest highly complex relationships between adolescents, literacy, and femininity. The power of fiction lies in the ways it engages with aspects of fantasy. Teen romance fiction especially enables insights into the ways many young women attempt to negotiate the relation of their fantasy lives to their actual lives. Romance fiction places some order and coherence on the unconscious and its fantasies. This poses both a challenge and opportunity for the teachers of young women, many of whom are immersed in the worlds of popular fiction. In two provocative final essays. Sandra Taylor and Bronwyn Davies reflect on the implications of the previous chapters for helping readers think beyond dominant constructions of femininity. Both chapters take into theoretical account the powers of desire and fantasy in developing feminist strategies for change.

Sandra Taylor raises broader theoretical questions relevant to developing a feminist classroom practice based in a cultural studies perspective. This entails students analyzing and creating texts that move them beyond traditional ways of thinking about gender. A first step for teachers is to rethink the patterns of power and control in the classroom that privilege their perspectives over students' experiences. This means bringing to the fore the meaning of gender relations in students' lives and creating spaces for students to connect individual experiences to larger historical and cultural contexts. Another requirement is for teachers to recognize the many ways in which popular fiction speaks to the concerns of young women. One of the reasons teen romance novels are so lucrative and popular with young women readers is that the books explore some of the dilemmas they face today. Therein lies the difficulty educators may encounter when encouraging the deconstruction of popular series novels.

The previous chapters have shown how these books speak to readers on the level of consciousness and desire. Change at that level is arduous and often resisted. Taylor's discussion of the difficulties of 'raising consciousness' and developing feminist reflective practices is sensitive to both students' and teachers' perspectives. The practical strategies and feminist cultural politics Taylor proposes stem from a comprehensive understanding of the risks, challenges, and necessity of change. Taylor returns attention to the necessity of taking struggle beyond the realm of literacy and into the larger society.

In the final chapter, Browyn Davies vividly demonstrates the difficulties of rethinking gender as suggested in Sandra Taylor's chapter. Her study presents a compelling poststructuralist argument for the necessity of students' access to discourses which hold that there are multiple and diverse ways of being and knowing. Such discourses provide the means for critiquing a gender system which creates rigid divisions between women and men that make it difficult to imagine alternative possibilities and constructions. That feminist books *per se* do not automatically evoke feminist responses in readers is quite clear from her analysis of the responses of six Australian sixth grade girls and boys to a traditional and a feminist fairy tale. This chapter provides glimpses of the ways by which girls and boys construct their gender subjectivities in opposition to one another through conversation. These readers' struggles with *Snow White and the Seven Dwarves* and *Princess Smartypants* disclose a range of conflicting responses resembling a 'battle of the sexes' over dominant and alternative gender discourses. In this literacy event, the teacher questions and challenges the students' responses, providing them with the space and conceptual tools for exploring the complexities of gender. This kind of feminist pedagogy, according to Davies, can move students toward a position that considers the possibility of femininity and masculinity residing in a single person. Davies argues that this is a step towards transcending dualism and finding one's way towards multiple genders and multiple subjectivities.

Texts of Desire thus marks out a future chapter for transformations of gender, literacy, and schooling. As Taylor and Davies note, to reconstruct the world, we must rethink and rewrite it. Only then can one desire differently. As texts, these chapters represent the writers' desires for a different world for both young women and men.

Acknowledgment

The author thanks Toni Wright for assistance in the preparation of this chapter.

References

BUTLER, J. (1990) *Gender trouble: Feminism and the Subversion of Identity*, New York, Routledge.

CROSSEN, C. (1988) 'Book publishers finds lucrative niche in soap opera series for teen-age girls', *The Wall Street Journal*, February 11, p. 25.

FOUCAULT, M. (1980a) *The History of Sexuality*, London, Allen Lane.

FOUCAULT, M. (1980b) *Power/Knowledge: Selected Interviews and Other Writings, 1972–1977*, New York, Pantheon Books.

GRAMSCI, A. (1980) *Selections from the Prison Notebooks*, New York, International Publishers.

HENRIQUES, J., HOLLOWAY, W., URWIN, C., VENN, C. and WALKERDINE, V. (1984) *Changing the Subject: Psychology, Social Regulation and Subjectivity*, Methuen, London.

HUNTWORK, M.M. (1990) 'Why girls flock to Sweet Valley High', *School Library Journal*, March, pp. 137–40.

LANES, S. (1981) 'Here come the blockbusters — teen books go big time', *Interracial Books for Children Bulletin*, **12**, pp. 5–7.

LAPLANCHE, J. and PONTALIS, J.-B. (1973) *The Language of Psycho-Analysis*, New York, W.W. Norton.

LAPLANCHE, J. and PONTALIS, J.-B. (1986) 'Fantasy and the origins of sexuality', in V. BURGIN, J. DONALD and C. KAPLAN (Eds) *Formations of Fantasy*, London, Methuen, pp. 5–34.

LONGHURST, D. (1989) *Gender, Genre and Narrative Pleasure*, London, Unwin Hyman.

LOVELL, T. (1987) *Consuming Fictions*, London, Verso.

LUKE, A. (1988) 'The non-neutrality of literacy instruction: A critical introduction', *Australian Journal of Reading*, **11**, pp. 39–43.

MITCHELL, J. (1975) *Psychoanalysis and Feminism*, Harmondsworth, Penguin Books.

RADWAY, J. (1984) *Reading the romance*, Chapel Hill, NC, The University of North Carolina Press.

WALKERDINE, V. (1984) 'Someday my prince will come: Young girls and the preparation for adolescent sexuality', in A McROBBIE and M. NAVA (Eds) *Gender and Generation*, London, Macmillan, pp. 162–84.

Chapter 2

Retailing Gender: Adolescent Book Clubs in Australian Schools

Dianne Cooper

Introduction

Picture this scene in a year five classroom. You and your girl-friend — both avid readers — eagerly await the latest book club brochures each month. Your teacher passes out the flyers to each student in the class. You both scan the glossy colours, searching for your favourite series. Your friend finds it first. She reads excitedly the blurb of the new book in the series of *The Baby-Sitters Club*. You just know that you have to add it to the thirty-four you have bought and read in the last two years.

Particularly as it occurs in many social institutions like churches and schools, reading is not a neutral, apolitical activity. It involves the ideological transmission of gendered culture — the teaching and learning of modes of thinking and of behaving, and indeed of reading. In schools and homes alike, books are channelled to or from children according to their gender. Many girls pass from fairy-tales to adolescent romance, finally to reach the possible worlds of adult romance. Girls' reading histories thus serve to prepare and position them *vis-à-vis* stereo-typic and patriarchally defined forms of 'femininity' (Christian-Smith, 1990).

This progression ensures a steady market for particular genres of discourse, a 'hunger for redundancy' (Eco, 1979). Compulsive dependence on sameness characterizes the consumption of texts of popular culture. Readers, particularly girls, are driven by a compulsion for the predictability and sameness of these texts (Christian-Smith, 1988; Kress, 1985), a phenomenon which has not escaped a growing multinational publishing industry which increasingly has targeted the youth market. The selective traditions of popular culture — romance texts for girls and science fiction for boys, fairy tales for young girls and dinosaur books for young boys — perpetuate and reproduce gendered 'reading' and readings intergenerationally.

This chapter draws upon theory and methods from political economy, critical linguistics and social semiotics to investigate how this situation comes about. It focuses on Australian school book clubs — and their advertising texts — as a key institution in the construction of reading and subject positions of reader/consumers, thus tracing the textual production of gender from publisher to classroom to reader.

The Power of Publishers

Reading and literary choice cannot be divorced from the culture, politics and economics of the industry of publishing. Books do not come to the notice of readers accidentally. It is according to publishers' policies, ideologies and economic practices that certain books are published and promoted and others are rejected. In most instances a book's potential to return quick profits, rather than literary merit *per se*, ensures publication, marketing expenditure and wide distribution. With policies that emphasize profits at the expense of artistic or literary merit, I here want to document how publishers capitalize on the production and reproduction of gendered reading practices.

In the last few decades the publishing industry has become more and more the private province of the mega-mogul — the conglomerate which owns or has controlling interests in the paper-mills, printers, distribution outlets and the media used to promote and publicize the end product. When one firm is bought out by another it invariably becomes the creature of the buyer, adopting its economic and editorial policies, and frequently its staff at the expense of original personnel. In the case of conglomerates, management is rarely composed of literary people. As a consequence, management interests are more oriented towards profits and quick turnovers which largely preclude the risk of publishing unknown authors or experimental texts (Coser, 1979). Editors in such organizations have three masters to consider: the reader, the advertiser, and the stock market (Bagdikian, 1980). These considerations, and the changing structures within publishing, have led to changes in editorial practices, policies and ideologies. Such changes have profound effects on what is published and indeed, on what authors write. Changing societal trends such as the incremental increase in saleable information, growth in literacy, increased concentration on formal higher education, and a boom in mass entertainment has resulted in great changes in book publishing in the past twenty years. The publishing industry has followed the lead of other culture industries and is now characterized by international and/or corporate ownership with multiple diverse holdings (Coser, Kadushin and Powell, 1982).

The American-based Scholastic Inc. is a prime example of this trend towards multiple product diversification. This multinational company is a leader in the production of children's paperbacks, including teenage fiction and romance series, and books based on juvenile licensed characters. The corporation is also heavily involved in the publication of classroom text and film materials, television programs, video films, computer software, computer magazines as well as thirty-two classroom and professional magazines (Scholastic Inc., 1985). In addition, Scholastic Inc. was awarded an Emmy for the Outstanding Children's Entertainment Special of 1983, with the dramatization of the screen play adapted from the Scholastic book *The Great Love Experiment*. Scholastic Inc. also achieved a hit with the prime-time television show *Charles in Charge* — also sold to Australian television organizations — which spawned a Scholastic paperback and screenplays under the same title. The profitable success of this program led Scholastic Inc. to invest further in Scholastic Productions and to produce a wide variety of programs for television and cable-television viewing, as well as the home video market.

Book clubs, book fairs and educational conferences together with traditional commercial venues, thus provide wide outlets for Scholastic products. Scholastic's name, traditionally associated with quality educational materials, grants institutional authority to its products and hence a targeted mass market that is already familiar with the 'name' and its implied association with the institution of education.

Editorial policies and practices are largely mediated by the type of book the organization publishes, the size and social/political/economic status of the market-audience to which it is targeted. Indeed, market constraints and editorial policies largely combine and have an impact on the type of texts published and the texts authors write (Apple, 1986). In this complex multinational political economy, culture gets commodified according to the political and economical trends of publishing houses.

Trade books represent financial capital to most publishers and include, for example, juvenile books, escape fiction such as Gothics and romances, Westerns or adventures, tie-ins with film or TV, as well as cookbooks and most self-help and how-to books. The usual outlet for trade books are bookshops, chainstores, supermarkets, airports, bookclubs, and 'anywhere a bookrack can be squeezed in' (Coser *et al.*, 1982, p. 60). They usually have very large print runs and are targeted to the 'lowest common denominator of reader in order to attract the largest possible audience' (Coser *et al.*, 1982, p. 61). Hence the commodity function of popular literature is realized in its marketability — its mass exchange for profit. The consumer is reified as an object of the industry — an industry that actively creates a desire for its product. The product, in turn, becomes the object of the consumer's pleasure, interest or needs. It is from practices which build on the desire for redundancy (Eco, 1979), that markets for series books such as the teen and adult romance are based. From these practices many gendered reading habits are formed and perpetuated. Moreover, it is from these practices that most gendered reading and subject positions have their origins, are maintained and reproduced.

The predominance of 'closed' texts in children's reading preferences means they are subjectively constructed to rely on 'highly fixed [textual] schemata' (Luke, 1989, p. 71) that transforms reading into a process that delimits interpretation. But rather than the sameness creating boredom, the 'narrative of redundance' builds in the consumer, a 'hunger for redundance' (Eco, 1979, p. 120). In many cases the messages contained in these books are passively accepted by readers. Such uncritical acceptance ensures cultural reproduction along patriarchally gendered lines. Publishers of generic texts have largely constructed readers in the roles of passive receivers of knowledge from the beginning of their relationships with literature (Heath, 1989). It is not surprising therefore, to find that many students choose to read formulaic and gendered materials both inside and outside the school environment — reading that builds on the redundancy of closed texts. Such materials construct subject positions that are non-critical and ideologically disempowering (Kress, 1986).

Much text publishing is not aimed at the needs of students as consumers *per se*, but rather is designed to impress and meet the criteria of those who select educational texts on behalf of students — teachers, principals, curriculum developers and state department personnel (Lorimer, 1986). Because of the huge cost involved, however, the multinationals ultimately control what educators can select. Furthermore, in this particular patriarchal subculture of publishing, it is generally males who head these corporate organizations and males who make the editorial decisions and determine what is published and therefore what is available for selection.

Multinational infiltration into Australian publishing has impacted greatly upon the texts prescribed for student use and, in addition, to texts consumed for recreation and personal interest — including those available through book clubs. The greatest problems confronted by Australian-based publishers are the small base market, escalating international competition, and the changing outlet structure of markets. With profits the prime concern of publishers, books that might initially be unprofitable but are important works are difficult to get published (Whiteside, 1982). Australians own less of their publishing world than foreigners, particularly foreign-based conglomerates and multinationals (Wilson, 1992). Since non-Australians monopolize the publishing industry, foreign policies, ideologies and economic practices influence what is published and when it is released in this country. Books without mass markets are pushed aside in favour of, for instance, teen romance series with market recognition and instant appeal, and which return high profits to publishers.

The implications for the production of gendered texts and reading are multiple. With the majority of trade and school texts emanating from multinationals and conglomerates predominantly controlled by patriarchal hierarchies, a 'selective tradition' of knowledge, ideology and culture is transmitted to consumers. Within this masculinist tradition, texts are institutionally sanctioned, and thereby naturalized, legitimated and authorized. Since males dominate the hierarchies of the industry, masculinist philosophies — based on economic business principles — decide what the populace, including women and juveniles, can read, should read, or want to read (Apple, 1986).

A further implication is that since most publishers' policies are profit driven, they tend to invest in fewer books and aim for high volume sales, thus reducing the choice and options of consumers. It also means that small publishing enterprises which have attempted to present innovative literature or literature which represents a feminine world view — women's knowledge — are silenced through acquisition, merger or takeovers, or are so undercapitalized that they are unable to compete with the conglomerates/multinationals. Through the resultant published text, culture is commodified, and consumers — and in this instance, child consumers — are constructed into subject and reading positions 'that reflect the ideological categories of the economic and social system into which the child readers are being socialised so closely, and indeed mirrors the world of advertising' (Kress, 1985, p. 77).

Known profit-making genres continue to command the most attention under present marketing practices — the teen romances and 'series' genres, for example. As a result, these genres continue to be marketed and promoted, and placed in strategic positions in retail outlets and marketing brochures of book clubs. It is through strategies and policies based on economic factors that genres promoting gendered cultural traditions continue to find their way into schools and children's personal and public libraries. In this way, the power of the publishing industry can be seen to influence reading choices.

Currently, Ashton Scholastic must be included among the foreign-based publishing institutions successfully and profitably operating in Australia. Ashton Scholastic continues to expand its Australian market and is, according to

Australian Bookscene (1988–89, p. 40) 'probably the largest distributor of children's paperbacks in Australia'. What follows is a case study of this publisher/distributor which centres on its provision of literature to Australian primary school children.

Ashton Scholastic: An Overview

Although many of its publications are sold through commercial institutions, Ashton Scholastic's four children's book clubs have established themselves as important reading links between home and the institution of schooling. Book fairs and educational conferences also provide a lucrative outlet for the company's commodities, which appear to benefit greatly from an implied and actual association with educational institutions and authorities.

Analyses of company documents filed with the New South Wales Department of Corporate Affairs make clear that despite the single token share held by the managing director, Ashton Scholastic Pty. Limited (Inc. NSW) is foreign controlled and *de facto* foreign owned. The parent company, Scholastic Inc., is a multinational conglomerate with diverse interests in media and publishing. Foreign operations of Scholastic consist of wholly owned subsidiaries in the United Kingdom, Canada, Australia and New Zealand. These international companies are profitable and provide multiple avenues which allow Scholastic to broaden its reach to young people through the juvenile trade outlets — including book clubs. Scholastic Inc.'s *1984 Annual Report* states that 'The Company's international subsidiaries established record levels of sales in local currencies. Although performance was good in local currencies, the continued strength of the US dollar reduced profits when translated into US dollars'. Apparently, profits made in international divisions are channelled back to the parent company in the United States. It is clear that profit justifies and motivates decisions such as the selling off of hardcover publishing interests Four Winds Press, and Children's Choice. It is also the driving force behind the increased investment in the electronic media as well as the introduction of new romance series for adolescents.

Ashton Scholastic has a long history of involvement with Australian schools through children's book clubs; its ongoing relationship began in 1967. The responsibility for the current operations of Ashton Scholastic Book Clubs in state schools rests with the school principal. He or she determines whether or not the school will participate in the book clubs and also oversees the management of clubs. There are no apparent standards, criteria or provisions to guide or restrict book club operations. Indeed, Ashton Scholastic holds a monopoly over the commercial sale of books (and associated products) within Australian schools. In the state of Queensland, Ashton Scholastic is the *only* commercial enterprise to gain access to Queensland state schools to sell its merchandise.

Ashton Scholastic's unrestricted freedom coupled with the apparent lack of departmental control or monitoring may influence the standards of literature offered to children through Ashton Scholastic Book Clubs. It may also be responsible for the large proportion of Ashton Scholastic and its imprint products among the selections from which children are able to choose. This is despite the assertions of the Promotions Manager that 'Ashton Scholastic Book Club books are selected on the basis of being the best books available from *a wide range of publishers*' (I. Perriman's emphasis, personal communication, November 22, 1988). However, 'Ashton Scholastic publish Australian children's books to ensure a high percentage of local [Australian] books'.

That Ashton Scholastic is a subsidiary of Scholastic Incorporated, an American company is reflected in the books available through Australian school book clubs. A cursory glance of books published by Scholastic (US) and its imprints 'Ashton Scholastic' (Aust.), 'Apple', 'Little Apple', 'Vagabond' (all US), 'Hippo' (UK, copublished and distributed by Pearson-Penguin), and 'Studio Publications' (NZ), listed in book club brochures in 1989, reveals that far from being Australian or 'quality', a large number are serial-type books that build on redundancy. These start in Lucky, the book club for lower primary children, with the Apple, Paperback series *Peanut Butter and Jelly* and Scholastic's *Baby-Sitters Little Sister* — both aimed at girls. Arrow Book Club, aimed at middle primary students, offers the serial books *The Gymnasts* and *Animal Rescue Farm* as well as Apple Paperback books which focus on family relationships and 'growing up' — all intended for girls. Star Book Club is targeted at upper primary school students. Scholastic publications (or their imprints) included among Star selections are *The Baby-Sitters Club, Going on Twelve* (*Thirteen, Fourteen, Fifteen* and *Sixteen*), *Anastasia*, and a range of what Ashton Scholastic categorize as 'family' and 'animal' books — all aimed at girl readers — and *Secret Agents Four, Hauntings* and 'suspense' — books targeted at boys. The predominance of this type of literature offered through book club brochures suggests that Ashton Scholastic, by introducing formulaic literatures early in children's reading history, are able to build on them in the ensuing years, and thereby maintain a steady market for commodities that hook children into a particular style of reading — one that, as we have seen, builds on redundancy (Eco, 1979). Research supports the insidiousness of this practice. A study of year ten girls' reading habits revealed a high correlation between formula fiction read in earlier years and the reading of formula fiction books, including romance, in later years (Altus, 1984).

Currently, the most frequent criticism facing the company in Canada, the US and Australia, concerns the quality of books offered to children, and in particular, to adolescents. Keresey (1984) maintains that the reputation of Scholastic for supplying quality educational materials has been tarnished by the controversy over the romances and their editorial policies. Other researchers have criticized the quality of Scholastic publications, particularly those marketed to girls (Altus, 1984; Christian-Smith, 1986, 1987, 1988, 1989, 1990; Knodel, 1982; Lam, 1987; Vickery, 1989; Willinsky and Hunniford, this volume). All have commented on the distribution network and the implied educational endorsement that the commodities gain through their association with the institution of schooling.

> Scholastic's educational connections have supported their enterprises in a variety of ways: providing almost comprehensive market research, and an extensive promotional and distribution network which enables competitive pricing and an identified audience for future sales, and implied educational endorsement. Schools seem to have provided the very means by which teachers' and librarians' views can be bypassed (Lam, 1987, p. 14).

Given Scholastic's claim that they provide 'quality books to children', it is somewhat ironic that Scholastic should be the first publisher to produce an adolescent romance series, *Wildfire*, in 1979. This decision followed research which alerted the company to the possible market potential of teen romance books (Lam, 1987). The huge financial success of *Wildfire* led to additional series: *Wishing Star* in 1981, and *Windswept* in 1982. All these series have been distributed by book clubs in the USA, Canada and Australia. *Sunfire* historical romances — building on the success of *Wildfire* romances — followed in 1983, as did *Point*, which currently features in Australian book club brochures. These series are '*every bit as pernicious as the adult counterpart*' (Altus, 1984, p. 129). Yet the appeal of these series does not lie solely with their intrinsic literary and cultural merit. Institutions such as schools 'mediate' student taste and reading practices. In what follows I examine two key questions. How do books hook children? How does classroom authorization occur?

Retailing Gender: The Classroom as Market Place

Each of Ashton Scholastic's four book clubs is promoted and operated to appeal to different age and reading levels. However, because of access restrictions and difficulties, no book clubs exist in Australian secondary schools. This is a key reason for the discontinuation of the Teenage Book Club and for its inclusion as a feature of 'Star' Book Club.

Book clubs operate through the cooperation and collaboration of teachers who serve as sales representatives for the various clubs. Great use is made in brochures and advertising blurbs of terms such as 'former teacher', 'former children's librarian', 'practising school teachers', and so forth. This has the effect of legitimating and authorizing the commodities by their implied association with educational authorities and institutions.[1] Arguments presented to parents through a form letter constructed by Ashton Scholastic, remind them that 'the child who reads widely at home has distinct advantages — the home reader has a wider knowledge, a broader vocabulary, more ideas, and a greater facility in speaking and writing.' The rhetoric contained in this 'letter' must make many parents feel they are depriving their child of the potential to achieve if they do not support their child and the school by buying from the book club. Parents may be further troubled with emotive sentences which personally address them as concerned members of the school such as: 'our school receives free books from the book club (one for every ten ordered by the children) which allows us to regularly update our library with just-published and favourite books.' This letter goes on to extol the 'specialness' of 'owning your own books' and to state that there is 'no better way to encourage reading than to allow children to own their own books'. Signature by the participating school's principal or classroom teacher gives the letter further local institutional authority.

Book clubs thus function in schools through Company practices which rely on teachers as economical sales agents to handle all aspects of sales of its commodities. In effect, the company has acquired without cost, a vast network of sales agents throughout the nation. Its related marketing techniques entail teachers' *de facto* endorsement and sanction of commercial products, as part of an enterprise that sells gendered materials to children. A key moment in this distribution and authorization sequence is the distribution of Ashton Scholastic advertising brochures to children. The purpose of the brochures is to sell to a child audience (and/or their parents) a range of reading matter and other adjunct materials such as calendars, diaries, stickers, and so forth, at a price lower than retail prices. In addition to discounted retail prices, Ashton Scholastic at times offers consumers incentives to buy their products. These include the chance to get something 'free' or to 'win'. For instance, in the October (1989) edition of 'Star' Book Club Student News, purchasers of Scholastic's *The Baby-Sitters Club* 'double dynamite pack' had the chance to enter a 'Meet-the-Author' Competition. The prize was a trip to California for two to meet Ann M. Martin, the series's author. In the same issue, patrons purchasing Scholastic's *1990 Diary* — where the entry form was to be found — had the opportunity to vie for an all-expenses-paid trip to Disneyland with spending money. In both instances the opportunity to compete was dependent on purchasing a commodity.

Not only are there incentives for children, but Ashton Scholastic also offers inducements to teachers to promote and/or buy its commodities. They are lured with 'free' books and other merchandise. As well, teachers have the opportunity to win prizes to benefit their students and their school. 'Win-an-author' for 'your school' for a day were the prizes advertised in two issues. Computers were also offered to teachers as incentives to increase sales of books promoted through book club brochures.

The distribution of book club brochures in schools has institutional approval which grants the products legitimacy and an implied authoritative recommendation. The dominance of Ashton Scholastic in the retailing of reading materials in schools is controlled by the Department of Education which, by sanctioning the operation of book clubs, additionally grants texts sold within schools' institutional sanction. This multinational company has been operating in Queensland schools for the past twenty-three years. It apparently has operated to the satisfaction of the State Department of Education which prescribed the system under which the company operates.

The production of brochures published for book club consumers constitutes an expensive advertising expenditure involving a series of separate procedures using a wide range of skills and expertise that are both labour and time intensive.[2] That this textual medium has resulted in the sale of over 47 million books is testimony to the success of the procedure in producing and reproducing reading positions that have continued to construct 'desire to own' in child readers. How is this want and desire created? Texts operate within genres and discourses. Texts, then create subject and reading positions. These positions are closely interrelated. Brochures for children construct reading positions, which are in turn, influenced by the complex economics underlying the production of those texts. The processes that ensure a child readership begin in publishing institutions where decisions are made about what is published, in what form, and how it will position readers as consumers. The advertising literature sets up reading positions that accept, naturalize and neutralize the ideologies inherent in the texts. Subjectivities of many readers are shaped and formed from interaction with such literatures. Furthermore, reading positions and subjectivities are formed for consumers of book club advertising media before books are purchased, before books are read. The culture and commerce of these texts presupposes the gender of their audience and also delimits possible readings. The potential effect is to influence children towards ingrained gendered reading. However, the express purpose of book club brochures is to mediate child consumerism — want for the product(s) advertised.

In the brochures, the editorial synopses accompanying each book are themselves mini-narratives which consist of propositions — events or facts chained together by semiotic frames.[3] They are reflective of a larger semiotic epistemic frame,[4] the macroproposition structures[5] of the books themselves. Yet they are a selective part, one which is elicited selectively to sell a commodity to children. The characteristic structures of these narratives link events into sequential chains by the use of transparent signifiers[6] of coherence and order, which generally have an indication of closure (Hodge and Kress, 1988). The narrative frame 'serves to signify the stability of the status quo' (Hodge and Kress, p. 230), but its structure generally shows some disturbance that interrupts the equilibrium which must then be restored or rearranged so that a new state of equilibrium is attained. This is achieved by a resolution, or suggestion of a possible resolution to the problem. The brochure analysis entailed study of the propositions and the textual devices used to construct the child reader into particular reading and subject positions. Rhetorical questions are a textual device utilized in many mini-narratives in Scholastic brochures, textually operating as commands to addressees (Hodge and Kress, 1988). Here, as in TV 'preview' advertisements for coming episodes, rhetorical questions have a dual imperative force: to answer the question, one has to buy the book. For example, the illustration of R. Cusick's book *The Lifeguard*, is accompanied by the narrative in Figure 1:

Figure 1: Mini-narrative from bookclub brochure illustrating the use of advertising textual devices.

THE LIFEGUARD — R. Cusick. 212 pages.

Kelsey's summer holiday is turning into a *nightmare!*
First there is a note from the girl who's missing.
Then there's the man in the lighthouse who won't leave Kelsey alone.
And there have been a number of suspicious drownings.
At least she has the lifeguards to protect her . . . But do they always save lives?

RRP: $4.95 $3.50

'Do they always save lives?'; to know the answer requires that you read further, to read further requires that you purchase.

Modalities are an important editorial textual device used to express the values society places on particular behaviours and actions (Hodge and Kress, 1988). Various genres instruct the reader about who, what and how to be in given social situations, occasions and interactions (Kress, 1985). Girls reading a series of texts such as *The Baby-Sitters Clubs* are constructed by reading positions which instruct them to be sensitive and responsive to others' problems and needs, to help them find solutions, to act collaboratively as one of a group, rather than independently, to value the social rather than the natural environment, and social/emotional actions rather than physical actions. Figure 2 illustrates the helping behaviour, focus on beauty, and the 'winning' element that is exemplified in this series.

Figure 2: Text from bookclub brochure, Issue 1, February 1989

LITTLE MISS STONEYBROOK ... AND DAWN — Ann
Martin. 152 pages. Baby-Sitters Club No. 15.

Mrs Pike wants Dawn to help prepare Margo and Claire for the Little
Miss Stoneybrook contest.
So what if Margo's only talent is peeling a banana with her feet!
Dawn's going to help them win.
The only trouble is . . . Kristy, Mary-Anne, and Claudia are also helping
others, too . . .

RRP: $ 3.95 $3.00

A device common to every book or adjunct product and shown in Figures 1
and 2, is the slash signifier, negating the retail price, and its replacement
discounted price. This powerful symbolic erasure of a (imaginary?) higher price
positions the reader with an act of choice — to buy through book club or to pay
the full retail price at a commercial retail outlet. In constructing the juvenile
reader, the book club editors use other signifieds in the semiosic plane. As well as
the rhetorical question, these include capitalizations, exclamation marks, ellipses
and dashes. All these devices and the referential signifieds operating in the
accompanying pictorial illustrations combine to dramatize the messages contained
in the plane of semiosis with the intention of creating a desire to own the
publication.

Coser *et al.* (1982) suggest that book clubs thrive by repeating successful
formulas with little change, preferring to rely on the known and commercially
profitable rather than to risk the new or innovative. Ashton Scholastic appears to
rely on genres which have been financially successful over the years: science
fiction; adventure (mostly for boys); family; romance; relationships; animals;
adolescent problems (all mostly for girls); mystery; ghost/suspense; 'classics', and
non-fiction — mostly nature books. Families and relationships are themes which
occur frequently among the books offered for sale to bookclub readers. However,
it seems that this area is one that concerns girls only, despite the fact that many of
the relationships involve male characters. In books within these genres, females
are the protagonists. They invariably are the passive recipients of others' actions;
the solution to their problems appears to lie in the formation of friendships with
others, or in restoring friendships with those who have had a causal part to play
in the problem. Physical beauty figures as a positive attribute, but can be
compensated for if it is marred or is deficient, by making others happy or caring
for others, or as in the case of one protagonist, adapting and coming to accept
oneself — imperfections, faults and all. *The Baby-Sitters Club* series are included
in the genre of 'family/relationships'.

In Western cultures, literature constitutes an important cultural commodity.
Children glean a great deal of their cultural knowledge from this commodity.
Literatures, as cultural products, not only embody and express ideologies, but are
themselves products of it (Williams, 1978). Children's texts are commodities of
the culture industries. These industries exist within a complex political economy
of corporate production (Apple, 1986). Since literatures, such as *The Baby-Sitters
Club* and adolescent romance, are cultural commodities of the culture industry

of publishing, it can be argued that publishers sell gender roles and behaviours. More specifically, the selling of gender roles and behaviours in school authorized book clubs is a facet — albeit neglected — in the total capitalization/economy of gender. Other facets include commodities like Barbie dolls, Cabbage Patch dolls, rock music and videos, cosmetics and fashion. All these facets contribute to the reproduction of culturally defined gender roles and behaviour. These factors which contribute to gender reproduction all have their genesis in corporate production.

Children are influenced in their selection of books by the fabric of socio-cultural factors. Consequently, they often choose those books which adhere to traditional concepts of gender appropriateness. Marketing and advertising are factors which play a pivotal role in these selections.

Power and the Construction of Reading and Subject Positions

Reading and writing involve asymmetrical power relations (Kress, 1986). In reading, the author is always invested with more power than the reader or consumer of text. The writer constructs the text and has the power to influence the field in which the reading will take place. For example, *The Baby-Sitters Club* books, like the romance text, are written to a formula dictated by publishers (Christian-Smith, 1989). These publishing formulas generate a variety of new texts. However, these new texts reproduce old meanings which in turn reproduce existing power structures between males and females. Thus the permanence of unequal cultural and social practices is assured. The way a genre is read is dependent upon its narrative features and the social, cultural, discursive literary history of its consumer (Kress, 1985). However, if it is read for little else than pleasure — which is precisely how these texts position the reader — the ideologic effects of the text pass unnoticed. Readers, constructed by the text through repeated experiences with the genre, may come to read it as compliant subjects. Such compliances reinforces the ideological messages of the text and its unproblematic 'naturalness'.

Genres, including the adolescent romance, adult romance and series such as *Mr Men*, *Trixie Belden*, *Asterix*, *The Baby-Sitters Club*, and other so called 'pulp lines', are successful because of their insistently repetitious generic nature. Oppositional readings are possible, but readers of these genres tend to conform to the pressures that are exerted.[7] The constantly insistent demands of a discourse have both short and long-term effects. In the short term a reading position is constructed, which indexes how to read a text or a set of texts. That instruction is also an instruction to act in certain ways, to take stances, to conform or adapt. In the long term, subject positions are constructed which fix a range of actions and modes of thinking and being which instruct participants on how to behave in the various roles and situations faced or assumed in life. It is from interaction with discourses that reading positions and subjectivities are created. 'Control of genre conveys at the same time the possibility of control of the reader, and with it the possibility of an effect on the formation of individuals' (Kress, 1985, p. 115).

How is the reader constructed in book club brochures? The discourse of book club brochures reflects the policies and ideologies of the institution of their source, and sets out to retail commodities to consumers — children. This is a carefully orchestrated and researched product in which an image has been constructed of the typical male child consumer and the typical female child consumer (Kress, 1985). The structural forms, the meaning systems, of these texts are not arbitrary, but the result of social and professional routines of editors within publishing institutions and their track record in the market place.

Book club brochures communicate particular messages to readers through semiotic codes, modality markers and signs. The brochures include a range of meaning systems: visual, symbolic, and textual. No meaning code stands in isolation, but is influenced by the context of the situation and in all its interconnected meaning systems (Hodge and Kress, 1988). That is, the structural form succeeds in constructing want through the creation of particular (gendered) reading positions. What appears in these brochures are titles in genres with appeal to the interests of this clientele, and at prices that are within their reach.

Visual Codes

A number of print conventions are used in book club advertising brochures to catch the attention of consumers. Semiotic markers, cues, and other semiotic devices assist to construct gendered images and messages for readers in pictorial texts. The visual semiotics are gendered in terms of the colours used, the portrayal of male and female characters, the settings they are depicted in and the things they do. These findings are further reinforced by the textual semantics of the editorial synopses.

Advertising techniques exclusive to particular series or genres operate as a 'symbol package' (Rotzoll, 1985) to entice children to them and to influence their growth. They work on the formulation outlined by Voloshinov (1973) that: 'the form of signs is conditioned above all by the social organization of the participants and also by the immediate conditions of their interaction' (p. 21). In this instance the 'participants' are potential consumers; the 'conditions of interaction' are those of commodity sales through the genre of advertising. For example, all books in *The Baby-Sitters Club* series feature the same semiotic signifiers and modality markers, making their visual design the metasign for the series. On all books the iconic symbol and the imprint label 'Apple' are printed in the top left-hand corner — two signifiers synonymous with Scholastic publications. In the opposite corner, in tiny print are the prices of the book in Canada and the US. The price in North America is a type of corporate 'signature' — a signifier of an *authorized* source.[8] It connotes that these books are international — that purchase of these books is a joint act with other 'baby-sitting sisters' around the world. The act of reading and the ideological messages transmitted are 'normalized' through this international sisterhood which succeeds in producing and reproducing gendered reading and subject positions multinationally.

On the top of each book, balancing just above the illustration, is a set of children's building blocks, arranged in three tiers, each with an impressed capital letter spelling out *THE BABY-SITTERS CLUB* in thick red block-type. Children's blocks here are symbolic of children's play, so the association between them and the title printed in the blocks, signifies in redundant fashion, the function of the Club — looking after and playing with young children, or fulfilling roles that can be seen as preparation for adulthood within a patriarchal social system. The solid square frames that constrain the illustrations have the effect of providing limits not only on the possible readings, but also on the environment of characters depicted within them. These tidy frames create an implied closedness (Luke, 1988), a limitation or restriction on the movement, the environment and the universe of the baby-sitters and their charges. Their tidiness and regularity also signifies intimacy — the values of the domestic, the feminine (Hodge and Kress, 1988, p. 135). The books' titles have the same regularity. They are always placed below the realistic cover illustration. Each word is printed in a contrasting colour to that of the pastel frame in which the print and illustration are situated. The title appears to be of little importance. Relative to the rest of the print, it is considerably smaller than the series's name, the author's name, and even the apple of Scholastic's imprint label. The emphasis, then, is on the series name itself which operates as a metonym signifying to girls the 'nature' of the book. There appears to be little need to give a title since readers construct the rest of the syntagm from the parts given — the series name and other symbols on the books' covers, including a single statement or rhetorical question printed in small lower-case within the illustration, which explains the semiotic plane. These together represent the major theme of the book. Thus the series name, *The Baby-Sitters Club*, embedded in children's building blocks, as well as the illustration are the focal metasigns for the genre rather than the book's title, which because of its small print, must be considered of lesser significance in the construction of the reader.

Readers of visual text read the modality cues in a 'reasonably predictable fashion' (Hodge and Kress, 1988, p. 128), and although visual texts may have more possible ranges of readings than verbal texts, they are nonetheless constrained and limited by the modality markers which facilitate particular readings while resisting others. If this is indeed the case, it is likely that girls — and boys — are reading the realism of *The Baby-Sitters Club* illustrations as reality. Moreover, many girls identify with their reading of the modality markers simply because they are so 'real' and appear to represent reality, a reality which implies group membership or belonging and a 'natural' affinity with children. Boys read the signifiers as representative of what girls do, of what girls are. Realism in the visual code corresponds with truth (Hodge and Kress, 1988, p. 130). Hence, the modality markers in these visual texts serve to signal affinity with the real world, and in so doing, naturalize the relationships and activities of the characters. The ideological message of the text is therefore built into the modality scheme which, in turn naturalizes a set of ideological configurations and relations.

Drawing on the modality cues and transparent signifiers it is possible to construct the baby-sitters of Ann M. Martin's Club. In the brochure illustrations, all the 'baby-sitters' are middle-class, slim, well dressed, have long hair, clear skin, and smile incessantly. One of the protagonists is of a different racial background to the others, who are stereotypically white. The children they tend to are also white, normal, clean, well-dressed, and obviously middle-class. The visual characterizations construct subjectivities for children with images of life that are far removed from the reality of the real world. They reproduce ideologies which suggest modes of behaviour that characterize what it is to be a baby-sitter and romanticize the role by neglecting any mention or visual images of negative aspects, disadvantages or problems. In this way reading positions are laid out, while at the same time subject positions are constructed which describe ranges of action compatible with the discourse (Kress, 1985). In *The Baby-Sitters Club* books, semiotic transparent signifiers constrain and limit actions to within confined environments and so limit the readings and the subject positions.

The mimetic balance of gender representation reflects the semiotic conditions: the stories are about girls — the baby-sitters — to be read by girls. They construct a feminine image in the visual and written text. The hairstyles and modes of dress are visual signs of generation, class, and gender. They are signifiers of nature and energy which depict the baby-sitters as pure, natural and energetic. The close proximity of the 'sitters' to their charges connotes to readers the intimacy of female adolescents' relationship with children — a reproduction of patriarchal values and of the existing social order. Expressions of semiosis back up the logonomic rule that females look after children. The foregrounded realistic images of baby-sitters with children evoke a sense of realism which appears not only natural and obvious, but are without flaw or defect. From the tidy regularity of the covers, readers are constructed into a restricted universe that is peopled by adolescents and young children.

While some boys' books in the brochures feature realistic illustrations, they also show abstract, surreal and ethereal graphics. These realistic images project their power and are marked for masculinity by the solidarity of the character(s) and the modalities of the text that operate to negate any reference to the category female and also to draw a close affinity between the text and 'real' events. The transparent signifiers operating in texts for females — intimacy, domesticity, femininity — reflect high affinity but low status (Hodge and Kress, 1988). Male texts, conversely, reflect low affinity and high status — the epic, the public, the masculine. Similar differences are to be found in the flyers' written text.

Brochure Blurbs

All *The Baby-Sitters Club* books have social settings, and themes which revolve around helping behaviour. Family situations are common to all eight books advertised in the 1989 Book Club brochures. The editorial synopses — the mini-narratives accompanying each books' illustration — invariably begin with propositions that outline the social setting, an initial equilibrium, and are followed by a problem(s), and finally by propositions that indicate the resolution. For baby-sitters, this generally involves affect or the formation or restoration of social relationships which lead to the creation of a new equilibrium (Stein and Glenn, (1979).

For instance, Dawn, in *Little Miss Stoneybrook . . . and Dawn* (Figure 1), is 'wanted' to help prepare Margo and Clare for a beauty contest (setting/initial equilibrium). Dawn's problem lies with Margo whose 'only talent is peeling bananas with her feet!' The problem is further compounded by four other 'sitters', whose assistance has been similarly acquired to help other little girls to win (complication/further disturbance). Ellipses here — syntactically marking absence — are used textually to create desire in readers — in this case a desire to find out how Dawn moulds her charges into feminine beauties. Calibration with the pictorial text suggests that it is not peeling bananas with feet that wins beauty contests, but well groomed hair, feminine attire and appropriate stage behaviours. Use of the quantitative modal 'only' serves to reduce the value of this unique ability and implies that to win such a contest other talents are required and therefore must be developed. Hence girls are constructed by the text to devalue unusual talents and to develop more socially desirable and stereotypical feminine qualities.

The two media — pictorial and textual — naturalize the concept of competing against other girls for proof and recognition of feminine attributes. The implication is that one person will be deemed more feminine, more appealing, more attractive, and so forth, than other competitors who will be the losers, found wanting in one or more of these attributes. The text also suggests via ellipses and use of modals, that such qualities are attainable with the help of others and with the suppression of unusual talents.

The preceding paragraphs provide an example of visual and textual analyses using theory and methods derived from critical linguistics and social semiotics. They extrapolate the operants in advertising text synopses that create *want* in child consumers while also constructing reading and subject positions. Written texts, like all discourses, are sourced and produced in social contexts. They arise in social occasions and are the products of these occasions and processes. Like all commercial commodities, however, books are produced through a series of systematic processes to generate profits for their creators — publishers, distributors, advertising agents and authors. Editorial annotations address the child reader who buys books. They are published as commodities — commodities that are 'produced, sold and bought, consumed. They exist in a market, with advertising and promotion. This process constructs its own set of texts which mediate the narrative' (Hodge and Kress, 1988, p. 238). The language and the images are constructed with the child reader in mind and with a singular purpose — to create a desire to own a commodity or preferably multiple commodities.

The publishing industry depends for its existence on generating demands for its products. Book club brochures — which are representative of the genre of advertising — feature highly gendered visual and written texts. These narratives, furthermore, give expression to the meanings and values of the institution from which they arise. Hence it can be argued that Ashton Scholastic is committed to and operates within and under ideologies and principles of patriarchal, and therefore, gendered traditions.

Summary and Conclusions

I have suggested here that literature is not ideologically neutral or transparent, but provides readers with ways of exploring, understanding and building their worlds. From an early age children, often through the powers of advertising and promotion, consciously choose and read books with protagonists of like gender and they learn to identify with characters appropriate to their own gender and self-concept. This early childhood exposure to and selection of gender-differentiated literature and identification with same-sex characters is implicated in the reproduction of gendered reading positions and gendered literacy.

Research based on textual and thematic analysis of children's books confirms that much of children's literature presents a view of the world that routinizes gender: women in the kitchen, men outside; women sharing, caring or nurturing, men leading, directing and doing; the dominant powerful and active male, the submissive, powerless passive female; male the rescuer, female the rescued, and so forth. Gender roles thus have been commoditized, and the burgeoning corporate business of publishing has set about creating products that articulate gender roles and address gendered needs or desires. Commoditization has led to the development of a literature for children that fosters literary interest and desire on the basis of their gender. Indeed, mass capitalization creates desire at multiple levels. This desire is engendered into the product and runs at both a semiotic level and at a psychological level. The desire for the commodity gets conflated with the desire for romance.

Texts work to position consumers as particular readers within the terms of their ideological frameworks (Kress, 1985). Readers of traditional and contemporary children's literature are positioned according to gender. But the power of texts lies in their ability to command compliance in readers, in their ability to coerce readers to accept the ideological as 'natural' and to assume the reading position intended by the author. From such compliance, reading positions are constructed *vis-à-vis* particular genres and themes. Books, however, do not just fall into readers' hands by chance but find their audience through a network of commercial practices that guide, address, coerce and, I have suggested, constitute readers. The power of advertising texts such as Ashton Scholastic Book Club brochures lies in their ability to create a desire for ownership.

This study indicates that books, as commercial commodities with market potential, are diverted into audience-specific marketing venues including schools. Self-interest on the part of corporate power-brokers, manifest in mass consumption and company profits, surpasses or cancels the pretence to 'quality', 'diversity', 'art', 'children's interests', and so forth. In the market place, 'quality' has been turned into purchasing power, 'art' into saleable commodity, 'diversity' into marketability, and economic potential and literary excellence have been forsaken for the formulaic 'block-buster'. This procedure operates at the expense of minority or 'marginal' works. Such practices illustrate the selective tradition in action, the *de facto* control and diversity of literary censorship on the basis of social and economic forces. In addition, the school book club targets the classroom: a state-sanctioned site for the reproduction of a gendered tradition. Formula fiction is offered via Ashton Scholastic Book Clubs to children as young as 7. This introduction to formulaic reading positions girls — for whom most of this genre is aimed — for future discursive reading histories that depend on redundancy. From fairy tales, girls, on reaching schools, frequently progress to juvenile series such as *Peanut Butter and Jelly* and/or *Baby-Sitters Little Sister*, to the pre-adolescent *The Baby-Sitters Club*, to adolescent and teen romances, and finally to adult romances — all genres created, published and marketed by Ashton Scholastic. Thus girls are enticed by Scholastic promotions and hence learn to consume gender from an early age. Advertising engenders desire for a steady diet of 'romantic' fiction through to adulthood with what could be termed 'the "Barbie" of literature' — literature that reinforces beliefs and attitudes about being feminine. Luke (1988) describes this creation of consumer demand in readers as a process whereby:

> The culture industry creates in its audience a sense of dependency on the continuance of its conventions, codes and messages. In this manner, market demand is generated and sustained by the accessibility and ease

with which cultural products can be consumed. Hence, the need to produce further 'identical' (textual) products ... whereby 'appeal' is 'manufactured' figures prominently in modern publishing. ... The related consumption does not satisfy 'need', nor does it simply exhaust supply, but conversely generates greater 'wants' for and 'output' of similar, standardized products (p. 67).

It would seem, given the insistent pressure to maximize audiences and revenues, that there is a persistent tendency for publishers like Scholastic Inc. and Ashton Scholastic to create and promote desire for texts that are popular for their dependence on sameness and to neglect literature that has less 'unknown' commercial appeal. Books are merely commodities in the market place. But school literacy programs — particularly contemporary literature-based and whole language orientations — promote an ideology that reading and books are of moral, educational and aesthetic benefit (Luke, 1991). Reading and book consumption (and in the case of book clubs, sales) are mediated through free, publicly provided, teacher services in schools. The notion that reading is a valuable pastime and to be encouraged, and the commonly held tenet that reading anything is advantageous so long as children are seen to negotiate written text, are, however intentional or unintentional, key legitimations for the promotion of book club operations in schools and hence, the products they advertise. Apart from the semiotic and psychological desire engendered into advertising and the products themselves, what is also at issue here is that in consenting to become unpaid labour and therefore company representatives, teachers are seen to endorse gendered cultural products for the economic gain of a multinational company that at the same time is utilizing their position as classroom teachers. The question to be addressed is whether teachers should be involved at all in profit-making ventures of corporate business or indeed any business. Teachers' priority should be to assist students/consumers to explore, interpret and shape texts — to adopt critical reading positions and subjectivities in opposition to the desire that is generated by book club advertising that hooks readers, particularly girl readers, into a regular diet of gendered reading materials.

Notes

1 See Lorimer, 1986 for discussion on the legitimation and authorization process for textbooks used in schools and institutions.
2 See, for example, Helen Semmier (1988) for a detailed discussion on the many factors, processes and procedures publishers utilize to make a potential buyer choose their products from a catalogue or bookshop. See also Campbell, Griswold and Smith (1988) for a documentation on the effect of tradebook covers on the reading choices of elementary-age children.
3 Within the framework of Hodge and Kress semiotic frames are symbolic structures containing the signs and symbols — written and pictorial — of an episode/segment. Semiotic frames mark out or separate one episode from another in a similar way that a frame surrounding a painting marks a boundary between the art-work and the wall.
4 That is, the symbols and signs, knowledges, formalisms, practices, etc., that comprise the book from which the bookclub synopses are derived.

5 Each bookclub brochure synopsis is a précis or microproposition structure of the book which in its entirety is a macroproposition structure.
6 According to Hodge and Kress (1988) signs range on a continuum between transparent and opaque depending on how clearly they link the signifier and the signified. Hence the clearest links between the producer and receiver of text are transparent signifiers and the most vague or obscure are perceived as opaque signifiers. Most visual texts (comics, advertising, print media, etc.) act as transparent signifiers of semiotic activity.
7 See Linda Christian-Smith (1990) which provides elucidating insights on girl readers, particularly in relation to formula fiction romance novels.
8 See Roland Barthes (1977), especially his discussion and explanation on signifiers in advertising.

References

ALTUS, M. (1984) 'Sugar coated pills', *Orana*, **20**, pp. 70–90, 119–37.
'Annual return of a company having share capital' (1969 to 1988 inclusive), H.J. ASHTON and Ashton Scholastic documents filed with the New South Wales Department of Corporate Affairs, Sydney.
APPLE, M. (1986) *Teachers and Texts: A Political Economy of Class and Gender Relations in Education*, New York, Routledge and Kegan Paul.
AUSTRALIAN BOOK SCENE (1988–1989) 'Some publishing houses', pp. 40–54.
BAGDIKIAN, B. (1980) 'Conglomeration, concentration, and the media', *Journal of Communication*, **30**(2) pp. 59–64.
BARTHES, R. (1977) *Image-Music-Text*, trans. S. HEATH, London, Fontana.
CAMPBELL, K., GRISWOLD, D. and SMITH, F. (1988) 'Effects of tradebook covers on individualized reading choices by elementary-age children', *Reading Improvement*, **25**(3) pp. 166–78.
CHRISTIAN-SMITH, L. (1986) 'The English curriculum and current trends in publishing', *English Journal*, **75**, pp. 55–57.
CHRISTIAN-SMITH, L. (1987) 'Gender, popular culture and curriculum: Adolescent romance novels as gender text', *Curriculum Inquiry*, **17**(4) pp. 365–406.
CHRISTIAN-SMITH, L. (1988) 'Romancing the girl: Adolescent romance novels and the construction of femininity', in L. ROMAN and L. CHRISTIAN-SMITH (Eds) *Becoming Feminine: The Politics of Popular Culture*, London, Falmer Press, pp. 76–101.
CHRISTIAN-SMITH, L. (1989) 'Power, knowledge and curriculum: Constructing femininity in adolescent novels', in S. DE CASTELL, A. LUKE and C. LUKE (Eds) *Language, Authority and Criticism: Readings on the School Textbook*, London, Falmer Press, pp. 17–31.
CHRISTIAN-SMITH, LINDA (1990) *Becoming a Woman through Romance*, New York, Routledge.
COSER, L. (1979) 'Asymmetries in author-publisher relations', *Society*, November/December, pp. 34–37.
COSER, L., KADUSHIN, C. and POWELL, W. (1982) *Books: The Culture and Commerce of Publishing*, New York, Basic Books.
ECO, U. (1979) *The Role of the Reader*, Bloomington, Indiana University Press.
HEATH, S. (1989) 'Talking the text in teaching composition', in S. DE CASTELL, A. LUKE and C. LUKE (Eds) *Language, Authority and Criticism: Readings on the School Textbook*, London, Falmer Press, pp. 109–22.
HODGE, R. and KRESS, G. (1988) *Social Semiotics*, Oxford, Polity.
KERESEY, G. (1984) 'School book club expurgation practices', *Top of the News*, **40**(2) pp. 131–8.

KNODEL, B. (1982) 'Still far from equal: Young women in literature for adolescents', Paper presented at the annual meeting of the National Council of Teachers of English, Spring Conference, Minneapolis.

KRESS, G. (1985) *Linguistic Processes in Sociocultural Practice*, Victoria, Deakin University Press.

KRESS, G. (1986) 'Reading writing and power', in C. PAINTER and J. MARTIN (Eds) *Writing to Mean: Teaching Genres Across the Curriculum* ALAA Occasional Papers No. 9, pp. 98–117.

LAM, M. (1987) 'Reading the sweet dream: Adolescent girls and romance fiction', *The Victorian Teacher*, April, pp. 11, 14.

LORIMER, R. (1986) 'The business of literacy: The making of the educational textbook', in S. DE CASTELL, A. LUKE and K. EGAN (Eds) *Literacy, Society, and Schooling: A Reader*, Cambridge: Cambridge University Press, pp. 132–42.

LUKE, A. (1988) *Literacy, Textbooks and Ideology: Postwar Literacy Instruction and the Mythology of Dick and Jane*, London, Falmer Press.

LUKE, A. (1989) 'Open and closed texts: The ideological/semantic analysis of textbook narratives', *Journal of Pragmatics*, **13**, pp. 53–80.

LUKE, A. (1991) 'Literacies as social practices', *English Education*, **23**, pp. 131–47.

Perriman, I. (1988) Personal communication, November 22.

ROTZOLL, K. (1985) 'Advertisements', in T. VAN DIJK (Ed.) *Discourse and Communication: New Approaches to the Analysis of Mass Media Discourse and Communication*, Berlin, de Gruyter, pp. 94–105.

SCHOLASTIC INC. (1985) *Annual Report: 1984*, New York, NY, Scholastic Inc.

SEMMIER, H. (1988) 'Judging a book by its cover', *The Australian Author*, July, p. 15.

STEIN, N. and GLENN, C. (1979) 'An analysis of story comprehension in elementary school children', in R. FREEDLE (Ed.) *New Directions in Discourse Processing*, Vol. 1, Hillsdale, NJ, Erlbaum, pp. 53–120.

VICKERY, P. (1989) 'Teen romance: Through the looking glass', *Reading Time*, **33**(2) pp. 7–9.

VOLOSHINOV, V.I. (1973) *Marxism and the Philosophy of Language*, New York, Seminar Press.

WHITESIDE, T. (1982) *The Blockbuster Complex: Conglomerates, Show Business and Book Publishing*, Middletown, CT, Wesleyan University Press.

WILLIAMS, R. (1978) *Marxism and Literature*, Oxford, Oxford University Press.

WILSON, H. (1992) 'Marketing the canon: Australian publishing and literacy' in A. LUKE and P. GILBERT (Eds) *Australian Discourses on Literacy*, Sydney, Allen and Unwin, pp. 112–22.

Chapter 3

Girls and Reading: The Desire for Agency and the Horror of Helplessness in Fictional Encounters

Meredith Rogers Cherland with Carole Edelsky

The girls are 11 years old. There are eight of them around the table in the school lunch room, leaning on their elbows, looking at each other over the debris of sandwich crusts and plastic wrap and apple cores. Jerrica tosses her mane of hair and says, 'It's really good. It's about a brother and a sister who get married and have children.'

Karen interrupts. 'No, it was her *uncle*.'

Alisa leans forward. 'No, that was in the second book. My mother said!'

Lacey makes a face. 'Oh, yuck! Tell us the story.'

Jerrica takes a breath. 'Well, the grandmother and the mother lock the four kids in the attic. The grandmother puts hot tar on the girl's head, and they starve them so they have to drink each other's blood!'

Lacey gasps. 'Why did they give it that title?'

Jerrica explains. 'The kids made flowers in the attic because they could never go outside. They made flowers and a garden up there, and a swing. The grandmother said she'd give them food and shelter, but never love and kindness. Because they should never have been born.'

There is silence. Amanda straightens her back. 'My mom would never let me read a book like that. I mean, I'm just guessing, but I don't think she would.'

Jerrica says, 'Well, my mom said she didn't think it was right for me, but she let me read it. It took me two weeks to finish it.'

Alisa speaks. 'My mom said it was really, really good. She read it in two nights. But I just read the first chapter, cuz it made me sick. It's a true story, isn't it?'

Lacey is disdainful. 'No it isn't!' You don't think people would really *do that*, do you?'

Jerrica announces, 'I have *Petals on the Wind*, the sequel to this book. There are five in the series.'

'My mom has the whole set,' says Leah. 'She won't let me read them though, and she won't let me see the movie. She says I can watch it when I'm older. But I'd rather read the book. Can I borrow yours,

Jerrica? Books are better than movies anyway, because they tell more detail.'

    The bell rings. The girls rise, clear away their lunches, and walk back to the classroom.

This vignette portrays a few moments in the lives of children for whom the reading of fiction is a daily social practice. These children use the reading of fiction to learn about the culture in which they live, to enact that culture, and to resist it. They are avid readers of fiction, much of it mass-marketed for preadolescent girls (the *Sweet Valley* series by Francine Pascal and the *Baby-sitters Club* series by Ann Martin are popular, for example), but they also read traditional children's literature recommended at school, young adult novels from the public library, and popular novels available to them at home. This chapter will focus upon one dynamic in the girls' explorations and constructions of *gender* through their fictional reading. That dynamic is their desire for agency in the world and their perceptions of the culture's counter to that desire for agency: horror in the form of violence against women in fictional texts.

    The vignette is taken from the data for an ethnographic study conducted over the course of one year in an elementary school in a small, affluent, middle-class community near a major Canadian city (Cherland, 1990). Seven girls, ages 11 and 12, members of a group of forty-two sixth graders at that school, were the focus of the study. Four types of data were collected to answer the research question, 'What does reading fiction mean to these sixth grade girls?' Data included field notes based on over 400 hours of participant observation; transcripts of ethnographic interviews with the girls, their parents, and their teachers; transcripts of the children's literature response groups; and dialogue journals in which the researcher and the children wrote to each other about the books they were reading.[1] Inductive analysis of the data produced several themes, one of which was that the girls read fiction to enact cultural beliefs about gender.

    The research report that followed attempted to present the girls' perceptions of and meanings for their world and for their reading, while taking account of the broad structural constraints that shape those more subtle perceptions and meanings. Because the study both focused on local meanings and at the same time attempted to account for the influence of larger social structures (like patriarchy), it can be called 'critical ethnography' (Anderson, 1989).

    Not everyone would agree, however, that this study was anything more than traditional ethnography. For instance, Lather (1986) distinguishes between research that operates out of an interpretivist/phenomenological paradigm and research that uses a critical, praxis-oriented paradigm. The latter is concerned both with producing emancipatory knowledge and with empowering the researched. This study did not empower the researched. The conclusions of the study were not shared with the girls, so that they could examine their reading practices critically to better understand and control them. Gitlin, Siegel and Boru (1989) suggest that the American educational left must not separate understanding from application in ethnographic research. While this study did not apply its understandings in the research site, it did make use of feminist and critical educational theory in interpreting data.

    These interpretations of girls' reading offer only one type of critical explanation for what happens when girls read. Like Christian-Smith (1987, 1989) and Gilbert (1983, 1987, 1990), they emphasize social and cultural contexts for girls' reading and the influence of these contexts upon readers' constructions of texts. But where Gilbert and Christian-Smith have emphasized the ideological nature of the text and its role in the reader's construction of stereotypical femininity, this work focuses upon the broader, cultural forces present both in texts and in contexts which work to maintain social inequality through girls' reading. Walkerdine's (1984) work focuses more closely on the mind of the reader in interaction with the text, and on the roles of fantasy and desire in girls' reading. Taylor (in press) is concerned with the implications of these analyses for a feminist classroom practice.

All these studies have to some extent made use of critical educational theory, which like feminist theory has been concerned with the relationships among individuals, social categories (ethnicities, genders, ages), and an oppressive social structure (Weiler, 1988). Critical educational theory is concerned with the reproduction of oppressive social structures through public institutions like schools, and with individuals and collective resistance to that cultural reproduction. It often seeks to explain the role of human agency, or will, in cultural reproduction and in cultural change.

Anthropologists also use the notion of 'agency' to refer to a culture's approved ways of acting upon the world, of producing an effect within the community. Hoskins (1987) has, for example, described the complementary forms of male and female agency in the Kodi culture of Eastern Indonesia. It can be argued that mainstream North American culture subscribes to ideas of complementary male and female agency much like those of the Kodi people, who believe that women exercise agency in the private sphere of home and family, while men exercise agency in the public sphere. The belief that the two genders complement each other is consistent with the belief that they are opposites. The gendered division of daily activity serves to demonstrate and teach these gendered forms of agency (Thorne, 1986).

Critical educational theorists have frequently used the word 'resistance' to mean the action of individuals and groups by which they assert their own desires and experience and contest the ideological and material forces that are imposed upon them by the culture (Weiler, 1988). People exercise agency to resist the imposition of forces that work to construct their places within the society. McRobbie (1989) has suggested that 'negotiation' may be a better term for the processes by which individuals come to terms with these forces. Similarly Anyon (1984), in a study of school girls' attitudes toward contradictory gender role ideologies in the world around them, has suggested that the girls she studied both *resisted* those roles as they accommodated them and *accommodated* those roles as they resisted them. She writes:

> The dialectic of accommodation and resistance is a part of *all* human beings' response to contradiction and oppression. Most females engage in daily conscious and unconscious attempts to resist the psychological degradation and low self-esteem that would result from the total application of the cultural ideology of femininity: submissiveness, dependency, domesticity and passivity.

In this study the word 'resistance' is used to name the processes by which girls negotiate their own meanings for the cultural scripts they encounter in fiction.

This chapter, then, treats girls' reading as a social practice. It considers individual meanings for reading, but in light of the broad structural constraints upon them. It uses the concept of agency and perspectives from feminist and critical educational theory in making its analyses. Finally, it emphasizes the role of the culture, and concerns itself with cultural reproduction and resistance at work in girls' reading.

Reading Fiction as 'Improper Literacy'

This study draws upon the work of Lankshear and Lawler (1987), who argue that we must try to understand the nature and role of existing forms of literacy within established patterns of structural power and the pursuit of human interests. They believe that the actual form that literacy takes in daily life is shaped and defined within the process of competing groups struggling to meet their respective interests. They suggest that, when we look at literacy, we look at whose interests are being served and whose aspirations are met.

If we look at girls' extensive reading of fiction as a form that literacy takes in daily life, we can then look to see how it is shaped by competing groups in the struggle to serve their own interests. Publishers constitute one of these competing groups, peddling an easily produced commodity to a lucrative market of 12-year-old girls. Parents and teachers constitute another (sometimes two others) of these groups. They offer fiction as an approved activity, but only for girls. This form of literacy separates girls in one more way from boys of the same age.[2] Reading fiction keeps girls quiet and happy at home. In this way, girls' reading of fiction serves the interests of adults teaching the culture's beliefs about female agency to girls. Reading fiction isolates and entertains girls waiting to grow up and begin a life of service.

Reading fiction is in this sense a form of 'improper literacy', to use Lankshear and Lawler's term. It is a form of literacy practiced by a subordinate group that may actively undermine that group's own interests and positively promote the interests of the dominant group. This is one way to understand how reading fiction functioned for the mothers of 'New Town', the community featured in this study, who read to escape housework and loneliness and boredom. In the broadest terms, reading fiction anesthetized them and helped them endure their lot. Reading fiction can be seen as a part of the process of a group's subordination.

This analysis is vastly oversimplified, however. It takes no account of the active consciousness of the women or the girls themselves, of the people who do this reading of fiction. And if reading fiction does play a role in the preservation of patriarchy, the process by which it does so is certainly not as straightforward as the above analysis implies. Reading fiction for the girls of New Town both supported and contradicted the idea of 'improper literacy'.

The Desire for Agency in Girls' Reading

The sixth graders of New Town were struggling to live their lives more independently. They were learning to keep track of their homework, their gym equipment, their lunch money and their book order forms. They were learning to stay clean and well groomed, to contribute labor to the maintenance of their households, and to meet their obligations to the community organizations they joined. They were learning and practicing these things with varying degrees of success, moving in and out of states of determination and rebellion. They said, 'I have so much more to do this year. Life was easier in fifth grade.' They worked toward growing up and yearned to *be* grown up.

The sixth grade girls of New Town were using their reading of fiction to explore the possibilities that surrounded their own roles as agents in the world. They often imagined themselves in roles that were in conflict with the roles their families imagined for them, regardless of either the presumed power or passivity of those roles. Alisa, for example, resisted her mother's vision of her attending law school. Other girls resisted their parents' vision of them as grownup 'good' girls (Walkerdine, 1984) who would behave decorously, please others, and serve their husbands. Even when the fictional texts they read suggested one model of female agency, girls sometimes read those texts to explore another.

For example, the *Baby-Sitters Club* books by Ann Martin do not seek to promote social revolution. These are stories of middle-class, preadolescent girls who live in the same neighborhood and support each other cheerfully in their dealings with parents, teachers and the families for whom they baby-sit. The girls in these stories are 'good' girls; Their struggles with parents are low key. The girls who belong to the Baby-sitters Club beautify themselves diligently, do their chores conscientiously, love their families well, and serve the children of their community faithfully. This is one model of 12-year-old female agency that promotes a comparable model of adult female agency. But the New Town girls read these texts in another way. They saw the baby-sitters making money that they then used to achieve their own ends. They saw the baby-sitters shaping the action around them so that things worked out the way they wanted them to. They saw girls their age acting as agents in their own right.[3]

The Desire for Agency in Daily Life

> Karen's face is grim. She pulls her chair up to the table where the literature response group is about to meet. She speaks across the table to Jerrica. 'Did you hear what happened to Lacey in Social yesterday? Mrs Johns was absent and we had a sub. We were working on our reports and the sub came around to see what we were doing. Lacey showed her her report — and the sub wrote all over it! She drew arrows on it and crossed out things and she changed it all around. Lacey was so mad! If it had been my report, I would have killed her.'

For the sixth grade girls of New Town, life was full of situations over which they had no control and in which they had no choice. They could negotiate with teachers, but when a substitute arrived they had to put up with whatever she or he chose to do. Certain features of their lives were imposed by their parents: Sunday school and church attendance were imposed by parents. Often music lessons were too, and children practiced not because they wanted to but because they had to.

The children actively resented these things, but they realized they had no choice in the matter. Children had to cooperate because they were dependent people. Cara described the situation thus:

> My Mom and Dad are really the most important people in my life. I like
> my brother, but he's really not important to me at all. We both depend
> on Mom and Dad. There isn't much that we could do to help each other.

The girls would have loved more control in daily life, and they looked
forward to the day when they would have it. Jerrica said,

> I was helping my mother get supper the other night, and she said to me,
> 'Jerrica, some day you'll be able to fix your husband a nice supper.' I got
> so mad, so I said to her, 'Oh no you don't. *He's* gonna fix *my* supper!

Julie said that when she grows up she won't be doing all the housework. It isn't
fair that girls have to do it all, and she isn't going to stand for it. Gilligan *et al.*
(1989) suggests that at 11 girls are 'resisters', especially prone to notice and question the compliance of women to male authority. The New Town girls enjoyed
imagining themselves as adults who exercised choice and asserted themselves.

The desire for agency was visible in the girls' readings of their library books
and of books assigned by the teacher. Lacey read *The Secret Garden* and said she
didn't like the way Colin in the book bossed Mary around. She said, 'If I was
Mary, I'd just tell him to stop it.' When the teacher asked the children to follow
their reading of *The Book of Three* with an activity in which they 'gave gifts' to
the characters in the book, the girls enjoyed the idea and thought long and hard
about what to give Eilonwy. Finally Karen hit upon the perfect present: 'Let's
give Eilonwy a sword! Like she always wanted to fight and everything. She
didn't want to be considered just a little girl.'

When the girls recommended books to each other, they often recommended
stories of female agency as 'good books' for that reason. Samantha recommended
Kid Power to Alisa, saying, 'It's about a girl who needs to earn some money, so
she starts her own business.' Karen recommended *Julie of the Wolves* to everyone,
saying that Julie was so smart and independent. And Jerrica enjoyed a book about
the aftermath of nuclear war because the ending showed the children managing to
survive and able to secure help for their injured mother.

The girls exercised agency wherever they possibly could in their daily lives.
Amanda, for example, who had been strictly forbidden by her mother to see the
movie of *Flowers in the Attic*, arrived at Nicole's birthday party to find that
Nicole's parents had rented *Flowers in the Attic* for the evening's entertainment.
Amanda chose to say nothing and watch the movie. Marcia and Julie often chose
to 'hide' and read when they were supposed to be doing household chores. They
willingly paid the consequences for this defiance later. All of the girls would
sneak reading in school when they were supposed to be 'doing schoolwork'. In
resisting the teacher's assignment of their time and exercising choice in what they
would and would not do, the girls were exercising agency in their/daily lives.

The Desire for Agency and the Series Book

The girls who read series books seemed to find in them a complete and real world
that was 'continuous' with their own world (Radway, 1984). Francine Pascal's
Sweet Valley Twins and *Sweet Valley High* series presented the adventures of

Elizabeth and Jessica, the Wakefield twins, in a world of shopping malls, television programs and junk food that was perfectly familiar, in spite of the fact that the series is set in California. The fact that the world of the series could be treated as a real world made it easy for the girls to think of the characters in series books as real girls, with problems similar to their own. The grade six girls of New Town read series books, as they watched each other, for cues as to acceptable ways to behave, and for examples of ways to be in the world. Desiring agency for themselves, the girls desired agency for the girls in their series books. They admired them for exercising agency when and where they could. Walkerdine (1984) suggests that young girls fantasize about the texts they read in order to fulfill their desires. The New Town girls did seem to imagine themselves exercising agency as they read series books.

Tanya sits at her desk, her math homework finished, reading her *Sweet Valley High* book. The cover says that it is Book no. 50: *Out of Reach*. The picture on the cover shows an attractive Oriental girl with an athletic towel around her neck looking pensively off to one side. Blonde and beautiful Elizabeth Wakefield stands beside her, looking at her supportively. The sentence on the cover below the picture reads, 'Will Jade Wu have to defy her father to get what she wants?'

Tanya reads intently, turning the last few pages slowly. She finishes, sighs, and closes the book. 'That was an excellent book,' she says to the girl across from her. 'She did it.'

Jerrica and Marcia and several of the other girls read *Sweet Valley High* books faithfully. They all admired Jessica Wakefield, and enjoyed her independence even when she was severely punished for it. Marcia explained in her dialogue journal:

May 1, 1989

Dear Mrs Cherland,

Characters can be boring at times, but Jessica never is. My favorite character is Jessica because she always does these neat things and always takes risks. In *All Night Long* Jessica took so many risks and it had a lot of adventure, too. It was about Jessica going out with a college guy who had a Ferrari (some sort of car). He invited her to a beach party with all these other college students. When she gets there, she starts drinking beer and they are smoking pot. Then he takes her to an abandoned shack and tries to abuse her. She started screaming so he took off to his cottage and left her there in the dark. She made her way back to the cottage, and all his friends are still there, but she can't get home, and a telephone isn't within ten miles. So she is forced to stay overnight there. When Elizabeth finds out that her sister hasn't been home, she has to be Jessica and Elizabeth at the same time.

Truly yours,
Marcia

Marcia enjoyed reading about Jessica's risk-taking, even when it nearly ended in disaster. Elizabeth frequently rescued Jessica from one awful situation or another, and Marcia loved it. And Jessica Wakefield did enjoy herself through the exercise of her own agency. Her life wasn't all trouble. Jessica almost always chose short-term happiness and instant gratification over long-term well-being, and Elizabeth always saved the situation in the end. It appeared to the New Town girls that Jessica made wise choices.

Not all the grade six girls enjoyed *Sweet Valley High*. Those who did may have enjoyed the fact that Jessica and Elizabeth were older than they were, and therefore seemed so much more powerful. Most of the grade six girls preferred the *Sweet Valley Twin* series where Jessica and Elizabeth (the same characters) were 12 years old. Their characters were the same; Jessica was selfish and Elizabeth was saintly. Elizabeth repeatedly rescued Jessica from the awful situations she got herself into.

Alisa responded to the *Sweet Valley Twins* books as Marcia responded to the *Sweet Valley High* books: 'I love it when she gets into trouble. Those are the books I like.' Getting into (and out of) trouble required the exercise of agency.

The *Baby-Sitters Club* series offered less 'excitement', but it still seemed to meet the girls' need to feel more confident and capable. In this series a familiar group of characters faced challenges to their baby-sitting success that were not too dangerous but that were rather real, and that were always overcome. The featured baby-sitter was always shown to be clever and competent and well-liked by all. The Baby-Sitters Club reader, who could say with Lacey, 'I feel like I *know* those girls,' was reassured that she too could be useful and could contribute something to the world of material production. The *Baby-Sitters Club* characters were not 'used' as baby-sitters. Instead they did something praiseworthy, challenging and worthwhile that gave them agency.

The *Baby-Sitters Club* books that the girls of New Town read both promoted traditional gender values and subverted them. The baby-sitters of the books did embody the traditional feminine virtues of nurturance and service. At the same time, however, they were capable and clever and often assertive. In *Mary Anne Saves the Day*, for example, Mary Anne was sweet and timid and largely controlled by her father at the beginning of the story. She was allowed by her father to meet with her girl friends and to baby-sit until 9:00 p.m., but she was not allowed to wear makeup or to assert herself in any way. When one of her baby-sitting charges became ill, Mary Anne demonstrated that she was a capable person by caring for the sick child and getting help. Her father's attitude toward her then changed. Mary Anne was both the compliant female child and the effective agent. She did not rebel, and yet she successfully demonstrated her capabilities and convinced her father to remove his restrictions. Girls reading this book saw a worthy individual triumph over the gender restrictions of the culture at large, and they learned to believe that it is possible to do so.

Radway (1984) suggests that romance reading for women may be 'combative' because by reading the woman temporarily refuses the otherwise constant demands of her family. Reading series books may have been 'combative' for the New Town girls because by reading the girls could temporarily escape the constant demands upon them to be 'good'. When they read, they *were* being 'good'.

Radway also points out that romance reading may be 'compensatory', in that by reading the women make up for the emotional deprivations of their daily lives. Perhaps series book reading for the girls was also 'compensatory' in that by reading and identifying with characters, the girls could feel more powerful than they were allowed to feel in the real world.

Horror: The Denial of Agency

The New Town girls, reading to explore the possibilities for female agency in the world around them, valued the stories that showed those possibilities. They resisted, or renegotiated, the cultural messages that conveyed images of female passivity and submissivenes. But the New Town culture continued to reproduce itself. The great majority of girls were growing up to keep their places in the gender hierarchy and did not attempt to subvert the social order. There seemed to be cultural controls upon the girls' desires for agency. The data for this study suggests that horror and violence in fiction offered disturbing fantasy experiences that muted and countered the desire for agency. Horror and violence were made attractive when the culture associated them with sexuality, the desire for agency was made to feel dangerous, and the cause of cultural reproduction was served.

Reading fiction served as the site for fantasizing about agency, but it also allowed for other kinds of fantasizing too. One powerful motif the girls encountered in their fictional reading was that of the sexual aggressor and victim. Michelle Fine (1988) has suggested that while adolescent boys are treated in our culture as sexual agents, girls are treated as sexual victims, and this ideology of aggressor and victim is reflected in the language of sex education curriculum materials. It is certainly present in fiction for children. When girls seeking stories of female agency encounter these, they can become profoundly upset.

> 'This is that book I was telling you about.' Samantha pushes it across the library table toward me. It's a paperback with a picture on the cover of a schoolgirl who might be 12 sitting nervously in a dentist's waiting room. The title is *The Trouble With Wednesdays*. The spine is labelled YA. It must be from the Capital City Public Library. I turn it over. The back cover says, 'This book is about learning not to let grownups abuse you.'
>
> 'It's good,' says Samantha quietly. 'But at first I didn't like it. I got to Chapter Eight and I really felt bad about it. I cried. I gave it back to my mother and said. "Take this back to the library!" So then she read it, and she said I really should finish it. So I did.'
>
> 'What's wrong with Chapter Eight, Samantha?'
>
> 'It was gross. I really didn't like it. I felt too sorry for the girl . . . You can look at the book, if you want to.'
>
> Samantha returns to class and I turn to Chapter Eight. The girl in this story has been going to the orthodontist every Wednesday afternoon and he has been molesting her, feeling her and rubbing up against her. She hasn't been able to get her parents to listen and believe her explanations of what's wrong. She feels sick and powerless.
>
> I flip to the final pages. She does get her parents to listen. They help her. She feels better as the story ends.

Brownmiller (1975) has suggested that the existence of the act of rape inspires in women a mind set that makes them fearful of men as a group, and that that fear helps support male control of society. The presence of the agressor/victim motif in stories for children may work in the same way. The message is clear. The threat of male sexual violence is always there in the world — and the threat is for all women.

Awareness of that threat is signalled in the girls' language. Samantha thought Chapter Eight in *The Trouble With Wednesdays* was 'gross'. Alisa and Lacey thought *Flowers in the Attic* was 'gross'. Cara thought it was 'gross' when Daniel forced his kisses on Miyax in *Julie of the Wolves*. The girls seemed to use the word 'gross' to mean nauseating and extremely unpleasant, and they used it to refer to violent and/or sexual events in stories.

This is not to say that violence and sex in stories always triggered this reaction. The girls were interested in sex and didn't seem to fear it. Violence did not offend them either. Something other than sex and violence called for the use of the word 'gross'. We would suggest that the word 'gross' was called for when someone was powerless to resist violent treatment and abuse. When that powerlessness and abuse was associated with sexuality, the girls perceived it for what it was: a gendered threat. The girl in *The Trouble With Wednesdays* did nothing to bring on her victimization. It was just waiting for her there in the orthodontist's office. She found out. It isn't really possible to take care of yourself.

Countering Resistance to the Culture with the Gender Threat

Horror as entertainment appeared frequently in the field notes for this study. Lacey and her family, for example, drove seven hours one weekend to a huge, well advertised shopping mall where they paid a ten dollars 'family fee' to see the medieval torture devices on display. At Halloween the girls' teacher casually brought the video of the Michael Jackson song 'Thriller' to school, thinking that the kids might enjoy watching it with their grade three reading buddies. In November Marcia stayed up past midnight reading *The Unloved* by John Saul. In December *Flowers in the Attic* came to school. One day, Jerrica brought her mother's copy. The next day, several of the other girls brought their mothers' copies. For two full weeks the girls could talk of nothing else. It was clear that horror stories had a presence in the school, and that this was due to the popularity of horror stories in Western culture at large.

Horror has been a part of popular culture since the turn of the nineteenth century. Twitchell (1985) suggests that we are currently in the midst of a revival of horror in popular culture. The genre is everywhere: in music videos, in books, in painting, on television (almost half the made-for-TV movies in North America are 'terror-jerkers'), and even in breakfast cereals ('Count Chocula' and 'Frankenberry'). What does it mean? Twitchell creates a Freudian analysis to suggest that horror monsters frighten us because they are acting out those desires that we fear; that may well be. It is clear, however, that the classic horror stories of Count Dracula, Frankenstein's mother, the Phantom of the Opera, and werewolves are all stories of male aggressors who seek female victims, and that the pleasurable emotion horror excites is a form of fear.

Twitchell (1985) writes that in preparing to undertake his book on horror he watched hundreds of hours of film and video that was much like pornography. It was rife with misogyny, incest, rape, and aggressive antisocial behavior directed against women. He notes that in the horror movies of the 1930s sexual violence was never displayed on the screen, 'but it was always there; we're just now getting a good look at it' (p. 70). Modern horror films include such genres as 'slice and dice' and 'stalk and slash' films, in which women are pursued, stabbed and dismembered. Twitchell quotes Gene Siskel, film critic for *The Chicago Tribune*, who believes that it is not coincidental that these films have proliferated in the years in which the Women's Movement has flourished. These films have a clear message: women should get back in line.

The New Town girls often enjoyed reading horror stories. Horror was accessible entertainment; They could read the horror novels their parents bought and watch the horror movies their parents rented. They could find 'scary' and 'spooky' books in the school library. Indeed, the girls said they loved 'scary' books as much as they loved 'sad' books. But 'scary' library books were in many ways quite different from horror movies, and the girls did sometimes encounter horror stories that upset them profoundly. What was the difference?

The Horror-in-Literature Continuum

Jerrica said, 'I love to read scary things that give me the shivers in bed. Have you ever read *Blind Date*? I don't know who the author is, but it was pretty scary.'

Alisa said, 'I love mysteries and scary books. But not too scary, because then they give me bad dreams. *Deadly Rhyme*, that book about the mystery in the boarding school that I gave you to read, that one was just right.'

What do Jerrica and Alisa 'love'? Walkerdine (1984) has shown how fiction for girls presents fantasies through the use of textual devices which engage with the desires of the reader. She suggests that readers live through fictional fantasy experiences which are real in psychic terms. The data for this study show that the New Town girls desired agency, and that the fiction they read allowed them to fulfill that desire for agency through fantasy. It may be that 'scary' books and mysteries also allowed them to fulfill desires for adventure and excitement. There may also be, for some girls, connections with the desire for sexual experience and fulfillment. Jerrica and Marcia, for example, were fascinated by *Flowers in the Attic*. They pored over all the books in the series. It would not be wise to overlook the fact that these novels contain sexual scenes between the two older children that are designed to be both sentimental and titillating. Episodes of abuse alternate with episodes of self-conscious nudity, declarations of devotion, and lengthy expressions of physical affection that are meant to be erotic. The mix of the sexual and the violent may have led these young readers to associate the two. It may be that the threat of violence was enough to awaken the sexual association in the minds of the New Town girls.[4]

The New Town girls were fascinated with the details of this plot, but also felt revulsion. Lacey said, 'At first I liked *Flowers in the Attic* because everyone else did. But it turned out to be so slow to read, and really disgusting. I quit reading it.'

Clearly, there are broad differences among texts. The mysteries and the scary books the girls enjoyed so much are distant relatives of the 'stalk and slash' horror movies. Like the horror movies, they often featured an element of threat directed at a girl or woman. In the girls' novels the female protagonist often found herself in a graveyard at night, in a murky fog, or in a dark old house. There was always the possibility that something unnamed and unknown might jump at her. But in these books, that happened very rarely. And when something did jump out at her, it often turned out to be harmless: a friend who followed her there, or a bat on the wing.

The *Nancy Drew Files* were instances of this kind of 'scary book'. Cara described the Nancy Drew plots this way:

There's always some boy in the story who's trying to kill her or one of her girlfriends. He's always hanging around in the background some-where. Sometimes they even put him on the cover.

Alisa noticed this too. The Nancy Drew covers looked the same.

Nancy Drew, of course, always solved the mystery. That was always the same too. And although the grade six girls still occasionally read a Nancy Drew, they all felt they'd outgrown them. The focal girls for this study, all of whom read easily and well, had turned to the Young Adult racks for their mysteries. Many of these 'scary books' were highly satisfactory. But some were very upsetting. Samantha found *The Trouble With Wednesdays* on the Young Adult rack.

The Trouble With Wednesdays moved one step further along the horror-in-literature continuum in which the gender threat grew more and more explicit. In this book the female protagonist did *not* solve her problem through her own agency. Her parents solved it for her. In this way the book was like the *Sweet Valley High* books *Hostage!* and *All Night Long*, in which Jessica was faced with the possibility of rape, but was rescued by luck and by her sister Elizabeth.

Marcia enjoyed the Young Adult mysteries, but she also took an interest in the books that seem to be at the next step in the horror-in-literature continuum: the adult horror novel. Marcia read her mother's John Saul and Stephen King novels and enjoyed them very much. She said she preferred John Saul's books because they were more like mysteries, and things were always good at the ending. Evidently, it disturbed Marcia that Stephen King sometimes left things unresolved at the end of a story. The horror was not always eliminated, nor was it always fully understood.

The girls seemed to have different levels of tolerance for horror. Alisa and Samantha were perhaps the most sensitive to frightening things. Julie enjoyed mysteries, but said she read the beginning of a Stephen King novel at home and had a nightmare. Her mother warned her not to look at Stephen King again for a good long while.

Sometimes horror was *too* horrifying, even for Marcia, who had the highest tolerance for horror among the sixth grade girls. When Marcia's parents rented three Freddy Kruger movies (the *Nightmare on Elm Street* series) over the Christ-mas vacation, Marcia watched them all and was sorry she did. She spoke about it.

Freddy Kruger, like people burnt him and then he comes back and he's like a ghost, and he's got razor blades for fingers and he chops people up and when he was alive he used to take girls and he used to kill them in a broiler! ... After I saw that, I couldn't eat. It was disgusting. And I couldn't sleep for two weeks. Sometimes he comes back with you in your dream, and when you wake up he's still there. And he's in your house and stuff. . . . You're helpless.

If Nancy Drew was at one end of the horror continuum for children, Freddy Kruger was at the other. Different children could tolerate different kinds of horror, and it seemed that, like adults, they learned to tolerate more and more violence and gender threat as they moved along the continuum in their reading and viewing choices. What was it they felt in moving along the horror continuum?

It is likely that women and men feel different things in response to horror. Twitchell (1985) has studied the audiences at horror movies and reports that among the large proportion of teenagers in the audience, teenage women often call out warnings to the female victims on the screen. Some of the teenage men join them. But other teenage men and nearly all the older men in horror audiences call out encouragement to the stalker. The movie is nearly always filmed from the stalker's point of view.

If the horror audience is invited to identify with the monstrous aggressor, men who grow up in a patriarchal culture may be able to do so. They would then be able to find pleasure in the feelings of power and dominance and gratification that come to the horror protagonist. But it is not likely that women who grow up in a patriarchal culture would feel immune from the threat to the female that is central to the horror story. On the contrary, for women, it would be much easier to identify with her helplessness.

The New Town girls were best able to tolerate mystery stories in which the heroine was able to understand and control whatever threatened her. They were disturbed by tales in which the heroine had to rely on others for protection from threat. And they were truly horrified by senseless violence directed at helpless people.

Variations on the Theme

Flowers in the Attic is not a classic horror story. No weird monster threatens and stalks a female victim. Instead an ordinary mother is transformed into an emotionless, greedy madwoman who imprisons her four children in the attic. There she and her mother starve and mistreat them for a period of two years. *Flowers in the Attic* is a story of child abuse.

While the grade six girls at New Town School devoted themselves to discussing *Flowers in the Attic*, Meryl Streep's new movie *Cry in the Dark* was released. This movie told the story of an Australian woman accused of murdering her baby. That week a child abuse case concluded when a lawyer was convicted of beating his 5-year-old daughter to death. *People* magazine had covered the trial. M.H. Clark's novel *The Cradle Will Fall* appeared in Marcia's desk at school. People seemed to be fascinated with stories of child abuse. Perhaps stories of child abuse are a new form of horror.

If so, they are not gendered horror stories in the same way that classic horror stories are gendered. They do not confine themselves to male aggressors and female victims. They are still stories of aggressors and victims, of the powerful preying upon the powerless. These grade six girls, who routinely read fiction and helped themselves to their mother's books, tried hard not to see themselves as powerless people, but they knew that as children they were nearly powerless in relation to the adults in their lives. Boys, as children, were powerless in this way too. But the New Town boys were not reading and discussing and dwelling on stories of child abuse in the same way the girls were. Reading fictional stories of child abuse may have reinforced girls' feelings of powerlessness much as other kinds of horror stories did.

Pornography associates the sexual and the violent. While horror mixes sex and violence and is intended to provoke fear, pornography mixes sex and violence and is intended to provoke sexual arousal. It becomes hard to distinguish between the 'stalk and slash' subgenre of horror and most extreme hard-core pornographic films where women are chained and slashed and put through meat grinders. It is interesting to note that in recent years more pornography has been produced involving children.

The New Town girls did not seem to have access to hard-core pornography. They did, however, have access to horror stories where the powerless were exploited. They were learning to enjoy horror. They were being encouraged and they were encouraging each other to move along a continuum of horror stories that began with female characters who could understand and control what threatened them and ended with victims who were horribly abused and finally obliterated.

Conclusion: Desire for Agency and the Gender Threat

The children of New Town were acquiring the beliefs about complementary agency taken for granted in their culture. They looked forward to being grown up, because it appeared to them that grown-ups had the ability to exercise power, to act and produce an effect on the world. Grown-ups seemed to be instrumental in shaping the world around them and these children at 11 would like to have been. They felt their lack of instrumentality keenly. Children of both genders desired agency.

The desire for agency develops as older children begin to understand their own powerlessness at the hands of adults and become less able to take it for granted. The culture promises agency to children as a part of adult status, but it promises gendered forms of agency. Generally speaking, boys expect to grow up to become men who will act as agents in the world at large, and wield economic and political power. Girls expect to grow up and become women who will act as agents within the family and wield power in personal relationships. It is not surprising that female children are not entirely satisfied with that arrangement. They too would like to grow up to have a wider influence in the world.

Reading fiction was an approved activity for 12-year-old girls in New Town. Romances and girls' series books promoted the notions of female agency approved by the culture at large. But this did not mean that girls passively accepted those notions of female agency. The girls of New Town sometimes resisted the culture's notions of female agency. They *used* their reading of fiction to explore other types of agency and to imagine themselves using other forms of power.

But, as Lankshear and Lawler (1987) have suggested is possible, in reading fiction they also used literacy in a way that worked against their own best interests. Their reading became a form of 'improper literacy'. Through their reading they not only fantasized about exercising agency; they also repeatedly engaged with aggressor/victim motifs that inspired feelings of horror and revulsion in response to images of violence and powerlessness. They became, in all likelihood, less able to act upon their desires for agency.

Walkerdine (1984) throws light upon this psychic conflict, which arises in response to cultural messages implicit in the fiction girls read. She suggests that when girls read fiction, 'the positions and relations created in the text both relate to existing social and psychic struggle and provide a fantasy vehicle which inserts the reader into the text' (p. 165). Girls can imagine themselves as powerless, as victims.

Reading fiction is one site in which children can confront their culture and construct its meanings for their individual lives. Reading fiction is a social practice through which children seek to understand their own places in the world. The New Town girls took the books the culture produced for them and used them to try on and analyze forms of behavior that went beyond what was culturally approved for them. They accepted and they resisted.

But the culture countered that resistance by providing horror stories. Horror may mean different things to women and to men and to people of different ages. To the sixth grade girls of New Town, it seemed to convey messages of female helplessness at the hands of a pervasive and gendered threat of violence. The threat was gendered because the violence was associated with sexuality in the horror stories and in the culture. The girls learned to associate violence and sexuality when sexual titillation was included in the mysteries and the horror novels they read. And so mysteries and horror stories (some of them) were fun to read.

But Freddy Kruger was still disgusting. The message of powerlessness and helplessness that the extremes of horror conveyed were too painful for the girls to tolerate. And yet, at the age of 11, they were taking in the message in gentler forms: Girls are not free agents. Moving in the world is dangerous. There are forces out there that will get you if you don't watch out.

Notes

1 The reader is referred to Cherland (1990) for a more complete description of the study, and for a detailed discussion of the methodology and the issues it has raised.
2 Thorne (1986) discusses at length the separation of girls and boys in elementary schools, especially in the upper elementary grades. She makes the point that dress and demeanor and *activities* have more to do with the cultural meanings of 'girl' and 'boy' than do their physical characteristics or their sexual behaviors. Cherland (1990) found that many activities in New Town were considered more appropriate for one gender than the other, perhaps because the genders were seen to be opposites. Sports for the most part belonged to the boys. Reading fiction for the most part belonged to the girls.

3   Ellsworth (1984) explains how, in a similar way, a group of feminist women interpreted a film for their own purposes and in opposition to the interpretation intended by the film's makers. She found that these women, sharing a common political orientation and beliefs about women's oppression, formed an interpretive community in considering the film *Personal Best*. They opposed the film industry's suggested pre-reading of the film and inflected it with their own oppositional readings. The data for this study show that the New Town girls also formed an interpretive community and developed their own oppositional readings of mass-marketed fiction.

4   Adrienne Rich (1970) has said, 'When you strike the chord of sexuality in the patriarchal psyche, the chord of violence is likely to vibrate in response, *and vice versa.*' (The emphasis is ours.)

References

ANDERSON, G.L. (1989) 'Critical ethnography in education: Origins, current status and new directions', *Review of Educational Research*, **59**, pp. 249–70.

ANYON, J.M. (1984) 'Intersections of gender and class: Accommodation and resistance by working-class and affluent females to contradictory sex role ideologies', *Journal of Education*, **166**(1) pp. 25–47.

BROWNMILLER, S. (1975) *Against our Will: Men, Women and Rape*, New York, Simon and Schuster.

CHERLAND, M. (1990) *Girls and Reading: Children, Culture, and Literary Experience*, Unpublished doctoral dissertation, Arizona State University, Tempe.

CHRISTIAN-SMITH, L.K. (1987) 'Gender, popular culture, and curriculum: Adolescent romance novels as gender text, *Curriculum Inquiry*, **17**(4) pp. 365–406.

CHRISTIAN-SMITH, L.K. (1989) *Going Against the Grain: Gender Ideology in Selected Children's Fiction*. Paper presented at the annual meeting of the American Educational Research Association at San Francisco, March.

ELLSWORTH, E. (1984) 'The power of interpretive communities: Feminist appropriations of *Personal Best* (Doctoral dissertation, University of Wisconsin, 1984) *Dissertation Abstracts International*, **45**, p. 1225.

FINE, M. (1988) 'Sexuality, schooling, and adolescent females: The missing discourse of desire', *Harvard Educational Review*, **58**(1) pp. 29–52.

GILBERT, P. (1983) 'Down among the women: Girls as readers and writers, *English in Australia*, June, pp. 26–27.

GILBERT, P. (1987) 'Post reader-response: The deconstructive critique', In B. CORCORAN and E. EVANS (Eds) *Readers, Texts and Teachers*, Montclair, NJ, Boynton/Cook, pp. 234–250.

GILBERT, P. (1990) *Fashioning the Feminine: Reading Dolly Fiction*. Paper presented at the 15th Australian Reading Association National Conference at Canaberra, April.

GILLIGAN, C., LYONS, N.P. and HANMER, T.J. (Eds) (1989) *Making Connections: The Relational Worlds of Adolescent Girls at Emma Willard School*, Troy, NY, Emma Willard School.

GITLIN, A., SIEGEL, M. and BORU, K. (1989) 'The politics of method: From leftist ethnography to educative research', *Qualitative Studies in Education*, **2**(3) pp. 237–53.

HOSKINS, J. (1987) 'Complementarity in this world and the next: Gender and agency in Kodi mortuary ceremonies', in M. STRATHERN (Ed.) *Dealing with Inequality*, Cambridge, Cambridge University Press, pp. 174–206.

LANKSHEAR, C. and LAWLER, M. (1987) *Literacy, Schooling, and Revolution*, New York, Falmer Press.

LATHER, P. (1986) 'Research as praxis', *Harvard Educational Review*, **56**(3) pp. 257–77.

McROBBIE, A. (Ed.) (1989) *Zootsuits and Second-hand Dresses: An Anthology of Fashion and Music*, New York, Unwin Hyman.

RADWAY, J. (1984) *Reading the Romance: Women, Patriarchy, and Popular Literature*, Chapel Hill, University of North Carolina Press.

REED, T. (1989) *Demon Lovers and their Victims in British Fiction*, Lexington, University of Kentucky Press.

RICH, A. (1979) *On Lies, Secrets, and Silence: Selected Prose, 1966–1978*, New York, W.W. Norton.

TAYLOR, S. (In press) 'Some further thoughts about "girl number twenty": Feminist classroom practice and cultural politics', *Discourse*.

THORNE, B. (1986) 'Girls and boys together . . . but mostly apart: Gender arrangements in elementary schools', in W.W. HARTUP and Z. RUBIN (Eds) *Relationships and Development*, Hillsdale, NJ, Erlbaum, pp. 167–83.

TWITCHELL, J.B. (1985) *Dreadful Pleasures: An Anatomy of Modern Horror*, New York, Oxford University Press.

WALKERDINE, V. (1984) 'Someday my prince will come: Young girls and the preparation for adolescent sexuality', in A. McROBBIE and M. NAVA (Eds) *Gender and Generation*, Houndmills, McMillan, pp. 162–184.

WEILER, K. (1988) *Women Teaching for Change: Gender, Class and Power*, South Hadley, MA, Bergin and Garvey.

Fiction Mentioned in the Text

ALEXANDER, L. (1964) *Book of Three*, New York, Dell.

ANDREWS, V.C. (1982) *Flowers in the Attic*, New York, G.K. Hall Paperback.

ANDREWS, V.C. (1987) *Petals on the Wind*, New York, Pocket Books, Inc.

BURNETT, F.H. (1938) *The Secret Garden*, New York, Harper and Row.

CLARK, M.H. (1983) *The Cradle Will Fall*, New York, Dell.

GEORGE, J.C. (1972) *Julie of the Wolves*, New York, Harper and Row.

GONZALES, G. (1986) *Deadly Rhyme*, New York, Dell.

MARTIN, A. (1987) *Mary Anne Saves the Day*, New York, Scholastic.

NATHANSON, L. (1987) *The Trouble with Wednesdays*, New York, Bantam.

PASCAL, F. (1989) *All Night Long*, Lakeville, CT, Grey Castle.

PASCAL, F. (1986) *Hostage!* New York, Bantam.

PASCAL, F. (1989) *Out of Reach*, Lakeville, CT, Grey Castle.

PFEFFER, S.B. (1977) *Kid Power*, New York, F. Watts.

SAUL, J. (1988) *The Unloved*, New York, Bantam.

STINE, R.L. (1986) *Blind Date*, New York, Scholastic.

Chapter 4

Sweet Dreams: Gender and Desire in Teen Romance Novels

Linda K. Christian-Smith

> It's just when you're reading you're in some other world, well, not really, physically, I mean but you imagine you are. Sometimes I feel like I am the person going on dates, having loads of fun (Annie, a 12-year-old White middle-class American romance fiction reader).

When I was the same age as Annie, my world revolved around the current novel I was reading. I had exhausted the books in the children's section of the public library some years earlier and was thrilled to find the titles I had dreamed about reading someday in my junior high school library. I read several books at the same time, going from novel to novel as I desired. For hours at a time, I lived in other worlds, becoming Elizabeth at Sir William Lucas's ball, imagining my awkward adolescent body moving with the grace of a well-brought-up young English woman. Instead of my usual spurning of dresses and frills, I took pleasure in the satin and lace of my ball gown. For weeks I dreamed of finding a local Mr Darcy who would take me away from my small stifling Midwestern United States hometown. With the change of a book I became Captain Nemo, roaming the seas without home and warmth, but with a passion born of oppression. As Nemo, I was powerful, brilliant and in control of my life. I no longer needed a Mr Darcy to shape my destiny. I also imagined myself as the dead Mrs Nemo, resurrected in my imagination to navigate the sub and right all wrongs in partnership with the man I loved. The language of fiction shaped my desires and positioned me in multiple gender discourses then and now. Although Annie, myself, and the other young women readers I discuss in this chapter are separated by several generations, there are threads connecting our experiences with fiction.

While reading we dream of identities and pleasures beyond what is possible and escape everyday realities. This is especially true of fictional forms like the teen romance novels Annie reads, which encourage fantasies of love and sexuality and allow young womens' passions an expression. According to Kaplan (1986, p. 117), reading is 'a sexually divided practice' which explores power relations, shapes desire, constructs femininities, and demarcates sexual differences. Popular fiction often confirms conventional femininities that carefully circumscribe women's possibilities. It may also contain fissures in the texts and oppositional elements that invite readers to 'read against the grain', thereby reflecting on sexual differences and traversing the female/male gender dualisms (Christian-Smith, 1990). Teen romance fiction has other dimensions. These books are not innocent sagas of hearts and flowers, but are an 'area of negotiation' in the ideological struggles in the United States for young women's hearts, minds, and desires.[1] These struggles are personal, economic and above all, political.

When Annie and other young women read American teen romance novel lines like *Sweet Dreams, First Love, Crosswinds,* and *Wildfire,* they become parts of a fictional world where men give meaning and completeness to women's lives and women's destinies are to tend heart and hearth. If girls have interests other than boys in these books, the interests are subordinated to the important task of getting and keeping a boyfriend. To this end, girls spend hours before the mirror transforming themselves into visions of beauty. The 'Cinderella' and 'Sleeping Beauty' metaphors endlessly repeat themselves as boys give girls completeness at the moment of the first kiss. Girls are constructed as objects of other's desires with few desires of their own. Although in more recent titles an occasional career aspiration and questioning of boys' actions are allowed, these are mostly 'window dressing' to accomodate changing social relations.

If this attitude sounds somewhat anachronistic in these times of women's supposed independence and parity with men in the United States, one needs only to recall these late twentieth-century truisms. Most American women still earn less than men, many women clock in from 9 to 9 between paid work and house-work, and that marriage and baby carriage are still the social experiences having the most currency for women.[2] The past ten years of the Reagan and Bush administrations have done much to perpetuate conventional gender sentiments through their pro-family policies and endorsement of traditional views of women associated with the New Right (Hunter, 1985). George Bush's veto of the 1990 Civil Rights Bill and his economic policies advantaging the rich continue the conservative legacy of Reaganism and the building of a conservative cultural and economic consensus. According to Hall (1985), a key factor in building this consensus is tapping into the needs, fears and desires of the public. The New Right has been quite successful in articulating fears over women's growing independence and changes in family form and authority relations (Hunter, 1984). However, the desires of many women for financial independence, political power, and more equitable relations with men represent counter-currents in this era of conservativism. The tensions and contradictions surrounding these struggles for popular consent are being played out in young women's reading of romance novels such as *P.S. I Love You, Love at First Sight,* and *Against the Odds.*

In this chapter, I discuss how teen romance novels constructed the gender, class, racial, ethnic and sexual subjectivities of twenty-nine middle and working-class young American women, ages 12 through 15, from diverse racial and ethnic backgrounds. Through reproducing and analyzing the words of these readers, I demonstrate how they negotiate the relation of their fantasy lives to their lived experiences and attempt to refashion the latter through imagining other possibilities. I discuss the relation of romance novel reading in schools to readers' future expectations as women and analyze how the political climate of the larger society and the classroom shape and constrain the production of meaning and desire. I begin by providing a context for romance fiction in schools by linking the recent political events in the United States discussed above with the romance publishing industry.

The Politics of Popular Fiction

Coward (1984, p. 13) notes that being a woman means having one's desires constantly shaped, courted, packaged and lured by discourses that often sustain male privilege. It means being the object of desire of the corporate sector which spends several billions of dollars yearly to woo women to consume. Young women are not exempt from these campaigns. Whenever they pick up teen romance novels, they enter the world of a 500 million dollar a year industry (Market Facts, 1984) whose stock in trade is fantasies of love and cultivating conscious and unconscious desires to be cherished and for clothes, videos, CDs, and cosmetics. Teen romance novels are 'packaged desire'. The word 'packaged' best describes teen romance fiction as they are the product of astute mass-marketing from cover to cover. The rise of teen romance novels to the third most widely read young adult genre in the United States (Market Facts, 1984) in only ten years is part of two intertwined stories in which desire is wedded to politics.[3] Teen romance fiction appeared at the moment of the shift in the political climate of the United States to conservativism. I am not implying an outright conspiracy here. Rather, many segments of the culture industry, particularly publishing, have been acquired by multinational corporations[4] whose interests are politically conservative. These interests make their way into publishing through business practices and the very content of books (Christian-Smith, 1986).

In 1981 Ronald Reagan was elected president of the United States. In the same year, the first new teen romance series, *Wildfire*, a proven seller in school bookclubs, became available in the bookstores. The concept of romance fiction written for teens dates back to the 1940s and 1950s, when Betty Cavanna, Maureen Daly, and Rosamond du Jardin wrote books focusing on young women's first love experiences. The new romances have reappeared in the midst of several large-scale mergers within educational and trade publishing that have had the effect of endowing profit and loss sheets with a new importance (Coser, Kadushin and Powell, 1982). Other changes are apparent. Editors in the old-fashioned sense are no longer key people. Rather, professional managers with business or legal backgrounds now occupy key decision-making positions. A consistent worry expressed by insiders in publishing is that this business mentality may be narrowing the range of books published, making it difficult for initially unprofitable but important books to be published (Turow, 1978; Whiteside, 1981). Teen romances are a response to dominant publishing interests that center on profitability and instant appeal (Retan, 1982).

One way in which publishers today increase their profit margins is to culti-vate constantly new reader markets, and develop new books for existing ones (Shatzkin, 1982). Harty (1979) notes that the schools have historically constituted a lucrative market for publishers. According to *Publishers Weekly*, in 1984 the schools spent 695.6 million dollars on books, making the schools the third largest account — only surpassed by general retailers and college bookstores. Although textbooks comprise the bulk of these sales, the trade division is growing steadily as more schools use these general interest books for instruction along with or in place of textbooks.[5] Teenage romance fiction is a case of publishers developing new readers and books within a steady market. It is the product of school book club (TAB) market research conducted by Scholastic Inc., a leader in the el-hi (elementary and high school) market, regarding which books were most frequently ordered by young women readers (Lanes, 1981). Teen romance novels such as Silhouette's *First Love* are written to a formula specified by Silhouette Books through a 'tip sheet' (Silhouette Books, 1981). These guidelines specify romance with some sensuality, although 'not graphic detail'. The plot should focus on 'the disparity between the heroine's romantic fantasies and reality, and her own desire to define herself as a person'. No slang or dialect is permitted and values should be 'humanistic'. The aim is to give teens 'a good, light read that includes young characters, contemporary situations and universal themes' all within ten chapters. The schools are further connected to these romance novels as important points of distribution.

Pick up a Troll or TAB school book club order flier or a catalog of adolescent tradebooks for the classroom and you will see teen romance novels on every page. Teen romance novels are components of a highly lucrative segment of educational publishing, the Hi-Low market, which is comprised of books with 'interesting' content and limited difficulty of reading aimed at 'reluctant readers'.[6] Reluctant readers are often students who may be able to read, but refuse to because they are disinterested in reading materials, or have some actual reading difficulties (Otto, Peters and Peters, 1977). Aulls (1978) suggests that reluctant readers can be best taught to read using Hi-Low materials. Series romance fiction shares all the characteristics of many Hi-Lows, especially the differentiation of content on the basis of gender. For example, Scholastic's *Action* books feature mystery and adventure for boys and romance, dating and problem novels for girls. The demand from teachers and librarians for reluctant-reader materials has increased in the wake of the recent national debate about both the imputed difficulty of many students in learning to read, and their boredom with standard reading texts such as basals.[7]

However, the appearance of romance fiction has not been without controversy. Lanes (1981) notes that in her interviews with educators, parents, and librarians general reactions ranged from annoyance to rage. Romance fiction has been criticized for its 'limited roles for females' and their depiction of 'a narrow, little world' in which virtue is rewarded with the right boy's love (Lanes, 1981). The most vocal critics, The Council on Interracial Books for Children, claims that the books teach young women to put boys' interests above their own, encourage young women to compete against each other for boys, and depict the life of suburban White middle-class nuclear families (Harvey, 1981). Others identify the new romance fiction with the political ideology of the New Right.[8] Conservative elements have criticized the teen romances for promoting promiscuity through the sexual tension between girls and boys in the novels that stops at the first kiss. The novels keep readers excited and turned on sexually (Madsen, 1981). Still others have criticized the way in which romance fiction gets into the hands of young readers — primarily through school bookclubs (Pollack, 1981).

Despite these controversies and adults' misgivings, teen romance fiction remains a force to be reckoned with. It is immensely popular with young women readers, and is important in constructing young women's femininities and desires.

The Research Context

During an eight-month period in 1985–86, I studied teen romance-fiction readers in three schools in a large American Midwestern city that I will call 'Lakeview'.[9]

Once dominated by the automobile, farm-equipment and alcoholic-beverage industries, the economic crisis of the late 1970s left its imprint on the city and surrounding communities. Plant closings have transformed Lakeview from a smokestack blue-collar city to one of empty factories and glittering strip-malls. Most new businesses are in the service sector, such as fast-food and insurance companies, which employ the bulk of the working and middle-class teenagers, women and men in Lakeview.

Lakeview School District is a large district that draws students from the inner city and some of the outlying areas that were annexed to the city thirty years ago. My sites of research were Jefferson Middle School and Sherwood Park Middle School, two outlying grade 7–8 schools, and Kominsky Junior High School, an inner city grade 7–9 school. Students were bussed or walked to Jefferson and Sherwood Park. A majority of Kominsky students were bussed to school. At the time of the study, Lakeview was in the process of converting the junior high schools into middle schools. Jefferson and Sherwood Park each had about 300 students. Sherwood Park's student population was mostly White. Like Sherwood Park, Jefferson was predominately White, but had some Black and Chinese students. Kominsky's over 700 students broke down into about one-half White, one-quarter each Black and Hispanic, with a small Vietnamese and Asian Indian population. Both Jefferson and Sherwood Park split their students into three tracks (low, medium and high)[10] for reading instruction. Reading placements were based on the results of the following: district-wide and individual-school standardized reading test scores, teacher recommendation, and students' previous grades. Kominsky and Sherwood Park also had an additional reading support service through the federally funded Chapter I program, which enrolled one-half and one-quarter, respectively of their students.[11]

In order to study romance-fiction readers I used a variety of methods combining ethnography with survey research.[12] An initial sample of seventy-five young women from the three schools was assembled through interviews with teachers and librarians regarding who were heavy romance-fiction readers and by personal examination of school and classroom library checkout cards and book club order forms.[13] A reading survey[14] was given to all seventy-five young women. From this survey, I was able to identify the heaviest romance-fiction readers, some twenty-nine young women, whom I interviewed individually and in small group settings. These twenty-nine young women had five teachers for reading in the three schools. I observed these classes and interviewed these teachers. This chapter stems from the written reading survey of the seventy-five young women, and from observation of and interviews with the twenty-nine young women and their five teachers.

Teen Romance Fiction and School Daze

Who reads teen romance fiction? My reading survey shows that at Jefferson and Sherwood Park, the novels tended to be read by White middle-class young women aged 12 through 15, and to a lesser degree, by Black, Hispanic and Asian young women at all three schools.[15] At Jefferson and Sherwood Park, romance novels accounted for 36 percent of all books checked out from school libraries and ordered through book clubs as compared to 25 percent at Kominsky. This is in keeping with recent book industry surveys that have placed romance fiction within the top three kinds of books that adolescents read, superseded by mystery and adventure books (Market Facts, 1984). Another characteristic of readers concerns how readers were grouped for reading instruction. The twenty-nine heaviest readers of romances were identified by school personnel as 'reluctant' or 'slow' readers and were tracked into remedial or low ability reading classes.[16] In the three schools, the girls who most often read romance novels were also reluctant readers. These twenty-nine girls were barely passing their courses. They were characterized by counselors and teachers as being more interested in boys than in academics, as young women who would have difficulty completing the remainder of their schooling and who would in all probability, marry early and be young mothers.

The twenty-nine young women's five reading teachers provided much insight into the complexity of teen romance fiction in schools. Three teachers were aware of the national controversy surrounding these books, and all felt some degree of apprehension regarding their use. The contradictory position of teachers is nicely illustrated by the observations of Mrs M (Kominsky) and Mrs K (Sherwood Park), both White middle-class teachers:[17]

> I feel guilty about letting the girls order these books through TAB [a school book club]. I read a couple of them once. They are so simple and the characters in the novels are stereotypes. You know, Mom at home in her apron, Dad reading the paper with his feet up. But the girls seem to like the books, and the classroom sure is quiet when they're reading them.

> The girls just love them [romance novels]. I see them reading their books in study hall and even in lunch. Can you believe that! I'm just happy that they are reading, period.

The romance-novel reading in these teachers' classrooms was the outcome of factors indicating the delicate interplay of readers' desires to have power over one aspect of their schooling. The teachers' overwhelming desire to see students reading and reasonably interested in books generated Mrs K's idea that 'any reading was better than no reading'. Teachers were also under tremendous pressure from the administration to improve students' measured reading scores. In the case of the Chapter I teachers, Mrs K and Mrs M, those scores were key ingredients in retaining yearly federal funding of their programs, and by implication, their jobs. All five teachers conceded the difficulty of keeping order in classrooms where students resisted instruction. Securing students' consent to read voluntarily made teachers' lives in the classroom 'tolerable'.

Most romance novel reading occurred during independent study, which was in great abundance as instruction was mostly organized around individual-learning models to provide for the specific needs and interests of each student. This was especially the case in Sherwood Park and Kominsky. During the usual classroom period in each school, students read or worked on skill sheets. Student and teacher interactions were mostly limited to correcting skill sheets, updating reading folders, giving directions, and answering procedural questions. Students mostly read privately and rarely shared their reading with their teachers or other students.[18]

Although most books were student-selected, teachers attempted to influence book choice by categorizing books as 'quality'[19] award-winning books[20] or 'fluff' books, like romances. That students did not automatically accept teachers' authority regarding book choice is illustrated by Mrs B, a White middle-class Kominsky Chapter I teacher, and four of her students. As a strong advocate of 'quality' teen literature, Mrs B's room was crammed with an array of 'quality' paperbacks, magazines, and newspapers. No romance fiction was to be found in this classroom library. The young women brought romance fiction from home or libraries, and often bought them from mail-order book clubs. Mrs B more or less tolerated the romances in her classroom. This tolerance was the outcome of both pressure from the administration to show reading gains and protest from the four young women.

Of all the teachers, Mrs B felt most apprehensive about granting any legitimacy to romance fiction. She fit the romances into her 'quality literature' perspective by striking a bargain with her students: for every romance novel read, a student must read another type of book. The reality was that Mrs B hoped to draw the interest of the young women away from the romance fiction so that they would expand their reading to 'quality' books. This tension was revealed in Mrs B's exhortation during weekly library visits to 'choose something good, something you'll want to stick with'. When students inquired into the reasons behind Mrs B's dislike of romances, she neither offered any explanation nor encouraged any critical dialogue with romance-fiction readers about their reading.

Four of Mrs B's students took matters into their own hands by fiercely championing romance-novel reading. Tina, a White working-class student, quoted Mrs B's words 'Read something interesting', to defend her choices. Tomeika and Jan, Black and White students from middle- and working-class backgrounds, respectively, supported their reading tastes by citing their mothers' devotion to the books. White middle-class Carol saw romance fiction as something truly pleasurable to read, in contrast to teacher-selected books:

> I like *Sweet Valley High* because the books Mrs B [my pseudonym] picks are so long and boring . . . I read a story about a girl stranded on this island and how she survives. [perhaps Scott O'Dell's *Island of the Blue Dolphins?*] It was interesting, but doesn't have much to do with my life. Get real! How many girls are stranded on islands in 1985? At least with *Sweet Valley* the stories are fun and I learn a lot about boys.

Finally, all four young women would continually languish over teacher-selected books, mutilating the pages and covers, and complaining how boring the books were. Or they would retire to the 'book-nook' and covertly read their favorite romances, which they had stashed among the floor cushions.

Romancing Readers

An amazing amount of romance-fiction reading was done by the twenty-nine young women. Allowing for the fact that some young women were more avid readers than others, the young women as a whole read an average of six romances a month at home and school.[21] However, these young women were not indiscriminate in their romance-fiction reading — that is, not just any romance novel would do.

Most of the young women were loyal to certain individual authors such as Stella Pevsner, Ellen Conford, Norma Fox Mazer and Francine Pascal. High on their lists were also romance-fiction lines such as Silhouette's *First Love* and *Blossom Valley*, Scholastic's *Wildfire* and Bantam's *Sweet Dreams* and *Sweet Valley High*. These novels were favored because they provided an easy and cheap way of securing books, through a book club. More important for Silhouette readers was the fact that Silhouette publishes a newsletter soliciting letters from readers. The young women viewed the newsletter as important because in the words of Val, a working-class Hispanic student at Kominsky,

> They [Silhouette] care about what we want in books ... I wrote once about a book I hated. I even got a letter back from Mrs Jackson [an editor]. Funny thing, nobody ever asks us our opinions about nothing.

That these opinion polls are part of Silhouette's sophisticated marketing program does not detract from the positive impact they had on these young women. The overall effect was to provide them with the experience of having their voices heard.

Why Young Women Read Romance Novels

In many ways, young women's reasons for reading romances (Christian-Smith, 1990) compare with those of adult romance-fiction readers in Radway's (1984) study. In both studies the reasons combined elements of fantasy, knowledge and pleasure. Underlying each of these elements is desire, the yearning to be recognized, possessed, powerful, and the longing for the other. Teen romance fiction as fantasy organizes desire and directs young women's desires towards an object of the opposite sex.[22] The seventy-five young women felt that romance fiction offered the following benefits:[23]

1. Escape, a way to get away from problems at home and school;
2. Better reading than dreary textbooks;
3. Enjoyment and pleasure;
4. A way to learn about romance and dating.

The fantasy of escaping problems emerged over and over again. Some young women recounted how romance novels provided them with the dream of a world different from their own: no family problems and always a solution to any conflict. Mary Jo, a 14-year-old White middle-class student at Sherwood Park, commented that the romance novels portrayed the world as 'I would like it to be'. The happy resolution of family problems in the romances of Francine Pascal was especially appealing to 12-year-old Carrie, a Black middle-class student at Kominsky. Carrie said:

In her books things get all mixed up like fights and other stuff, but basically people still love each other. I'd love to have a family like the Martins [in *My First Love and Other Disasters*]. Sometimes when I read I kind of pretend that the family in the story is my family.

Precisely why romance novel reading was highly valued in school is evident from the words of Claire, a White working-class student at Sherwood Park: 'It's really a bore 'round here. Readin' Sweet Valley turns the worst day into something special.' Furthermore, romance novel reading provided the young women with the space to engage in something truly pleasurable and personal during the school day. The books left them with the same good feelings as meeting with their friends at lunch and in the halls. The companionship of other students and romance reading sustained them through an otherwise tedious school day. Romance novel reading was often preferred to textbooks. Nancy, a White middle-class student at Jefferson made this comparison between her favorite romance fiction series to her social studies book:

I'll read *Crosswinds* any day. The stories are really interesting. . . . Social Studies? The book is so boring and who cares about a bunch of dates and battles.

There was yet another aspect of the pleasure of the text. This involved the positive feelings that came from becoming romance-fiction heroines while reading. Without exception, the heroine should be, according to Tomeika and Marge, both Black Kominsky students, middle- and working-class respectively, 'pretty, smart, and popular'.[24] Being recognized as someone special, with the qualities of niceness, intelligence, and humor, was important to these young women. They were all aware of the social and academic significance of their placement in low-ability reading classes, and many of them felt that their teachers did not see them as intelligent or nice people. Their desires to identify with a smart heroine coincided with the young women's desire to have teachers and other adults recognize them as nice and capable, despite their academic placement.

The romance novels also were connected with the pleasure young women derived from imagining themselves as the heroine of one of these novels. Through their reading, they lived out much of the specialness and excitement associated with being the object of a boy's affection. Much of this desire seemed to hinge on their perception of romantic relationships in fiction as eminently satisfying, with all minor misunderstandings eventually resolved. However, very few of the young women envisioned romance in everyday life as anything like romance fiction. Pam, a 15-year-old White working-class student at Jefferson, sums up the feelings of several of the young women:

Nobody has these neat boyfriends. I mean, most of the guys boss you around . . . and bash you if you look at somebody else. But it's fun to read the books and think that maybe someday you'll meet a really nice guy who'll be good to you.

The novels operated at a distance from young women's own lives and provided a comfort zone where there were no consequences for risking all for love.

This process of identification was also evident when there was a mismatch between the young women's own lived romances and those they encountered in fiction. Marge, a Black working-class student at Kominsky, claimed that most of the romances she read did not accurately portray romantic relationships as she encountered them in everyday life. By the same token, Marge wished the boys she knew were more like the boys in the novels: 'treatin'' you good. Not bossin'' you 'round and tryin'' to hit on you all the time.' Marge went on to note that young women would probably always have to 'fight off' the unwanted attention of boys, but that it would be nice to dream it could be otherwise. Through romance novel reading, Marge and Pam fantasized the ideal romance. Romance-fiction reading allowed both of these young women to transform present and future romantic relations in imagination, according to their aspirations.

The romances stimulated a desire in shy young women and those not dating to find out what romance was about in a risk-free manner. Trina, a 13-year-old Chinese middle-class student at Jefferson, noted that 'sometimes the way guys are in the books helps us girls understand them a lot better.' This primer quality of romance fiction found favor with 13-year-old Marita, a working-class Hispanic Kominsky student. Marita's reading provided a valuable source of information about romance. Marita's family strictly controlled her whereabouts. Neither she nor her sisters were permitted to date until they were 17 and her older sisters were not open with her about their experiences. Marita related that several of her friends were in similar situations and depended on the romance novels for information.[25]

That's My Desire

Readers had very definite ideas about what made up a good romance novel.[26] These centered on characteristics of the heroine and hero. The good romance novel has the following qualities:

1 It is easy to read.
2 It does not drag.
3 Its heroine and hero are cute, popular, and nice, and have money.
4 It has a happy ending.
5 In it young women are strong and get the best of boys.

The appeal of many of the series romances is that they contain about 150 to 175 action-packed pages of easy reading. The young women placed a premium on these structural characteristics and on their ease in relating the books to their lives. Pat, a White middle-class student at Jefferson, explained that the novels 'are sure easy to read. I know all the words and don't have to skip any of 'em.'

This preference for easy reading had unexpected consequences for the young women, however. Mrs T, a White middle-class reading teacher at Jefferson saw a reciprocal, reinforcing relationship between the romances and the young women's status in the schools:

> Some of the girls show great impatience at reading books that are long or contain a great deal of exposition. That's why they like romance

novels. Sure, they like to read about boys — that's all they have on their minds. But they do like anything that's easy and doesn't make them think. The romances are mindless drivel.

Young women also had definite ideas about what constituted an ideal heroine and hero. As mentioned previously, according to Tomeika and Marge, the heroine should be 'pretty, smart, and popular'. The preference for a popular heroine was closely linked to these young women's personal desires to be liked by both sexes in their everyday lives. Another priority was to be cherished and treated well by a nice boy. Those characteristics that helped heroines attract boys were precisely the ones they wished for in their own lives. The ideal hero had some similarities to the heroine. He should be 'cute', 'funny', 'strong', 'nice', 'have money', and 'come from a good home'. While cuteness was certainly important, niceness and strength were indispensable. 'Strength' for these women, did not have to do with physical prowess, but rather stood for an array of attributes such as courage, initiative and protectiveness. The young women were repelled by teenage versions of the 'macho man' in books and everyday experience. As Karen, a White middle-class student at Sherwood Park explained, 'when I read a book, the guy has to be nice, has to be, he has to treat his girlfriend and everybody with respect.' This notion of respect has much to do with the hero's being attuned to the heroine's needs and feelings. In these young women's real lives, there was the occasional boy who reminded them of the romance-novel hero, but mostly the boys they knew did not measure up to this ideal.

According to several young women, romance fiction should end happily, that is, the heroine and hero should have ironed out their difficulties, and become once again a couple by the end of the story. The overwhelming preference for a happy ending closely relates to the romance novel's power to involve the young women vicariously in the developing romance. Several of the older readers, who were romantically involved themselves, looked to romance fiction to provide in fantasy the hoped-for outcome of their own romances. Patty, a 15-year-old White working-class student at Kominsky exemplifies this position:

> It would be nice to think that Tommy and me would end up like Janine and Craig [the couple from the popular *Blossom Valley* series], you know, married with kids and having a nice home, car, and money.

The saga of this fictional couple's romance, separation, and eventual marriage held out to this reader the possibility of living happily ever after.

The final quality of a good romance novel was that it had to have a heroine who is strong and assertive, especially toward boys. May, a Black working-class Kominsky student, strongly expressed this sentiment: 'I've got no patience with girls who let boys walk all over them. Believe you me, no boy mess with me or he be sorry.' Linked with preference for assertive heroines was a distinct pleasure in reading about heroines who 'got the best of boys'. In this regard, Victoria Martin of *My First Love and Other Disasters* (by popular writer Francine Pascal) was mentioned by several young women as a heroine whose courage and forthrightness they admired. This notion of 'besting boys', 'keeping them in line', was most often applied to situations where the heroine knew best, when the hero was treading on 'female things' or trying to compel the heroine to do things against her beliefs.

So far I have indicated the fluid and often contradictory quality of these readers' interactions with texts. I will now discuss the dynamics at work during reading that help create the femininities of young working and middle-class women, but also provide them with the occasion for pondering their social identities as well.

All I Have to Do Is Dream

I want to return to my earlier observations on the role of the text in shaping and packaging gender meanings. Although readers' life experiences are important in constructing meanings when reading, the text still exerts a measure of control over those meanings. In this regard, Iser (1974, 1980) claims that part of the text's control happens through 'blanks' or gaps in the text. Many times the threads of the plot are suddenly broken off, as happens between chapters, or they continue in unexpected directions. These textual features are another device to encourage readers to 'read between the lines'. The blanks call for combining what has been previously read with readers' life experiences and making predictions regarding further developments in the story. Teen romance novels are written to formula and characterized by predictability. Readers quickly cue into the framework of the novels and use the redundancy to read according to one reader, on 'automatic pilot'. The formula and the blanks are ways of packaging or funneling meanings. However, the blanks also stimulate constitutive activity on the part of readers. When young women readers encounter blanks in romance texts that involve matters of femininity, three things occur. The blanks stimulate readers' desires to find out what happens next. Readers are often offered versions of femininity, but are also given opportunities to think about them. In the case of teen romance fiction readers, the blanks situate readers within competing subject positions and stimulate the analysis of relations between women and men. I illustrate these processes by recounting the readings by three young women of Marshall's (1985) *Against the Odds*.

Annie, Marcy and Nancy, three White middle-class eighth-grade students at Sherwood Park, all in Mrs J's reading class, had recently read *Against the Odds*. This novel describes the struggles of four young women, Trina, Laurie, Joyce and Marsha, who are among a group of twenty-five young women registering as new students at the all-male Whitman High School. This school's ninety-year history as an elite all-male college preparatory institution is about to change under court-mandated affirmative action, and the four young women have decided to attend Whitman because it has the strong math and computer-science curriculum their old school lacks. The young women are initially greeted with protest signs of 'No Girls at Whitman High!', catcalling, and constant harrassment. The young women confront the troublemakers and establish themselves as serious students. Trina in particular wins the respect, admiration and affection of the most hardboiled of all the boys, Chris Edwards. The novel ends with the vision of a romantically involved Trina and Chris, and with the promise of a more gentle 'battle of the sexes'.

All the young women agreed that heroine Trina Singleton caused them to think about themselves as young women. They aligned themselves with Trina and suffered her perils and eventual triumph. Nancy clearly expressed these ideas in her comments on her favorite romance heroine:

That's gotta be Trina Singleton in *Against the Odds*. Trina is the kind of person I want to be 'cause she's not afraid to fight for her rights, while another girl might chicken out.

Against the Odds has certain blanks that invite completion as part of the developing story and characterization. At one point, Trina and her friends have a plan to revenge themselves for all they have endured and to put a stop to the harrassment once and for all. Readers are left to contemplate what this plan might be for several pages, and even then it is only gradually unfolded. Annie filled the blanks in this manner:

A: It was fun trying to figure out what Trina and the other girls would do to get back at those boys. I thought that they would sneak into the boys' locker room and do something to their sports equipment. Marsha had the guts to do something like that.

LKCS: Was that something you might have done?

A: Are you kidding? No way! I'd never have the guts. Well, you'd have to do something, that's for sure. Hmm, I'd probably start a rumor about the guys or every time me and my friends would see them we would make like we were talking about them. They can't stand that!

Marcy's responses to the same passage also set up a conflict between who she is and who she would like to be:

M: I figured Trina and Laurie would come up with something fantastic. I never thought in a million years that they would stuff confetti drenched in cheap perfume into the boys' lockers.

LKCS: Would you do that, get even in this way?

M: Well, I'd like to do something like that, to get even with some of the boys in my math class who are real pains. But I'd get chicken and probably just fume.

LKCS: Can you tell me more?

M: It's kinda difficult, I mean, well, I guess I don't want to be seen as a girl who's too pushy with boys. You have to be careful about that. But then you can't let the boys push you around. I don't know.

Annie's and Marcy's hypothesizing revealed several things about the packaging of gender. For both young women, the blanks allowed them to imagine a course of action that trod a path between what was possible given the story they had constructed and what they thought would be possible given their imaginations and subjectivities. The way Annie filled in the unwritten portions of the text reveals that gender tensions exist and that young women are not passive victims. Her predicted plan and subsequent response show a view of femininity that allows for collective action against boys, but sets limits on how forceful that action may be. Marcy adopts a position in relation to the text that sharpens a tension within her femininity when she admires that characters' plan, but expresses doubt as to her own ability to act in a similar manner. Like Annie, she refuses a discourse of female powerlessness and negotiates how assertive women should be when it comes to men. The narrative resolutions of these readers and the resolution offered by the text are conservative and indicative of the practices many romance fiction readers use to 'fight back' (Radway, 1984). This is not to downplay the importance of the young women's interpretations which demonstrate the ambiguous places women occupy.

As the twenty-nine young women read their romance novels, they constructed a story that put on center stage their desires, hopes for, and fears of romance. They construct the selves they hoped to become with a keen awareness of dominant social expectations. While reading the romance-fiction text, the young women's past and present positions within the school influenced the gender positions they negotiated. Their school identities as reluctant readers, and staff's assumption that they would not finish school fueled their desires to be seen as capable. In the young women's estimation, the ability to read and comprehend romance fiction became a symbol of 'competent' femininity. The young women's reading refuted, in their minds, the judgments made by school personnel about their competence. Equally important was each young woman's alignment with heroines and becoming the object of a boy's desires. These constitute the contradictory and at times fragmenting gender positions young women construct in the course of their reading.

The young women's romance novel reading indicated how gender was negotiated in classrooms. Their identification with the assertive heroines and pleasure derived from the romance novels fueled their attempts to continue their reading at all costs. The young women's vision of the romance novel as a vehicle for instilling a certain vitality into their reading classes as less boring and more meaningful material was an attempt to have their voices heard and a bid to secure some power and control over one aspect of schooling. In Mrs B's class, students introjected into the reading curriculum a text that operates on the fringes of accepted instructional materials, as evident in teachers' previous comments. These actions exemplify how some women students negotiate the 'given curriculum' in an attempt to win space for materials that have meaning in their lives.

With romance novel reading as a symbol of their femininities, the young women brought 'gender pleasures' into the classroom. McRobbie (1978) claims that young women's pleasure has always been problematic in schools, whether it takes the form of flirting, wearing sexy clothes, or openly primping in the classroom. In a manner similar to Radway's (1984) Smithton readers, the young women took pleasure in their ability to make sense of the novels and to articulate what these stories were about. This feeling of competence was not one they usually experienced in school. The young women's reading of romance fiction refuted in their own minds the judgments made by school personnel about their competence. The act of making meaning allowed them to refuse, if only momentarily, their identities as reluctant readers.

The young women constantly used the romance novels to escape temporarily the problems and unhappiness associated with school and general life difficulties. On the whole, the young women were barely passing their courses.

Many experienced the strain and uncertainty of the downward economic trend in Lakeview. Their glimpses of an economy in trouble did not prevent many of the young women from dreaming of a secure and comfortable future to be achieved through a good marriage combined with their own employment. Although many of the young women were aware of the disjuncture between that world and their own, the novels provided the space for them to dream and construct reality as they would like it to be. The novels therefore played upon many young women's desires and yearnings for a different present and future.

Romance fiction packages a version of gender relations based on hetero-sexuality. Readers often identify with heroines and discursively become the heroines. This is evident in the comments of 12-year-old Annie, quoted at the beginning of this chapter. Jenny, a 14-year-old Black middle-class student at Jefferson, describes the impact that one novel, Quin-Harkin's (1981) *Princess Amy* has had on her:

> My favorite part is when the girl and the guy first kiss. That gives me a squishy feeling in my stomach, sorta like I'm actually there, being the girl that's gettin' kissed.

The reader's endorsement of these relations between the sexes affirms traditional gender relations. The young women never disputed the desirability of hetero-sexual romance; they tried to capture it over and over in their reading of other romance fiction and wished for this specialness in their own lives. This was even the case when the young women's relationships with boys were fraught with conflicts to such a degree that the only satisfying romance they could imagine was one occurring in a novel.

How does this view fit with the strong assertive heroines the young women preferred to read about? In many ways, the young women's version of feminine assertiveness was a bounded one, one constrained within traditional views. These young women could certainly 'best' boys in everyday life and in the world of romance fiction, but the bottom line was that one could not be 'too pushy' because this could result in alienating boys and destroying any romantic pros-pects. The latter was clearly something the young women would not do, even when boys did not treat them well, as was the case with Marge, May and Pam, or in the 'get even' fantasy of Annie. Hence, the young women's conception of the proper relationship between the sexes featured some assertiveness, along with staying in the good graces of boys.

Young women's romance-fiction reading is characterized by this tug of war between conventional femininity and more assertive modes. This tension was an important factor in shaping their class subjectivities as seen in the young women's thoughts on their futures in the world of work and at home.

Material Girls

The twenty-nine young women's class positions were reinforced through their views on work, marriage and children which fed into their romance-fiction read-ing. Working for pay while in school was important for most of these young women, since it was the ticket to consuming, which improved their chances for romance. Marriage and children were on the distant horizon, along with jobs. The young women's reading tapped into their desires for material things, and centered the gender, class and racial aspects of their identities around consumption.

Beautification with an eye to romance underlay the young women's wage work and consumption. The young women saw a direct relation between appearance, popularity and romance. All the young women endorsed Trina's notion that 'pretty girls get nice boyfriends'. Although having a nice personality was equally important, attractiveness was 'something that a girl could not do without' according to Karen, a White middle-class student at Sherwood Park. These beliefs were validated in their everyday lives. Patty, a White working-class Kominsky student echoed the sentiments of many of the twenty-nine young women: 'the prettiest and most popular girls here have their pick of the boys.' These descriptions of the linkages between a girl's popularity and her beauty were similar to the ways teen romance fiction depicts heroines.[27] The linking of beauty with romance not only motivated the young women's consumption, but also provided the reason for working for pay.

All the young women were involved in various kinds of casual work, like baby-sitting and performing odd jobs to augment allowances or earn any spending money at all. A kind of 'Horatia Alger' earnestness dominated their efforts to earn pocket money. Their earnings were spent on movies, fast food, records and videos, with the greater part going for clothes and beauty products. With larger allowances, the White, Black, and Chinese middle-class young women baby-sat to buy what Black middle-class Tomeika described as 'little extras; or 'something extravagant' that her allowance would not cover. For the White, Black, and Hispanic working-class young women, consumption was on a more limited scale. Pam, a White working-class Jefferson student commented:

> We've never had a lot of money to spend at home. After my dad lost his job, it was really bad. I bought most of my school clothes this year. This summer I baby-sat almost every night and mowed lawns in my neighborhood until my asthma got real bad.

Pam was one example of an amazing entrepreneurship among the working-class young women to earn pocket money in the face of little or no spending money from parents. This not only involved the usual baby-sitting, but also doing odd jobs and paid domestic work in homes where they baby-sat. The young women in general had plans to continue working in high school in retail sales, clerical work, or the fast-food industry to have more spending money. They saw having a job as making the difference between doing without and having money to spend. This reality collided with the world of the teen romance novel.

The covers of these novels speak of affluence and even luxury through teen models clad in the latest teen fashions. Open to almost any page and you will find affluent teens who are the proud owners of TVs, videos and motorbikes. Although most of the heroines do casual work, their families are economically stable. Girls are again positioned as the objects of desire. This time it is the corporate sector wooing readers to become material girls as they immerse themselves in the affluent world of the teen romance novel. This universe was a different world for the twenty-nine young women with whom I spoke. The working-class young women glimpsed this world as bystanders. The designer clothes, elaborate homes and glamorous vacations were not for them. Several middle-class young women saw this world slipping away. During the recent recession in Lakeview, many of these women's relatives had lost well-paying jobs, like Pam's father, and were unemployed or working for drastically reduced wages. Austerity hit the middle class as massive white-collar layoffs continued. These glimpses of an economy still in trouble did not prevent the young women from dreaming of a secure and comfortable future. The romances, with their economically secure world, allowed these young women to realize their dreams.

The young womens' future plans included marriage, children, some further schooling, and work for pay.[28] Over half of the twenty-nine young women expected to marry before they were 20 and to work for a few years before having children. On the surface, they rejected the dominant vision projected by romance novels that married women are exclusively full-time mothers and house-wives. White middle-class Karen expressed the tension surrounding these young women's futures: 'Well, I'm gonna have to work for awhile to help out, but I want to be home taking care of my kids when they come.' The working and middle-class young women from two-paycheck families recognized the necessity of women in the workforce. However, along with this realization was a strong longing for the more 'conventional' life depicted in romance fiction. This tension was an outcome of their dawning knowledge of the difficulty of juggling house-work, children, and paid work. The young women's own considerable domestic responsibilities at home and their mothers' dawn-to-dusk work routine were sobering glimpses of what might be in store for them.

Places in the World

There is considerable negotiation between students and teachers regarding romance fiction in the classrooms at Kominsky, Jefferson, and Sherwood Park. In the larger institutional context, teachers were under mandates of state testing and pressured into demonstrating student growth in reading. These were factors in their decision to allow popular materials into the classroom. The five teachers also acknowledged that intensification of their workload, increasing numbers of students, and the immense amount of paper work for Chapter I teachers made it difficult to select materials carefully. Consequently, they strongly relied on the reputation of publishers. The selective rendering of experience in tradebooks and textbooks (Pollack, 1981) along with recent charges of censorship in school editions (Bridgman, 1984), makes this reliance politically problematic. The 'higher production quotas', increasing accountability, and intensification of teachers' work are expressions of capitalist practices and values within the schools (Apple, 1979). Romance fiction represents another aspect of this mentality within the schools. Gitlin (1982) observes that symbolic relations are becoming steadily linked to politics and economics. Consider the comments of Ron Buehl, *Sweet Dreams* editor, about marketing books the way jeans are sold (Pollack, 1981, pp. 25–28.) Teen romance novels not only sell millions like jeans, but are often a series of commercials for consumer goods promoting a way of life based upon conspicuous consumption. These are not only expressions of economic relations, but have political dimensions as well. Teen romance fiction's promotion of a highly affluent style of life is out of reach for many of the twenty-nine readers in this study and contradicts their current realities of families and women in economic trouble as the gap between the rich and poor has steadily widened during the Reagan and Bush administrations (Albelda *et al.*, 1990).

Popular romance-fiction reading encapsulates the tug of war involved in funneling young women's desires towards heterosexuality and securing their consent to the new conservative political consensus. Romance reading is evidence of readers' desires along with their fears and resentment of the power of men and the subordination of women. Readers' preference for strong heroines and impatience with passive ones represents their desires to transcend current gender stereotypes and imagine more assertive modes of feminity, which, however, stop short of confrontation with boys. Through romance reading, readers transform gender and class relations. Men cherish and nurture women rather the other way around. This, together with readers' collective rejection of a macho masculinity, represents their partial overturning of one aspect of current traditional gender sentiments. These readers did not unilaterally accept romance fiction's depiction of married women's lives as primarily domestic. In these books, paid work was undertaken only out of economic necessity. Readers' 'Horatia Alger' fantasy of feminine initiative represents the transformation of class relations by substituting breadwinning women for the homemaking June Cleavers of romance fiction. Along with this fantasy, there was a longing for a domestic life, one that emanates from these readers' dawning realization of the burdens represented by home and work. However, readers' final acceptance of heterosexual romantic love and its power structure undercuts the political potential of these insights. Romance reading in no way altered the young women's present and future circumstances, but rather was deeply implicated in reconciling them to their places in the world.

Popular-romance reading also involves political actions around authority relations in schools. As Tina, Tomeika, Jan and Carol wrested some control over their reading from Mrs B, they de-centered the teacher's traditional authority on the question of reading choice. Their actions contested the power of teachers to decide what is best for students. In many ways, their actions here exemplified the assertive femininity that the young women constructed as they read. They were able to substitute this mode of femininity for the compliant femininity expected in the classroom. The struggles between these young women and their teacher were ultimately over whose gender and class meanings had legitimacy. However, their actions were contradictory in that they hardened the young women's opposition to 'legitimate' texts and the official school knowledge they contain. Although the romance novels generated a high engagement with reading and provided readers with 'really useful' gender knowledge, this knowledge did not count toward achieving academic success. The twenty-nine young women remained categorized as reluctant readers despite the rich and complex interpretations they made of romance fiction. Teachers did not interpret their reading as competent because of the contradictory status of romance novels. They were not legitimate texts in teachers' eyes, despite student efforts to confer authority on them. Although teachers and students compromised (as in the case of Mrs B), teachers still dispensed the rewards upon which academic success rests. There are few such rewards for teen romance readers.

Teachers allowing readers to substitute romance novels for other instructional texts unwittingly contributed to the young women's opposition to the academic aspects of schooling. The absence of meaningful communication between students and teachers about their reading allowed many of the gender interpretations to remain in place. This practice militated against what is perhaps the most important aspect of learning from reading, that of making sense of books through discussion with others. While the very championing of romance novel reading momentarily empowered young women to assert a claim to a kind of schooling that would relate to their interests, it also had a dark side. Readers' resistances to the 'official' curriculum set in motion the possibility that these young women might graduate with skills that only qualify them for low-skill exploitative jobs or not graduate at all. In view of the movement of Lakeview toward a service economy featuring low-paying jobs, the limiting of these women to this kind of job seems likely. Keeran (1985) predicted that by 1990 service-sector industries would employ almost three-quarters of the workforce and that most of these workers would be women. Romance reading prepared these twenty-nine Lakeview students for entering the service-sector economy of the United States as middle and working-class women.

Conclusion

Popular romance-fiction reading exploits the many ideological strains that exist within the United States, and it represents the continuing struggle over women's places in the world. This fiction does not so much impose meanings on its readers, but rather constructs readers' gender, class, racial, age and sexual identities in complex ways. Volosinov (1973) has observed that language involves a 'struggle over meaning.' As the study of teen romance fiction demonstrates, this struggle is a political one that has long concerned feminists and other progressively-minded individuals. Although space does not permit a detailed account of the ways in which a political practice can be forged around popular texts,[29] it is important that educators help students to locate the contradictions between popular fiction's version of social relations and their own lives as well as to help them to develop the critical tools necessary to make deconstructive readings that unearth the political interests that shape the form and content of popular fiction. This means moving from a definition of reading as an apolitical, internal and individual activity to one of reading as a socially and historically situated political practice (Luke, 1991). Many reluctant readers read in a solitary manner without opportunity to share with other readers their impressions of books. Collective reading groups and group writing are a few ways of transforming reading from a silent to a social activity. The dominant practices for teaching reading are weighted towards the use of fiction as the primary texts, especially in the whole language and literature-based approaches. Often, readers are not given adequate instruction in how to read expository materials. For reluctant readers of the working class, this is a serious issue since expository materials are the 'discourses of power', the socially valued knowledge (Baker and Luke, 1991). Even though romance novels may give pleasure to readers and facilitate reflection, their knowledge will not help students secure diplomas, qualify for well-paying jobs and gain access to the dominant power structures.

The theory and practice of feminist pedagogy (Schneidewind, 1987; Shrewsbury, 1987) and that of Freire's and Macedo's (1987) political literacy approach represent points of departure for a 'politics of reading'.[30] Teachers and readers could discuss and write about their experiences of oppression within patriarchy and their moments of 'breaking out'. The feelings that romance fiction brings to the fore and the political and economic context of publishing are other areas to analyze. Politicizing text use is vital since much of the hegemonic power of ruling elites in the United States is consolidated through written forms, especially in this era of the close linkages between the media and the state (Apple and Christian-Smith, 1991). Since the control of publishing is in the hands of large multinational corporations, it is vital that political struggles continue to be directed toward the corporate sector, and that alternative presses be supported.

The sweet dreams of hearts and flowers spun by teen romance novels have considerable appeal to many readers and represent the next chapter in young women's education in romance[31] and the attempts of powerful elites to shape their conscious and unconscious desires. Romance fiction reading occurs at a time when young women are negotiating the relations of power and desire constituting their gender subjectivities. Despite the creative reconstruction of the texts by readers, this fiction is problematic for young women for developing their femininities from a range of characteristics rather than a few socially sanctioned ones. Teen romance novels are here to stay and continue to challenge students, educators, feminists, and change-oriented individuals in their quest to refashion women's places in the world.

Notes

1 These qualities of popular culture are discussed in Bennett, Mercer and Wollacott (1986), Giroux, Simon and Contributors (1989), Roman and Christian-Smith (1988).
2 See Stallard, Ehrenreich and Sklar (1983) and Plotke (1986) for additional discussion.
3 Refer to Christian-Smith (1990) for a more detailed history of teen romance fiction.
4 For an extended discussion of this topic see Apple and Christian-Smith (1991).
5 The growing implementation of literature-based curricula for reading instruction that features many trade books lends an added urgency to the critical examination of romance fiction and its use in schools.
6 Readability, or the difficulty of reading writing, is most often estimated through sentence length and word length. A number of the Hi-Lows that I have analyzed using readability measures are written at the fourth to fifth-grade level. Publishers routinely estimate readability and print it in terms of grade level on the copyright page of their books.
7 See Farr (1977), Flesch (1983), and National Assessment of Educational Progress (1976).
8 A more thorough discussion is contained in Christian-Smith (1990).
9 All names are fictitious.
10 The outlying schools tracked students in math, science, and language arts as well. Most of the girls in my sample were tracked together so they interacted with one another across a range of subject areas.

11 In 1965 Congress passed the Elementary and Secondary Education Act known as Title I (now Chapter I) as a part of its 'War on Poverty'. Chapter I's focus was improving the reading and mathematics knowledge of the poor and educationally disadvantaged. Although Chapter I funding has been severely curtailed of late, it still remains the major form of compensatory education within many urban school districts.

12 For a detailed discussion of the methodology and issues surrounding interpretive research, see Christian-Smith (1990).

13 I focus exclusively on school because access to homes was difficult.

14 Refer to Christian-Smith (1990) for the reading survey and a discussion of survey research.

15 There are very few romance novels in which characters are not White. Tracy West's *Promises* (New York, Silhouette, 1986) features Black main characters. However, the novel has no specifically Black cultural dimensions.

16 In the three schools, most of the heavy romance novel readers identified by the selection tools and staff happened to be students identified by school personnel as reluctant readers. No 'skilled' readers were found in the initial sample of seventy-five girls and the final sample of twenty-nine girls. While librarians and teachers acknowledged that some skilled readers read teen romances, they did not exclusively read them nor with the frequency of the twenty-nine readers.

17 All pauses and hesitations have been omitted.

18 There was very little communication between readers within the classrooms observed or outside of school on the topic of the teen romances. Because of court-mandated bussing of students, most of the twenty-nine girls did not live near one another and many did not attend schools near their homes.

19 Mrs B characterized 'quality literature' as a superbly told story, rich characters, and a concise 'literary' style. She did not view book quality as connected to the way women were represented.

20 The major adolescent book awards in the United States are the American Library Association's Notable Books, the Laura Ingalls Wilder Award, the Newberry Award, and The National Book Award.

21 The findings of the 1983 Consumer Research Study on Reading and Book Purchasing by the Book Industry Study Group found the average reader read 24.9 books for leisure or work over six months.

22 See Christian-Smith (1990) for more extensive treatment.

23 A close textual analysis of a sample of teen romance fiction, including several of the titles favored by the twenty-nine readers, is contained in Christian-Smith (1986, 1990).

24 The formation of the racial identity of the young women of color in this study is incomplete because of racial tensions in the schools that preceded and continued during the time of the study. For further discussion refer to Christian-Smith (1990).

25 The young women of color in this study were resigned to and expressed anger over the lack of Black, Hispanic and Asian heroines in the books. However, they felt that the books reflected the way women other than White are treated by society.

26 These characteristics are similar in content to the ones cited by adult women readers of romance fiction reported in Radway (1984).

27 Refer to Christian-Smith (1990) for more information.

28 See Christian-Smith (1990) for further discussion.

29 This topic is further developed in Christian-Smith (1990).

30 In calling for a combination of the the the two approaches I acknowledge the different traditions represented by feminist pedagogy and political literacy.

31 This concept is developed more thoroughly in Holland and Eisenhart (1990).

References

ALBELDA, R., MCCRATE, E., MELENDEZ, E. and LAPIDUS, J. (1990) *Mink Coats Don't Trickle Down*, Boston, Southend Press.

APPLE, M.W. (1979) *Ideology and Curriculum*, Boston; Routledge and Kegan Paul.

APPLE, M.W. and CHRISTIAN-SMITH, L.K. (Eds) (1991) *The Politics of the Textbook*, New York, Routledge.

AULLS, M. (1978) *Developmental and Remedial Reading in the Middle Grades*, Boston, Allyn and Bacon.

BAKER, C.D. and LUKE, A. (Eds) (1991) *Towards a Critical Sociology of Reading Pedagogy*, Amsterdam, John Benjamins.

BENNETT, T. (1986) 'The politics of "the popular" and popular culture', in T. BENNETT, C. MERCER, and J. WOLLACOTT (Eds) *Popular Culture and Social Relations*, Milton Keynes, The Open University Press, pp. 6–21.

BENNETT, T., MERCER, C. and WOLLACOTT, J. (1986) *Popular Culture and Social Relations*, Milton Keynes, Open University Press.

BRIDGMAN, A. (1984) 'A.L.A. study of book-club alterations prompts shifts in policy', *Education Week*, March 7, pp. 6–7.

CHRISTIAN-SMITH, L.K. (1986) 'The English curriculum and current trends in publishing, *English Journal*, **75**, pp. 55–57.

CHRISTIAN-SMITH, L.K. (1990) *Becoming a Woman through Romance*, New York, Routledge.

COSER L.A., KADUSHIN, C. and POWELL, W.W. (1982) *Books*, New York, Basic Books.

COWARD, R. (1984) *Female Desire*, London, Palladin Books.

FARR, R. (1977) 'Is Johnny's/Mary's reading getting worse?' *Educational Leadership*, April, pp. 521–7.

FLESCH, R. (1983) *Why Johnny Still Can't Read*, New York, Harper and Row.

FREIRE, P. and MACEDO, D. (1987) *Reading the Word and the World*, Granby, MA, Bergin and Garvey.

GASKELL, J. (1983) 'The reproduction of family life: Perspectives of male and female adolescents', *British Journal of Sociology of Education*, **4**, pp. 19–37.

GIROUX, H.A., SIMON, R. and CONTRIBUTORS (1989) *Popular Culture and Critical Pedagogy*. Granby, MA, Bergin and Garvey Publishers, Inc.

GITLIN, T. (1982) 'Television's screens: Hegemony in transition', in M.W. APPLE (Ed.) *Cultural and Economic Reproduction in Education*, Boston, Routledge and Kegan Paul, pp. 202–46.

HALL, S. (1985) 'Authoritarian populism: A reply', *New Left Review*, **151**, pp. 115–24.

HARTY, S. (1979) *Hucksters in the Classroom*, New York, Center for Responsive Law.

HARVEY, B. (1981) 'Wildfire: Tame but deadly', *Interracial Books for Children Bulletin*, **12**, pp. 8–10.

HOLLAND, D.C. and EISENHART, M.E. (1990) *Educated in Romance: Women, Achievement, and College Culture*, Chicago, The University of Chicago Press.

HUNTER, A. (1984) *Virtue with a Vengeance: The Pro-Family Politics of the New Right*, Unpublished doctoral dissertation, Department of Sociology, Brandeis University, Waltham, MA.

HUNTER, A. (1985) 'Why did Reagan win? Ideology or economics?' *Socialist Review*, **79**, pp. 29–41.

ISER, W. (1974) *The Implied Readers: Patterns of Communication in Prose Fiction from Bunyan to Beckett*, Baltimore, MD, The Johns Hopkins University Press.

ISER, W. (1980) 'Interaction between text and reader', in S.R. SULEIMAN and I. CROSMAN (Eds) *The Reader in the Text*, Princeton, NJ, Princeton University Press, pp. 106–19.

KAPLAN, C. (1986) *Sea Changes*, London, Verso.

KEERAN, R. (1985) 'AFL-CIO report: Service sector', *Economic Notes*, **53**, October, p. 4.

KELLY, J. (1983) 'The doubled vision of feminist theory', in J.L. NEWTON, M.P. RYAN and J.R. WALKOWITZ (Eds) *Sex and Class in Women's History*, London, Routledge and Kegan Paul, pp. 259–70.

KERESY, G. (1984) 'School bookclub expurgation practices', *Top of the News*, **40**, pp. 131–8.

LANES, S. (1981) 'Here come the blockbusters — teen books go big time, *Interracial Books for Children Bulletin*, **12**, pp. 5–7.

LUKE, A., (1991) 'The secular word: Catholic transformations of Dick and Jane, in M.W. APPLE and L.K. CHRISTIAN-SMITH (Eds) *The Politics of the Textbook*, New York, Routledge, Chapman, and Hall, pp. 166–90.

LUKE, C., DE CASTELL, S. and LUKE, A. (1989) Beyond criticism: The authority of the school textbook, in S. DE CASTELL, A. LUKE and C. LUKE (Eds) *Language, Authority and Criticism*, London, Falmer Press, pp. 245–60.

MADSEN, C.T. (1981) 'Teen novels: What kind of values do they promote?' *The Christian Science Monitor*, **18**, pp. B14–17.

MARKET FACTS (1984) *1983 Consumer Research Study on Reading and Book Purchasing: Focus on Juveniles*, New York, Book Industry Study Group.

McROBBIE, A. (1978) *Jackie: An Ideology of Adolescent Femininity*, Stencilled Occasional Paper, Birmingham, The Centre for Contemporary Cultural Studies.

NATIONAL ASSESSMENT OF EDUCATIONAL PROGRESS (1976) *Reading in America: A perspective on Two Assessments*, Denver, CO, Reading Report No. 06-R-01, October.

OTTO, W., PETERS, C.W. and PETERS, N. (1977) *Reading Problems*, Reading, Addison-Wesley.

PLOTKE, D. (1986) 'Reaganism and neoliberalism', *Socialist Review*, **86**, pp. 7–23.

POLLACK, P. (1981) 'The business of popularity', *School Library Journal*, **28**, pp. 25–28.

RADWAY, J. (1984) *Reading the Romance*, Chapel Hill, NC, The University of North Carolina Press.

RETAN, W. (1982) 'The changing economics of book publishing', *Top of the News*, **38**, pp. 233–5.

ROMAN, L. and CHRISTIAN-SMITH, L.K. (1988) *Becoming Feminine: The Politics of Popular Culture*, London, Falmer Press.

SCHNIEDEWIND, N. (1987) 'Teaching feminist process', *Women's Studies Quarterly*, **15**, pp. 15–31.

SCHOLASTIC INC. (1985) *Scholastic Inc. — An Overview*, New York, Scholastic Inc.

SHATZKIN, L. (1982) *In Cold Type*, Boston, Houghton Mifflin Company.

SHREWSBURY, C.M. (1987) 'What is feminist pedagogy?' *Women's Studies Quarterly*, **15**, pp. 6–14.

SILHOUETTE BOOKS (1981) *First Love from Silhouette*, New York, Silhouette Books.

STALLARD, K., EHRENREICH, B. and SKLAR, H. (1983) *Poverty in the American Dream*, Boston, MA, South End Press.

TUROW, J. (1978) *Getting Books to Children*, Chicago, American Library Association.

VOLOSINOV, V.N. (1973) *Marxism and the Philosophy of Language*, New York, Seminar Press.

WALKERDINE, V. (1984) 'Some day my prince will come: Young girls and the preparation for adolescent sexuality', in A. McROBBIE and M. NAVA (Eds) *Gender and Generation*, London, Macmillan pp. 162–84.

WHITESIDE, T. (1981) *The Blockbuster Complex*, Middletown, CT, Wesleyan University Press.

Most Popular Books Read by the Seventy-Five Girls (in order of popularity)

1 PASCAL, F. (1985) *Perfect Summer*, New York, Bantam's Sweet Valley High.
2 HARPER, E. (1981) *Love at First Sight*, New York, Silhouette's Blossom Valley.
3 HARPER, E. (1985) *Turkey Trot*, New York, Silhouette's Blossom Valley.
4 CONKLIN, B. (1981) *P.S. I Love You*, New York, Bantam's Sweet Dreams.
5 PASCAL, F. (1979) *My First Love and Other Disasters*, New York, Viking.
6 TYLER, T. (1983) *A Passing Game*, New York, Silhouette's First Love.
7 QUIN-HARKIN, J. (1981) *California Girl*, New York, Bantam's Sweet Dreams.
8 MARSHALL, A. (1985) *Against the Odds*, New York, Silhouette's First Love.
9 CONFORD, E. (1982) *Seven Days to a Brand-New Me*, Boston, Atlantic.
10 PEVSNER, S. (1980) *Cute Is a Four-Letter Word*, New York, Archway.

Chapter 5

Dolly Fictions: Teen Romance Down Under

Pam Gilbert

> . . . when quality young adult books are steadily improving, when serious authors who are skilled writers are publishing books with reasonably rounded characters, carefully constructed plots, and themes of genuine concern to adolescents, young women readers in droves are choosing instead books in which the writing is pedestrian at best, the characters range from plastic to cardboard, the plots are absolutely predictable, and the themes are almost exclusively 'boy gets girl', or rather 'girl gets boy'? (Knodel, 1982, p. 1)

> I thought about this and thought — oh, how embarrassing — I actually got hooked into a romance book (teenage romance reader in Gilbert and Taylor, 1991, p. 98)

The place that romance fiction plays in girls' lives remains, as various papers in this volume testify, a vexatious issue for researchers and educators. The issue is seen to typify many of the complexities associated with the status and nature of popular cultural texts: the power and ownership of patriarchal consumerism; the value placed on women's interests and women's experiences; the nature of reading and fiction in people's lives; and the school authorization of suitable classroom curriculum materials.

The issue becomes so particularly complex because the romance fiction industry is clearly a highly successful commercial enterprise, drawing its support from many different age groups of girls and women. Adult romance novels are translated and sold by the millions internationally (Thurston, 1987, p. vii), with special runs of some particular romance lines known to be as high as 500,000. In comparison with the average run for an Australian 'novel' of approximately 10,000, this is big business.

Given the significantly smaller commercial market from which it draws, teen romance fiction is similarly popular, even 'down under'. In Australia, Lam, for instance, cites comments by the national sales manager of Scholastic that even successful Australian children's writers like Joan Phipson and Colin Thiele can be outsold by a ratio of 3:1 with a 'good romance title' for adolescents (1986, p. 18), and the publicity and marketing manager of Bantam's distribution agency in

Australia similarly claimed that teen romances are the company's strongest
Australian sellers (Lam, 1986: p. 18).

American teen romance series like *Sweet Valley High* and *Sweet Dreams* (both
published by Bantam) have dominated the teen romance field for Australian girls
for some time. However in 1988 Australian Consolidated Press entered the lucrative teen romance series market with the launch of a new Australian series under
the extraordinary title of *Dolly Fiction*. The series was marketed as an extension of
Dolly magazine (hence the name): a popular teen magazine with an impressive
Australian circulation of approximately 250,000 issues per month. The series is
advertised widely in the magazine, and clearly trades on the expectation that,
through their reading of *Dolly* magazine, young women are already positioned
within a 'reading formation' (Kress, 1985) which promotes a particular version of
femininity compatible with the subject positions offered through *Dolly Fiction*.

Dolly Fiction follows the packaging patterns of the earlier young adult
romance series; the books clearly belong to a series (as is evident from the similarity of their covers, titles, and general lay-out) and they are numbered for easy
collection and consumption. The major difference with this series is that it obviously hopes to trade off the trademark *Dolly*, using the space that the magazine
currently occupies as a fashionable and contemporary 'voice' of teenage femininity. *Dolly Fiction* claims to offer girls more of what they 'loved' in the magazine.
'You just can't get enough!' is the advertising slogan.

'You Just Can't Get Enough': Femininity and Romance Fiction

As study after study of the dominant readings of teen romance fiction demonstrates (see Altus, 1984a, 1984b; Christian-Smith, 1987; Gilbert and Taylor, 1991;
Lam, 1986; Willinsky and Hunniford, this volume), such narratives position
readers to accept that what young women can't get enough of is heterosexual
love. Love becomes, in the novels, 'of itself a career' (Altus, 1984b, p. 128), and
the texts only acquire plausibility as a string of narrative events, if particular
versions of feminine subjectivity are recognized. In this way, as Cohan and Shires
(1988) claim in their discussion of the gendered nature of narrative, the romance
genre could properly be called a 'feminine' narrative, for:

> . . . it structures the meaning of gender difference through a narrative
> representation of female subjectivity in much the same way that mascu-
> line narratives such as the thriller and western structure the meaning of
> gender difference through narrative representations of male subjectivity.
> Though their structures differ, both feminine and masculine narrative
> genres rationalize the normative values of heterosexual relations — in the
> household (for the female) and in the workplace (for the male). In the
> case of feminine narrative, the story places gender in a field of
> signification so that, at the level of events and actors, representations of
> sexual difference acquire meaning by reinforcing the values of love and
> marriage, of emotional vulnerability and domesticity, and by making
> them appear natural, inevitable, and desirable as culturally legible signs
> of 'femininity' (Cohan and Shires, 1988, pp. 79–80).

The books usually focus upon the first meeting, the courting, and the final blissful culmination (in a kiss), of an adolescent girl's infatuation with a boy. The progress of the infatuation is constructed as the girl's dominant interest in life, often interfering with her school work, her hobbies, her family and with her friendships with other teenagers. All is seen to be sacrificed if the path of the love affair is to run smoothly, and girls in teen romance go to quite extraordinary lengths to achieve their goals.

However while the romance genre is dominated by the quest for 'love', love in the case of the teen romance usually means a single, 'steady' relationship with one boy. 'Clean romance is the appeal of these novels', claims Guiley (1983, p. 93): 'there's no sex in these books — physical encounters are limited to a few kisses and embraces'. Generally the teen romances are 'squeaky clean' in terms of direct reference to sexual behaviour, although some of the more recent post-AIDS romance novels extend the parameters of the physical encounters.

Physical sex is, however, generally not a dominant issue for the teen romance novel: discourses of female sexuality do not lie easily beside romance formations. In any of the more sexually explicit adult romance novels, it is discourses of male sexuality — quite often male pornographic discourses — which predominate. Snitow, for instance, argues that in the adult *Harlequin* romance novels, 'the joys of passivity, of helpless abandon, of response without responsibility are all endlessly repeated, savored, minutely described' (1984, pp. 268–9). Romance fiction structures incidents of male cruelty and callousness as plausible narrative sequences by linking them to heterosexual relationships. 'Cruelty, callousness, coldness, menace' are thus all equated with maleness and treated, Snitow suggests, as a necessary part of the package.

Not surprisingly, the character traiting possible in these 'feminine narratives' comes from a narrow framework. The women and men typically have no past and no context; such social formations are relatively unimportant in the dominant movement of the narrative. The romantic heroine is a known stereotype. In love with love, she is also inscribed by romance, and is preoccupied with her clothing, her hair and the shape of her body. She is also always attractive, although she may not initially think so and needs external reflection/verification of her feminine/romantic appearance. Usually she belongs to no ethnic group or religion, and exists in a buffered unreal social group where money and privilege are seldom discussed. Family circumstances are usually not described, nor are social values.

Heroes are traited from within a similarly narrow set of possibilities. Like the heroine, they are occasionally metamorphosed during the course of the fiction so that their full sensual attractiveness is revealed, but unlike the heroine, they are never really known and understood; their actions are often bewildering to the heroine. Snitow (1984) suggests that in the adult romance world all tensions and problems arise from the fact that male and female seem incapable of communicating with each other. The sexes, she suggests, 'find each other utterly mystifying' (Snitow, 1984, p. 260). The romance formula is then about bridging this gulf in such a way that the essential hardness and superiority of the male are not totally destroyed. He must become softer, but not 'too soft' if he is to be of service to the woman.

Other female characters are secondary to the romance and often serve as oppositional points of difference. 'Slags' and 'drags' (see Gilbert and Taylor,

1991, pp. 15–16) are the points of polarity for teen romances. Ugly, mannish or assertive women are un-'feminine', as are bitchy women who don't know how to treat their men, and flirts or sexually permissive women who flaunt their desire. Teen romances also often feature parent figures in stereotypical caring roles, epitomizing the fantasy of the loving marriage: the ultimate goal of the romance. Parents support the teenage girl's preoccupation with love, and mothers in particular worry for her if she has no boyfriend or no dates. Mothers also understand the pain of love, knowing that silent suffering in private is part of the 'game' of romance.

The romantic construction of femininity, then, seems to be connected to the heroine's quest for love — for domesticated male sexuality — and the resultant qualities of femininity such a quest is seen to demand. However the version of romantic femininity offered through formulaic fiction of this type is not static. Rather, as Thurston (1987) reminds us, it is constantly reshaped in response to market forces and perceived reader demand. However the limits of possibility of response to such shifting social forces are noticeable. As Christian-Smith observed in her American study of teen romance novels from 1942–1982 (1987), the codes constructing femininity (identified in this study as Romance, Beautification and Sexuality) stayed remarkably stable during the forty years covered. Changes were, Christian-Smith argued, 'not of a great magnitude'.

The changes are, however, significant in any analysis of the shifting ground of feminine subjectivity, because they reflect the constant re-shaping of acceptable subject positions for women, and indicate how social change is appropriated by patriarchal discourses. The fact that many romance series have floundered, that some romance writers are infinitely more popular than others, and that romance publishing houses spend huge sums surveying their readers for evaluation of particular titles (Guiley, 1983; Thurston, 1987), is testimony to the commercial necessity of monitoring the shifting social parameters of acceptable femininity. And this can be particularly noticed if the production of a new romance series is observed and described. In this chapter, the shifts that have occurred over twenty-four months to the first Australian teen romance series, *Dolly Fiction*, will be considered and critically assessed. How does a teen romance series first produced in 1988 construct teen femininity, and how do such constructions respond over time to social shifts in gender relationships?

Teen Romance Down Under: *Dolly Fiction* Arrives

In August 1988, Greenhouse Publications (a subsidiary of Australian Consolidated Press) announced a National Launch for September 14th to promote the first six titles in a new Australian series of teen romance fiction. Features of the promotion, such as a forty-eight copy dump bin, an eighteen copy counter pack, a special static display, perfumed bookmarks and national advertising in *Dolly* magazine, indicated reasonably clearly how the series was positioning itself similarly to comparable American teen romance promotions. By the same time in 1990, the initial six titles had become fifty titles, which had been promoted and released in similar ways. An initial release of one title a month increased once the series was established. In February 1989, with only twelve titles on the shelves,

Greenhouse Publications announced in *Australian Bookseller and Publisher* that over 200,000 copies of these first twelve had already been sold: big numbers for a new release series operating in a comparatively small Australian market space.

The series has directly grown out of the success of *Dolly* magazine: an Australian magazine aimed at the 13–20[1] age range, and holding down a key spot in the Australian magazine stakes for young women of this age. The magazine genre's potential to offer a multiplicity of reading positions and entry points for readers is well in evidence in *Dolly*, which is clearly a contemporary teenage girl's magazine. It offers texts on all forms of feminine body inscription (clothing, hair styling, makeup, dieting, jewellery and accessory collectibles, exercise and body shaping), on heterosexual female knowledge (as in 'When he's seeing his ex-girlfriend', October, 1990, or 'How to handle a guy who just won't take no for an answer', December, 1990, or 'What your guy's family reveals about his personality', March, 1991), as well as texts on drugs, parents, sex, music, film and media stars. *Dolly* provides an interesting and varied pastiche of texts, although the parameters of possibility are as would be expected. The 'Dolly reader' is positioned as uninterested in school, in feminism, in politics, in science, in technology, in craft, in nutrition, or in the more 'serious' forms of art, music, film or literature, by the absence of such texts from the pages of the magazine. Instead the 'Dolly reader' is positioned as the good-time girlfriend, who wants to know how to be 'hot' when she meets her guy.

Dolly Fiction comes as a series; each volume is numbered, and the covers have the same graphic format. As with American romance series, the covers feature a photograph of a teen model, often models who appear regularly in *Dolly* magazine. The model has the same hair and eye colouring as the book's heroine, and a photograph of her is placed centre on a single colour cover. The cover format changed in the second twelve months of publication, from the original single pastel colour cover, to a modernistic design in white and black. In keeping with the series nature of the books, DOLLY FICTION is printed in large capitals across the top of the cover, and the title and author in smaller print at the bottom.

Teen Romance as Dynamic: Changing Patterns in *Dolly Fiction*

Thurston has argued that the usual criticism made of contemporary romance fiction as 'the opiate of the female masses' is inaccurate and excessively generalized. Instead she argues that some of the adult romance genres portray a feminine consciousness 'that has to do not only with sexual liberation but also with economic liberation' (1987, p. 11). Thurston's reminder that romance genres are too easily lumped together and stereotyped is important, and most feminist readers are aware of the way in which generic forms associated with women have become culturally devalued. Feminist readers are also conscious of the dangers associated with critiquing the fictions which are obviously powerful and important in young women's lives. However one of the questions that needs to be asked is, is it possible to construct romance fiction — even within a broadened and more contemporary framework — that challenges and redefines romance ideology? As a way of addressing this question, two groups of *Dolly Fiction* — the first twelve titles released in 1988, and a more recent set of twelve released two years later — will be discussed and analyzed.

Titles 1–12: *Dolly Fiction* in 1988

The titles for the first twelve books in this series — when taken with the back and inside cover promotions — unambiguously positioned their readers for a formula romance.

1   *The Look of Love* by Margaret Pearce
2   *Broken Promises* by Katie Lee
3   *Good Timing* by Trisha Trent
4   *My Type of Writer* by Jaye Francis
5   *Who Do You Love?* by Marianne Vaughan
6   *I've Got a Secret* by Mary Forrest
7   *In Too Deep* by Linda Hollan
8   *She's a Rebel* by Mary Forrest
9   *Stroke of Luck* by Alice Adams
10   *Summer Escape* by Chris Kelson
11   *First Impressions* by Jaye Francis
12   *She's Got the Beat* by Gina Walsh

Interestingly, several of these title words can be recognized as puns once the back cover promotion has been read. *In Too Deep* has a windsurfing heroine, *Stroke of Luck* a swimming star, and *My Type of Writer* an amateur journalist. Despite this apparent playfulness, the titles, however, construct a typical concept of romance. They suggest that romance is observable (*The Look of Love*), and typified by a number of specific features, some of which include: luck in the 'game' of love (*Good Timing, Stroke of Luck*); secrets and promises (*Broken Promises, I've Got a Secret*); emotional intensity (*In Too Deep*); and a girl's need to keep an ever vigilant eye for a likely romantic scenario (*Summer Escape*).

The 'romance' follows a predictable narrative pattern in these first twelve texts. The narratives begin with a romantic/feminine novice, and turn on her metamorphosis — her transformation — into a romantic-feminine convert. The typical novice doesn't think she needs a boyfriend:

> . . . this year wasn't going to be easy. How was she going to juggle all the elements of her life, keep everyone happy, and pass her exams? At least, she thought thankfully, I haven't got a boyfriend to worry about (9, p. 2).

Or doesn't attract boyfriends:

> I've been told I'm attractive and maybe it's true, I don't know, but it doesn't seem to help me find a boyfriend (7, p. 2).

She thinks she is 'different' from other girls.

> Why, oh why was she so plain, and stuck with elderly parents, and treated like an outsider at school? (1, p. 5).

Fortunately not all parents are 'elderly' and unaware of the girl's needs. Most of the mothers in these novels are keen to see their daughters make the transition to romantic femininity.

Kyla giggled as she sat down at Emma's dressing table. 'Mum will be rapt'. she said happily, 'She's always reading fashion magazines and she loves to see me getting dressed up . . .' (6, p. 42).

The metamorphosis — the fashioning of the girl into the woman, of the pre-romantic child into the sexual female adolescent — hinges usually on one of three narrative movements in these first twelve novels. The novice may have to carve out her new romantic identity by inscribing her body romantically; she must be 'made-over' in the way that teen magazines make-over the ordinary girl into the desirable, 'feminine' girl. She may need a weight loss (1 and 3), and will almost certainly need different clothing and make-up (9 and 10).

Once 'made-over' — or if the girl was already romantically inscribed — a second plot shift is possible. The girl may be fooled by falseness, either from other 'bitchy' girls (1, 3, 6 and 8), or from irresponsible, non-husband material boys (5, 7, 10 and 12). The 'true' romance event will, however, ensure her safe passage through these murky waters and guide her towards a greater understanding of the acceptable faces of femininity. Jealousy, overt sexuality, public gossiping and vanity are outside the framework, as is association with boys who might jeopardize the girl's virginity and safety. The romantic girl — the feminine girl — is in search of the first awakening: the kiss. This marks her passage into womanhood.

Helping people with problems becomes the third, and most popular plot twist. Girls are 'worriers' who need to look after their girlfriends (11) and boyfriends (2, 4, 8). They are 'helpers' who unselfishly do what needs to be done for others to find happiness — usually romantic happiness. By helping others, they, too, often find their own romance. The feminine girl is unselfish, rather passive, and extremely considerate, and the slippage from feminine to romantic can be read through the positioning of narrative events in these first Dolly Fiction titles.

The traiting of the girls in the first twelve novels comes from a narrow syntagm of possibility. The girls have stereotypical families and stereotypical hobbies and interests. While the mothers' roles in all of the titles are not always mentioned, when they are, less than half of the mothers' work, even part-time, outside of the home. The jobs that are mentioned for mothers are nurse (6), library assistant (10) and union organizer (12). Three of the mothers are unambiguously located as full-time home people (1, 2, 5), and one of these is the classic, wicked, 'young' stepmother (2). While fathers may sometimes be constructed as organizing the evening meal (4 and 7), mothers are typically in the kitchen for the basic food preparation: cooking and serving breakfasts (8), baking biscuits and cakes to take on holiday (5), cooking and freezing a week's evening meals (4). Fathers read the financial pages (1), go fishing (5), play golf (2), develop a new business (8), supervise at a factory (12), or become infatuated by younger women (2).

While romance heroes in these books often drive cars, the girls always get driven, or walk, or ride bikes. In the sporting field, girls are similarly stereotyped. Apart from one girl who becomes a top wind-surfer (7), few others are sports-minded. One ice skates moderately well (once her new boyfriend teaches her) (12), and one is a champion swimmer (9). The girls are more frequently associated with the arts, the stereotypical field for romance. They are in school musicals (3), sing and play in rock bands (12), and write for the school newspaper (4). Girls in these romances sometimes find that boyfriends resent the time they want to give to their hobbies or sport (12) — although girlfriends are very understanding about the time boyfriends need for similar interests (1, 4, 7, 8). Unless boyfriends become committed, or are already committed, to the same hobby as the girl — as eventually happens in 9 and 12 — the romance flounders and the girl worries that perhaps she should forgo her non-romantic interest (12).

The girls spend most of their time talking to their friends, or planning what to wear, or what to say, in their next encounter with a boy. They are usually not doing well at school, and through the course of the novel, generally do less well because of the time they spend on their romantic plans. Conflicts with teachers and parents about homework not done or done badly are frequent features of the books (1, 3, 12). Typically the girl 'in love' cannot be rational and logical about her work; she daydreams, cries, locks herself in her room, or goes out to talk to her female friend. Being 'in love' causes a noticeable change in a girl's life.

> She *was* moody these days. Was love always like this? (9, p. 81).

> My brain felt like scrambled eggs and I couldn't think about my problems any more today. Because of my ups and downs (mostly downs), I hadn't been keeping up with my homework . . . (2, p. 90).

While she might initially resist 'love' —

> . . . falling in love is the pits. Whenever anyone falls in love, their brain seems to turn to mush and their conversation becomes as boring as the magazines in a dentist's waiting room (4, p. 2).

— she finds that it's inevitable.

> '. . . I really thought I must be immune to it. And now — well, they say that things like measles and mumps affect you worse if you catch them later in life. Maybe that's why this love virus feels so horrible.'
> 'No, it's always horrible,' said Marie . . . 'Half the time you're up in the air, and the other half of the time you're really down. That's just the way it is'. (4, p. 8).

Only a few of the girls have part-time jobs, and the money they earn is for 'make-over' jobs. In *Look of Love* (1), Clarinda realizes that without money 'the look of love' will not be possible.

> What did she need to turn herself into a new person? Money! Money for makeup and clothes and heaps of other things. Her elation faltered as she checked the contents of the piggy bank . . . She had never had any use for money. She didn't rush out buying records, or cosmetics or clothes . . . (pp. 9–10).

But she is about to. Fortunately Clarinda has one marketable skill: she is good at schoolwork. She begins a tutoring service, and when that doesn't provide quite enough money, she sells her schoolbooks.

She sacrificed her biology, geography, and one of her favourite poetry books to the secondhand shop. This gave her enough money for the mascara she wanted, and the layby on her first pair of jeans (p. 16).

In this particular novel, the heroine throws out her glasses, bleaches her hair, removes her orthodontic band, sheds fatty kilos, buys stretch jeans and mascara, and pretends she is not clever, in the metamorphosis from girlhood to romantic femininity. Blind, blonde and dumb, she then conforms more closely to what have seemed to her to be acceptable images of teenage femininity. Her boyfriend eventually convinces her that such excesses are not really necessary, so after humiliating herself publicly, the romantic heroine takes his advice and opts for a middle path: not *too* fat, not *too* mousy, only *a little* mascara. . . .

Careers, and life after school, are mentioned much more frequently for the boys in these stories, than for the girls. While boys curtail their social time because of their study (1, 3), or because they need to train for their professional sport commitments (7, 9), girls just get hopelessly muddled trying to balance even their romance plans with their school homework, and seldom have any long term plans. Not even the school dux (1), or the champion windsurfer (7), or the school swimming star (9), is career-focused. Girls typically don't think a great deal about their career options; there's too much distraction from romance. Take this particular example from *Who Do You Love?*

'What options are you doing at school next year?' he asked as his hand circled her shoulder blades. Jilly hadn't really thought about it. It felt good having him stroke the cream into her skin. Choosing options was the last thing on her mind.

'I don't know', she said. 'Maybe . . . astronomy.'

She sounded as though she was asking a question.

'Astronomy!' said Tom. 'I didn't know they were offering it. That'd be great. You know, there was an explosion up there in one of the galaxies hundreds of years ago. It left a black hole.'

'A black hole? What's that got to do with horoscopes?'

'Horoscopes? Oh, you mean astrology.'

'Astrology, astronomy, what's the difference?' (p. 72).

Only one of the stories suggests that the girls have plans beyond the kiss; in *She's Got the Beat* (12), Niva hopes to continue playing music with her boyfriend in a rock bank. By comparison, boys in these stories have plans to be professional windsurfers (7) or aeronautic engineers (5).

Boys know what they want, and they also know what girls want, consequently boys frequently play a significant role in the narrative's twist. For instance, they can actually help the girl construct her new image (3); they can tutor her when she falls behind at her schoolwork (1 and 3); they can save her from irresponsible boys (10); they can force her to keep up her training for a school swimming carnival (9). Many of the boys who will play the dominant roles are the 'old faithfuls' — examples of domesticated male sexuality — who have been part of the family scene for some time. They are the boys next door (1, 3), or friends of the family (5, 7): boys who know the girls for their true worth,

77

and are comfortable in the family setting. They present as possible and suitable partners.

Given these scenarios, it is rather difficult to see *Dolly Fiction* as a dynamic new series responding to the needs of women in the 1980s. None of the novels conclude with the heroine unpartnered. They unrelentingly portray images of adolescent femininity which tie girls to romantic inscription of their bodies for male approval; to complete absorption in the business of acquiring, preparing for and going on dates with boys; to reliance on male support, advice and financial backing; to disinterest in pursuing independent hobbies, sport, study, or career options. Becoming feminine, becoming romantic, becoming a *Dolly Fiction* reader, means accepting that there will be inevitable tension in pursuing independence, and that it might be best to find a 'good guy' who'll give you the best options *within this framework*, so that lost opportunities and forsaken goals are less keenly felt.

Titles 43–54: Dolly Fiction in 1990

A subtle shift in this framework has developed in the twenty-four months of *Dolly Fiction* publication, and the narrowness of character traiting and acceptable narrative transformation has noticeably broadened. The cover designs signal something of this shift in their move from pastel tones to black on white, but the general positioning of the books, within a romance/love story paradigm, is still quite clearly maintained through title and back cover promotion. The titles of the two most recent 'six-packs' of *Dolly Fiction* appear to signal the same resonances of the first twelve: love, trust, breaking up, bodily beautification, pride.

43 *Can I Trust Him?* by Lori Delahunty
44 *So Hard to Leave You* by Suzanne Lennox
45 *Understanding Jack* by Gerry Lapin
46 *When You're Pretty* by Alison Rhode
47 *What's Normal Anyway?* by Allie Melan
48 *The Desirable Alien* by Sarah Ferber
49 *Hot News* by Jenna Kinsey
50 *The Strangest Year* by Tegan Thomas
51 *Working It Out* by Gerri Lapin
52 *Best Friends* by Alice Adams
53 *Riding for a Fall* by Karen Miller
54 *Too Much Love* by Gina Walsh

As with the first twelve, there is the same playfulness of title in two of the texts. *Hot News* focuses on the infatuation of Stephanie for a TV newsreader she meets on work experience, and *Riding for a Fall* on an instant 'falling in love' by horse-rider Grace for a new mystery man at the Pony Club. The back cover promotions are also used unequivocally to frame the romance features of the texts.

> Susie's not too sure about Andy Reid, the American exchange student, at
> first — he just might be a total dag. Then again, he might not . . . It
> doesn't take long before Susie realises she's crazy about Andy — luckily,

he feels exactly the same way about her. In fact, they fall madly in love and Susie's never felt so fantastic in her whole life. There's one small problem though, in just a few months, Andy has to go back to America and Susie doesn't know how she'll bear it (*The Desirable Alien*).

As far as Grace is concerned, there are only two types of guys in this world: the ones who can wear jodhpurs, and the ones who can't. Dean Matthews is *definitely* one of the guys who can. When he turns up at Grace's pony club she can hardly believe it, and she falls instantly in love. Grace is convinced that she and Dean are meant for each other, but there's one small problem — her boyfriend, Pete! (*Riding for a Fall*).

However there is a difference in these more recent texts in the set of possible transformations open to the romantic heroines, and in the paradigm of setting and character the narratives draw upon. These texts extend the parameters of possibility by widening the range of character traits for young women and their mothers, by more directly confronting sexual relationships as part of romance, and by offering a slight shift in narrative closures away from the blissful single heterosexual relationship.

This seems to be in keeping with a 1989 advice circular for *Dolly Fiction* writers, produced by the series editor, Belinda Byrne. Byrne advises prospective writers of the texts that she wants this series to be different.

The stories *are* romances, but we believe we can examine other issues within the genre and still have books which are a good read, while having something worthwhile to say as well. We're talking positive role models here! . . . Our books can be funny — some of the best ones are — and they don't have to end happily, or with a kiss etc., although some form of positive resolution from the heroine is always preferable . . . We want to show girls interested in and pursuing things other than boys — some of the time anyway (Byrne, 1989).

These more recent twelve *Dolly Fiction* titles take up some of Byrne's requests, but there is clearly a limit to what can be considered 'positive role models', 'positive resolution', and 'things other than boys' within the paradigm of the romance genre. The restrictiveness of generic choice becomes apparent in these twelve, although there is no doubt that the set of options able to be drawn upon in the construction of the narratives — both paradigmatically and syntagmatically — has changed.

All of the novels still centre on a teenage girl's relationship with a guy, and in several of the stories, the narrative completely relies on these romantic events for its plausibility. Romance is the only narrative device in 53 and 54, and it is a key device in narrative progression in each of the other ten. In all twelve of these titles, the female protagonist learns something about love relationships with guys, and it is set of heterosexual activities that transforms her and provides the lesson.

One major transforming device occurs when discourses of heterosexuality are disrupted through challenges of male violence and male duplicity. For instance, in the first of these twelve titles (*Can I Trust Him?*), an incest victim has to be refocused on heterosexuality, and the novel closes with this transformation.

He laughed and kissed me again, this time really gently. 'Well I've loved you ever since I first met you, Andi.'
Suddenly the past had slipped away and there was only the future. And the present, of course, which was muscular and strong and had his arms tightly around me (p. 135).

Four of the other titles (44, 47, 49 and 53) similarly rely on the issue of 'trust' and a refocusing of attention on to the 'nice man' for narrative resolution.

The potential that the steadiness of a romance with a reliable guy has to steer girls through some difficult moments is also popular. *When You're Pretty* (46) does this most obviously, but it is also a narrative strategy in five of the other titles. Girls have to cope with relocation in a country town (44), with their mother's marriage to a younger guy (47), with a sister's death (50), with dropping out of school (51), and with losing girlfriends (52). Their relationship with a guy helps them through these difficult moments, although in 47 (*What's Normal Anyway?*), the girl does realize that the romantic relationship she had turned to is not one she should ultimately pursue.

Love is usually intermingled with familiarity and trust. As with the earlier *Dolly Fiction* titles, these newer ones similarly draw sharp lines between domesticated and dangerous romance. Dangerous does not usually imply sexual dominance, predominantly because the sexuality paradigm is barely introduced into these teen romances. The novel about incest (*Can I Trust Him?*) carries only the emotional traces of the aftermath of the physical act; the violence does not occur in the narrative. Incidents of unwanted physical advances are minor and typically dealt with in a pseudo-psychological way, by offering explanations of the prior events which have positioned the male offender within a paradigm of aggression. *Can I Trust Him?* and *What's Normal Anyway?* both work on this principle.

Domesticated romance/sexuality predominates. The familiar boy — usually known to the family and well-integrated into the girl's social life — is still the preferred romantic device, and in seven of these texts, the narrative turns to a certain extent on the teenage girl's gradual discovery of his true worth: the 'softness' within the 'hardness'; the feminine within the masculine (43, 44, 48, 50, 51, 52 and 53). In another two (47 and 49) the teenage girl becomes entangled with an older (implicitly more sexually experienced) guy, but in each case the 'dangerous' aspects become 'domesticated'. In 47 (*What's Normal Anyway?*) the girl realizes that the older guy is not for her and turns instead to familiar friends her own age. In 49 (*Hot News*) she discovers that the older more experienced male (a news-reader she meets on work experience at a local TV station) is gentle, warm and 'domesticated' after all. The only narrative to deal explicitly with sexual intercourse (*The Desirable Alien*) clearly positions the physicality in a domesticated framework of planned, monitored contraception; there is no lust, uncontrolled passion or dangerous emotional involvement. The couple are comfortable, familiar and relaxed, and it is the young woman who initiates the event.

I thought, I can't stand it any more. I said, 'Andy, I can't stand this. Can we go up to my room?' (p. 121).

The range of character traits now possible for the *Dolly Fiction* narratives has broadened and this is most noticeable in the field of gendered subjectivities now posited in the texts. The 'new woman' and the 'new man' have entered *Dolly Fiction*, although they jockey for space with some very traditional stereotypes. Teen protagonists are now shown as interested in social issues like wildlife preservation (44) and Aboriginal sacred sites (45) — the 'safe' politics of the environment. They are never, of course, linked with feminism, politics, abortion reform, or unemployment demonstrations. They are also shown exiting out of a romance with no apparently irrevocable damage (45, 47), although, again, they are never shown rejecting heterosexual romance as an inevitable aspect of adolescent life. In two of the narratives, the young women are noticeably independent and initiate several of the events in their romantic entanglements (47, 48). In the second of these, *The Desirable Alien*, the young woman, as suggested earlier, plans her initial sexual encounter with precision, even down to the purchase of condoms with her male partner. Again, however, these 'new women' are made to be with 'new men', and the independence and initiative they offer falls within conventional parameters of contemporary femininity.

The adult parameters have broadened in similar ways. The range of masculine character formations now includes nurturers (43), old hippies (44), politicized teachers (48), and single fathers (49). And the range of female subject positions occupied by 'mothers' has been similarly extended. The most significant shift has been to locate mothers in the public work force. In eight of these twelve titles, the mother is depicted as a worker, although the tensions of being a woman worker are often signalled. In *Riding for a Fall* (53), the teenage girl remarks:

Mum's a freelance book illustrator, and she works from home. It's the best of both worlds, really, because she has an independent income, which she says is absolutely essential for every woman, *but she's nearly always home when I get home from school* (p. 33, emphasis added).

The work that the eight women workers are engaged in is still stereotypically from 'feminine' fields. They are predominantly clerical staff (43, 44, 47, 48) or artists (50, 54), although one is a store buyer (51) and one a university academic (52).

The group of mothers also includes those who have had partners who were convicted of incest (43), those who were teenage mothers (44 and 47), those who leave their current partners and seek refuge in women's shelters (45), those who are in reasonably permanent *de facto* relationships (48), those who marry younger men (47), and those who are alcoholic (51). These women are used to construct a number of positive female scenarios: post-incest (43), post-teenage pregnancy (44), post-divorce (45, 48), post-marriage to a younger man (47). In *So Hard to Leave You* (44), the woman is constructed as an independent operator, taking herself and her daughter off to the bush in search of adventure and freedom. However the scenarios often become positive because the right man is found through which to construct a new relationship (43, 47, 48). Only two mothers are left without a male partner at the close of these twelve novels, and in one of these (44), there is a strong hint that a partner has been met and a relationship will ultimately result. The heterosexual relationship is still the dominant closing device.

A significant shift in these 1900 *Dolly Fiction* titles has been in their explicit reference to sexual intercourse. Whereas the first twelve titles lay totally within the 'squeaky clean' frame, one of these more recent titles addresses sexual inter-course in a reasonably explicit fashion, and two others introduce the possibility of sexual activity but stop short of using it as a narrative event. In *The Desirable Alien* (48), however, intercourse is planned and executed in the text, when Susie organizes her first sexual encounter with a visiting American exchange student.

This novel places sexual intercourse in a common-sense framework of practi-cality, almost as an instruction manual for safe sex. As Susie's friend says bluntly:

'I don't really think the love business matters too much either way, Susie. Just don't get AIDS, that's all, even for love' (p. 25).

And Susie says to her American boyfriend:

'Andy, we should make love sometimes, shouldn't we? I mean, we care enough, don't we?' (p. 88).

They eventually do, talking all the while about 'those rubber things' and 'the other stuff' that goes with them, and then post-intercourse Susie rings her friend to tell her:

'Jo. It's Susie. We did it'.

Practical friend's particular concern is:

'You're not ovulating, are you?' (p. 125).

The intercourse is very soft focus otherwise: no genitalia, no secretions, no moan-ing, no passion. Instead it was 'pretty amazing' and 'a bit unnerving'.

The narrative closures on these 1990 titles indicate that the shift that has occurred in the framing of the romance genre is still slight in terms of the domin-ant framing and shaping of the genre. While the kiss is not the only closure point, it is still dominant. Eight of the twelve end with the kiss or a clear indication that the heterosexual relationship is secure (43, 44, 49, 50, 51, 52, 53, 54); two close on the promise of a relationship yet to be confirmed (46 and 48); and two leave the girl unattached but happy that way (45 and 47).

However the female protagonist in these most recent titles is clearly more independent, more assertive and more contemporary. In general she is con-structed as approximately 16 years of age, as a schoolgirl in her last or second to last year of school, and as well in control of taking up preferred *Dolly* subject positions of trendy adolescent femininity through her attention to clothing detail, hair design, and knowledge of contemporary popular culture. She takes the initiative with sex, with relationships with guys, and with her family dealings.

In these twelve titles there is some reference to studying for exams, but on the whole the *Dolly Fiction* heroine is not interested in school. The female protag-onist in *Best Friends* is a possible exception; she is a computer expert and enters a software competition with her boyfriend. In *So Hard to Leave You* there is mention of how well-equipped and modern is Sophie's new bush school, but generally 'the school' does not figure as a place of any significance, or an event of any significance, in the girls' lives. Sometimes the girl protagonist studies with

her new boyfriend (47, 48, 52), although the opportunity to be together —
particularly in *The Desirable Alien*, where the couple are able to continue their
sexual relationship uninterrupted at a study retreat at the beach — is the predomin-
ant motive.

Schooling is also introduced as problematic for your women, but not in
ways that might be expected. In *Working It Out* (51), Holly is described on the
back cover promotion as 'sick of being hassled at school', but the 'hassling' seems
to stem from the early behaviour of a feminist teacher. Part of Holly's trouble
with school is constructed as arising out of an incident she had in primary school,
where the teacher mocked a 'show and tell' she gave about her new pair of Barbie
and Ken dolls.

> I remember being really excited, but instead of congratulating me, Ms
> Stevenson, my grade teacher, groaned. 'Won't parents ever learn? Not
> another Ken and Barbie set.'
>   I blushed bright red . . . and flew out of the room and hid in the
> toilets for the rest of that morning. Apparently Ms Stevenson used the
> opportunity to sound off about Ken and Barbie. 'Some dolls are bad
> news,' she explained. 'Using these . . .' she held Barbie out to the class,
> '. . . uh . . . dolls as a role model sets up ridiculous expectations in young
> people's minds. They think they ought to look like this' (p. 22).

Ms Stevenson's ideology is rejected by this *Dolly Fiction* text. In the novel's
construction, the class is mystified by her statement, and the incident becomes a
key factor in the positioning of Holly as a potential drop-out. It is eventually
through the intervention of a male teacher counsellor — not a feminist teacher —
that Holly is able to return to school to study art.

Romance Fiction and Social Regulation: Reading the Shifts in *Dolly Fiction*

The differences between 1988 and 1990 *Dolly Fiction* texts are noticeable, but the
significance of these differences, in terms of reframing the gendered nature of
romance fiction, needs, as this chapter has argued, to be read with caution.
Novels from both groups still clearly position their readers — 'frame' their reader
— to expect romance ideology. This is obvious from the promotional material
used, the cover design, and the back cover introduction of both sets of texts. By
their links with *Dolly* magazine, readers of *Dolly Fiction* are also clearly positioned
within a reading formation that links romance ideology with the discourses on
teenage femininity that prevail in the magazine. While the textual extension of
the magazine is a set of fiction that explores romance, romance is inevitably
associated with, and seen as compatible to, the dominant reading positions of
fashionable femininity constructed in *Dolly* magazine.

However the shifts that have occurred over the twenty-four months indicate
what flexibility romance fiction has in its response to contemporary versions of
teenage femininity and heterosexual relationships. It is clearly possible to construct women in more authoritative, public and independent subject positions,
and it is clearly possible to discuss sexual activity with *Dolly Fiction* readers, but

it is clearly not as possible to construct narrative transformations that reflect such authority and such independence. In both sets of fiction, the narratives predominantly achieve closure by the kiss, and, in this regard, the second set of twelve are just as consistent as are the first twelve. Consider these closing frames for five of the more recent titles:

'You know I'm crazy about you,' I said . . .

He nodded. 'I feel the same.'

I couldn't believe it. He felt the same! I felt like laughing or crying or both, but I didn't.

I said, 'How about kissing me, then?'

And he did (44, p. 126).

'Hello, Steph,' he said. His arms slid around me. It felt wonderful . . .

We kissed. Long and slow . . . (49, p. 148).

That was the moment of truth. And the truth was that things could never be the same as they were before. Both of us had learnt so much about each other . . . about our weaknesses and strengths and how much we missed and needed each other . . . But the wonderful thing was, we knew we were meant to be together. I guess I don't have to tell you how happy I felt right them . . . (51, p. 148).

I'm truly in love for the first time in my life. Luke seems to be pretty happy too — at least, he grins every time he looks at me.

And I love him to bits.

And that's about all really . . . (52, p. 141).

'Pete,' I said. 'I do love you. I realise now how much. Do you believe me?'

'I believe you,' he said softly. 'I love you, too.'

. . . and then we kissed again. I was so happy (53, p. 144).

The narrative pattern clearly still relies upon the intervention of the romance hero for substantial movement. None of these twenty-four titles have constructed a 'story' outside of a heterosexual coupling, and while some of the narrative events have more recently been broadened to include character, events and issues that have not always fallen within the paradigm of romance ideology, such characters, events and issues are read from within the dominant generic framework of the romance, and are thus subsidiary and satellite to the kernel events and the dominant narrative movement. The fact that women might now go to hear a one-woman comic (43), that mothers tell their daughters that an independent income is 'absolutely essential for every woman' (53, p. 33), that guys can work in child-care units (43), that fathers and brothers can cook 49) that women can marry younger men (47), that girls can initiate sex (48), or that a young woman might want to shake hands with a guy as a 'token of equality' (45, p. 6), does not significantly alter the limited parameters of social action possible in these novels.

Despite their superficial accommodation to contemporary social shifts, these texts are still firmly located within the parameters of romance fiction, and as such they structure gender difference through various narrative representations of femininity. By rationalizing the normative values of heterosexual relations, such stories place gender in a field of signification so that, as Cohan and Shires argue, 'representations of sexual difference acquire meaning by reinforcing the values of love and marriage, of emotional vulnerability and domesticity, and by making them appear natural, inevitable, and desirable as culturally legible signs of "femininity"' (1988, p. 80).

Dolly Fiction has undoubtedly broadened its parameters and its scope in its first two years of operation, and the range of gendered subject positions constructed through the texts is now more contemporary and less stereotypical. The difficulty lies in the generic nature of these texts, and it is here that the limitations of textual possibility can be most keenly felt. While the generic pattern draws so strongly upon romantic discourses for its parameters of possibility, the narrative sequences constructed within this framework are necessarily limited in the possibilities of gendered subjectivity that they can represent.

This limitation becomes of key importance. 'Stories', as Cohan and Shires argue, 'structure the meanings by which a culture lives' (1988, p. 1), and it is stories such as these *Dolly* fictions which inevitably define parameters of possibility for many young women; they are certainly limited in the 'doll-like' versions of femininity they are able to construct. We need different stories for young women so that other cultural meanings — other ways of reading teenage subjectivity — can be legitimized and authorized. As was clear in the schooling extract referred to in *Working It Out*, or the working mother scenario of *Riding for a Fall*, various versions of feminism are very uneasily located within *Dolly Fiction*. The generic conventions of narrative movements and character traiting constrain discursive borrowings from feminisms.

The current field of signification that these teen romance novels rely upon for their plausibility as credible narrative sequences has flirted with alternative versions of femininity, but seems unwilling (perhaps conventionally and generically unable) to embrace them. Consequently, *Dolly Fiction* has still a long way to travel if it is to be able to draw from cultural paradigms which will be less restrictive and inhibiting for young women; if it is to provide, as Byrne would wish, a 'good read' with something 'worthwhile to say as well'. Fictions other than 'dolly' fictions are the good reads to which many young women still have little access.

Note

1 Marina Go, current Editor of *Dolly* magazine, claimed that this age range was her readership on a recent radio interview (*Offspring*, ABC, 10 April, 1991).

References

ALTUS, M. (1984a) 'Sugar-coated pills', *Orana*, **20**, 2, pp. 70–90.
ALTUS, M. (1984b) 'Sugar-coated pills: continued', *Orana*, **20**, 3, pp. 119–37.
BYRNE, B. (1989) *Dolly Fiction Series: Editor's Guidelines*.
CHRISTIAN-SMITH, L. (1987) 'Gender, popular culture and curriculum: adolescent romance novels as gender text', *Curriculum Inquiry*, **17**, 4, pp. 365–406.

COHAN, S. and SHIRES, L. (1988) *Telling Stories: A Theoretical Analysis of Narrative Fiction*, London, Routledge.

GILBERT, P. and TAYLOR, S. (1991) *Fashioning the Feminine: Girls, Popular Culture and Schooling*, Sydney, Allen and Unwin.

GUILEY, R. (1983) *Lovelines: The Fun, Quirks and Trivia of Romance*, London, Zomba Books.

KNODEL, B. (1982) 'Still far from equal: young women in literature for adolescents', Paper presented at the annual meeting of the National Council of Teachers of English, Spring Conference, Minneapolis.

KRESS, G. (1985) *Linguistic Processes in Sociocultural Practice*, Geelong, Deakin University Press.

LAM, M. (1986) *Reading the Sweet Dream: Adolescent Girls and Romance Fiction*, Unpublished MEd thesis, University of Melbourne.

SNITOW, A. (1984) 'Mass market romance: Pornography for women is different', in A. SNITOW, C. STANSELL and S. THOMPSON (Eds) *Powers of Desire: The Politics of Sexuality*, London, Virago.

THURSTON, C. (1987) *The romance Revolution: Erotic Novels for Women and the Quest for a New Sexual Identity*, Chicago, University of Illinois Press.

Chapter 6

Reading the Romance Younger: The Mirrors and Fears of a Preparatory Literature

John Willinsky and R. Mark Hunniford

Fresh fun novels that teenage girls want to read and their parents will encourage them to read. Books that are touching, wholesome stories of the experiences teenagers everywhere need to understand and read about — first dates, first dances, first love (A blurb for Bantam's Sweet Dreams Series).

In 1984, Janice Radway published a detailed study of forty-two romance readers entitled *Reading the Romance: Women, Patriarchy and Popular Literature*. In her book, she deals with both the reasons why the women read romances and what they find there: to put it briefly, she finds that the books address 'an intensely felt but insufficiently met need for emotional nurturance' (p. 119), and that the women turn to these books as a means of 'denying the present' and 'identifying with a heroine whose life does not resemble their own' (p. 90). Radway sets these women's intensely pleasurable reading into the troubling context of a profit-driven publishing industry and a patriarchal society, both of which the romance serves all too well. The strength of her analysis is this double view, which has both depth, as she focuses on the responses of a small sample of readers, and breadth, as she describes the social forces at work in this simple act of picking up a book.

In this instance, we hope to complement her fascinating work with a parallel study of forty-two grade seven students who have on questionnaires and in interviews shown themselves to be avid fans of the young adult romance. With Radway as our guide, we wish to examine three areas which come together to create what might be termed the self-directed literacy of the young reader: a) the aggressive economy of literacy which produces the romance as the book of fashion for the young, b) the preparatory function which these books successfully serve for the students, and c) the limited nature of the life these romances portray for these keen readers.

This triple perspective has resulted in a long essay in three sections. The length and variety of perspectives seemed necessary to capture the broad nature of this literacy event; we have deliberately recast the reading act as something larger than those isolated moments in which students sit with the texts in hand. Though each section has its own theme and focus, the three taken together — that is, the production, the function and the content of the romance — mirror the nature of literacy beyond the school and, as such, reflect the site of certain apprehensions among educators. Which is to say that the mirrors and fears of this preparatory literature belong to both the young readers of the romance and their teachers as well.

We realize that this approach to literacy challenges both the more specialized models of reading and comprehension, whether of a reader-response of psycho-linguistic sort, as well as the traditional pattern of reporting on the reading act. We have treated this reading of the romance on the part of these grade seven girls as the point of entry into a culture of literacy production and consumption, an entry which cannot be divorced from life in the society at large. Many educators could happily see students move beyond isolated acts of text comprehension and into the very culture of literacy; in order to understand what that movement entails, educators need to remain curious about how this culture operates — how books are produced and marketed, as well as why they are read or rejected.

In the case of the young adult romance, our students have plunged ahead of us, headlong into this culture in a unique way. For the first time, these people, whom we would make readers, have become a major force in the publishing of books and it behooves us to know why. The three sections of this essay on the reading of the romance, then are underwritten by a concern with a sociology of literacy. In the area of literary production — the subject of the first section — the romance represents both the clever marketing of literacy in an age of consumerism and the continuation of a strong tradition in popular literature. These factors appear destined to determine the future of a literacy of pleasure. In the second section, we describe how the romances are serving girls in a different way than they serve adult readers, as reported in Radway's study. Rather than turning to the books as a way out of their world, as the adults in the Radway study had, these students, on the verge of full-blown adolescence, are turning to the books as a way of preparing to get into the world, at least as they imagine it to be. Finally in the third section, we describe how the romances represent both the power and the danger of a future found in literature, and as such bring us face-to-page with the things which books can still do very well.

I

'Oh, Lizzie, do you believe how absolutely horrendous I look today?' Jessica Wakefield groaned as she stepped in front of her sister, Elizabeth, and stared at herself in the bedroom mirror.

> *Double Love* (Williams, 1983, p. 1)

Radway's first point in taking up the way the romance works with the reader is to consider 'the institutional matrix' as she refers to the publishing business which produces and promotes the romance as the book of choice for these serious readers (pp. 19–45). Her description of the romance industry makes it clear just how different the making of these books is from what many of us hold to be the proper process of literary invention. Not surprisingly, the case with the junior version is little different. However, philistinism is not the issue here. Rather our project in this section is to provide a description of an industry which has success-fully found ways to create and sustain readers, to make the book an object of adolescent fashion. If we are to grasp the current nature of this literacy, we need to recognize that readers are responding to the thoughtful efforts of a publishing industry and not just to text they have before them.

The birth of the young about romance series can be set with unusual precision and confidence. In the fall of 1979, Scholastic Book Service launched its *Wildfire Romance* series (Jefferson, 1982, p. 613). To make this conceptual break-through to a junior romance series, the marketing people at Scholastic had to look no further than the flourishing figures for adult romances as well as the promising sales of individual romances in the school book clubs. To take the example of one major publisher of romances and a small source of Canadian pride, Harlequin in 1979 distributed 168 million copies worldwide. In the course of a decade, Harle-quin had created 'a regular readership of over 16 million women in North America' establishing the firm place of the romance as part of our reading habit (Harlequin, cited by Radway, 1984, p. 23).

The marketing people must have reasoned after Wordsworth, that the girl is mother to the women [romance reader]. Scholastic already had, by its own account, 70 percent of the school-age readers in hand through the collaboration of English teachers who serve as sales reps for the various Scholastic book clubs (Smith, 1981, p. 56). The people at Scholastic also knew that the shopping malls, with bookstore chains and drugstore bookracks, were the new suburban play-grounds of the adolescent. It was no publishing gamble. Over the first two years, the *Wildfire Romance* series sold over 2.25 million copies; first printings of the titles have been in the area of 100,000 copies (Smith, 1981, pp. 56, 61). Five years after their launching, our local bookstore in the mall has given over to the young adult romance an amount of shelfspace equivalent to the combined section of poetry, philosophy and religion!

If we are to understand how a reading audience can be so successfully and rapidly fashioned from among the young, we much recognize that the publisher, rather than the author, is responsible for this instance of literary invention. The strongest example of this creative urge in young adult romances is Cloverdale Press which has assisted a number of the large publishers by 'packaging' such romance series as *Sweet Valley High* (Bantam), *Sweet Dreams* (Bantam), *Caitlin* (Bantam), and *Seniors* (Dell). Mary Cullen, an editor with Cloverdale, has described the process in the terms of the modern business deal:

> We come up with the idea for a book or series, put together a proposal
> for the publisher, hire the authors (they employ over a hundred) and edit
> the manuscripts (cited in Sutton, 1985, p. 27).

The books have been packaged into the designer jeans of the book market, with their matching logos which the reader collects by number, from one to ninety-six and counting in the *Sweet Dreams* series. The reader can find the same familiarity of old friends and situations which they tune into weekly with sitcoms on television. As it turns out, the writing is as about as anonymous. *Double Love* (Williams, 1983) is the first title in the *Sweet Valley High* series, and on the spine and cover is said to have been 'created by Francine Pascal' (who also holds the copyright on the book and the series). Only on the title page does the writer Kate Williams get credit, which we took to be a foreboding welcome to a new age of authorship.

Obviously, the young adult romances are not the first instance of formula fiction and hired authors: first there was the Grub Street of writers for hire in Samuel Johnson's day and then many of us, many years later, spent some part of our youth chasing after the many-authored *Hardy Boys* and *Nancy Drew*. However, there are two distinctions to be made with this new 'grubstreet', as Johnson coined it. The young adult romance treats the young woman as a consumer of literature — no *Hardy Boys* spin-off to be purchased for daughters on birthdays — and as such the books are marketed with all the earnestness and flair of fast-food franchises. The point of comparison is the case with the young adult literature breakthrough of the 70s, the new realism of Blume, Klein, Danziger *et al*. These are author books rather than series books; they have won the literary hearts of librarians and teachers, if not parents of all persuasions. The authors would seem to have a social mission in the loyal representation of as much reality as young readers are believed to be capable of ingesting, though their works of realism were still found to be serving the young woman with stereotyping (Nelson, 1975) and gaps in that reality (Stanek, 1976).

Those shortcomings aside, the realistic novel, with all of its authorial integrity, has not been written to thoroughly appease the young woman reader, and that simple fact is what distinguishes it from the sheer reader-indulgence of the romance series. Realism is still bringing a message to young women rather than letting them feel as if they are there to be catered to, as the world must appear in the fantasy land of the suburban mall. The political climate over the last decade has changed and popular literary production has followed; where realism embraced the diversity and possibilities of conformism, the current mood is somewhat narrower and the times less tolerant. The romance with its strict adherence to formula, to the simplicity of ideals in physical beauty and fashionable coupling, is a political chronicle for these more conservative times. Finally, realism, in having achieved scholastic acceptance, now fails to pass as fashion, as something at the very edge of 'now'. Thus it might be claimed that the romance is shot through with a streak of realism which is in touch with the contemporary world of literacy and life in a different way. It sells accordingly, and has for the first time in the process shifted the weight of the juvenile market away from schools and libraries and into the hands of the readers themselves (Smith, 1981, p. 61). As the romance series is tuned to the current climate of consumption, we would do well to treat it, not as a perversion of our mission in literacy, but as indicative of a continuing appetite for the medium of the printed word which is well-met by the convenience and appeal of these packages in paper covers, these books in chains and malls.

This apparent literary cynicism on the part of the publishers in the pursuit of an unimaginative financial bottom-line over the dangerous headiness of art is not restricted to the publication of romances, adult or junior. Publishing for a profit has been a recurring theme throughout the history of the book, especially since the invention of moveable type. As Marshall McLuhan (1962) pointed out, Johann Gutenberg introduced the first instance of the assembly line, leading to mass production, which, in turn, made the book the first of the mass media.

Gutenberg understood these market forces and saw his future in publishing unadorned Indulgences as well as beautifully illuminated Bibles (Scholderer, 1963). The romance must be seen as contiguous with the history of the publishing enterprise, one which has always slipped about between economy and art, between investment and aesthetic, often in ways which made such distinctions difficult. Yet the special instance of the young adult romance is to have taken up the case of the young woman in our society, recognizing her impact as an independent consumer and 'maller'. She has proven to hold a generally stronger attachment than young men to literate activities, and her emotional vulnerability, in having to find herself in mirrors and boyfriends, is the stuff of which romances are made. In an electronic age amidst pronouncements of the book's imminent passing (Bell, 1985), the popularity of the romance attests to the book's surprising resilience in its stand against other media courting the young, a resilience based on specialized markets, economy, portability and elements of privacy and personal control. To speak of the Romance as symptomatic of the general decline in literacy is to display a selective ignorance of the history and force of popular reading (Davies, 1965; Illich, 1979). This persistent reading for pleasure has always been a mainstay of the publishing business.

Though the publishers can be portrayed as merely capitalizing on marketplace factors, we might also ask if they inadvertently do more for the readers. Do these books suggest to the girls an uplifting literature of their own, beyond wordy classics and hard edged realists; do they provide a vehicle for realizing both the limitations and the false ideals they find themselves thrown into with the onset of adolescence? Finally, do they contribute, as Radway convincingly argues in the case of the adult versions, to the reproduction of a patriarchal society which both creates the need for these vicarious pleasures and meets them in a way that perpetuates the inequities? The publishing industry has always shown an ability to swing with the current mood and in that way, we suppose, feed the temper of the times. The young adult romance publishing boom signals a rise in literate activities among the young which reflects a change in the marketing techniques of publishers and their reconceptualization of the young woman's need in literature. As Radway points out, the publishers are determined to create a market that is both predictable and easily serviced (pp. 40–44). Yet the publisher's power to create a flame where they believe there is a spark has limits; young readers do discriminate, as indicated by the failure of Bantam's *Circle of Love* series and Fawcett's *Coventry* series, both of which recently folded after an investment of several million dollars (Davis, 1984, p. 364).

We may wish to disparage the method of production as crass commercialism and the substance as dangerously given to stereotyping. But as educators with a strong interest in literacy, we also wish to better understand this political economy of reading and our role in it. We might begin by admitting that reading is a business for educators as it is for publishers. The ways in which our bottom-lines may differ — in why we would have them read — is a question which underlies this entire paper. We must decide if the publishers have bettered us in opening the pleasures of the text for the students. If what they have opened continues to disturb us, how are we to balance without closing that pleasure down?

The tendency among educators has been to remain ignorant of the production processes as beyond our literate interests. What we can learn about the production of these popular books would seem worthwhile sharing among ourselves and with our students as part of their education in the subject. The second step would seem to be to understand what it is students are taking from these books; there is more to them than marketing, though there is that in the first instance. How is it that these books serve so well? In her study of adult readers, Radway wrestles with both the conservative and liberating forces of literacy for the women who read the romance, but in fact this is a dichotomy which has always dogged the book (cf. Illich, 1979; Freire, 1983). In our study, we have found traces among the young readers of both acquiescent and questioning postures, as the books reinforce in the reader what they stereotype on the page, and as they provide a common forum for challenges and alternatives from readers who still have the final say after the cover is closed.

II

'I'm so gross! Just look at me. Everything is totally wrong. To begin which, I'm disgustingly fat . . .' with that, she spun around to show off a stunning figure without an extra ounce visible anywhere.
                                        Double Love (Williams, 1983, p. 1)

Our work with the students began with a survey of student reading habits in six classes of grade seven students in a junior high school. The school was located in a lower middle-class neighborhood with some subsidized housing and a fairly even mix between single-family and multiple-family dwellings. The neighborhood would seem to fall a little economically short of the one in which Radway did her study; her subjects were married and mothers for the most part in single-family homes, with about 20 percent having earned a college degree (pp. 56–7). Her subjects could be the mothers of our students and the women they could become. The students in our study were asked to identify their favorite type of reading from a selection of thirteen genres. The boys were split in their choices among war, adventure, and sports stories, while 61 percent of the girls selected romances as their reading material of choice. These forty-eight students were reduced to forty-two, to fully match Radway's sample, by a random process and given a modified version of the Radway questionnaire found in an appendix to her book. A small number of her questions were altered to reflect the omission of active sexuality in the young adult romances, and deleted where the demographic information was not felt to be pertinent. Finally, eight of the girls were taped during an interview based on issues raised in Radway's book and specific young adult romance novels.

The first parallel between these readers, young and adult, is the pattern of their reading habits (see Table 1). Romance readers of any age appear to be devoted to their texts and turn to them on a daily basis, the sort of reading habit schools have always looked to foster. Radway, on the other hand, is not so sanguine. She has cast this matter of frequency and repetition in the reading of the romance as a strong symptom of discontent rather than the triumph of literacy. While the adult readers she worked with felt strongly that this reading was a 'declaration of independence', 'combative and compensatory', Radway is inclined to declare this continuous turning of the pages a white flag of surrender to patriarchal forces (pp. 211–13). As we can see, Radway both represents the readers'

Table 1: *Reading habits of romance readers*

	Girls (n = 42)	Women (n = 42)
Read a romance every day	88%	88%
Read until the book is finished	29	26
Read until you are interrupted	48	71
Re-read the books sometimes	50	75

Note: Figures on the women's responses are from Radway, 1984, pp. 58–59. Reprinted by permission.

response to the romance and challenges what she sees as untenable in it. By the end of her study, she succeeds in setting the romance apart from both the novel and literacy, in general. Radway finds the romance closer to an oral-based fairy tale than the novel. Her concluding sentence envisions a world in which 'the vicarious pleasure supplied by its reading would be unnecessary' (p. 222). It should be clear by this point that we are not so inclined to set this reading as far off from what the rest of us do with books. Still, we do want to make a number of distinctions with the particular case of what girls are doing with the young adult romance.

Radway establishes that the women find a consolation in the romance, using it to set up a quiet, private space, rather than using their discontent to raise a public voice against the inadequacies of a social structure which deprives women of both status and nurturance. This reading of the romance is a means of finding themselves in the books, rather than remaking who they are in the world, a finding which sustains itself in the pleasure of returning to these books on a daily basis. The experience may be vicarious but not the pleasure. But reading fiction is generally like that and, we suppose, philosophy is too, at least according to Boethius. With the young readers in this study, whom we found as given to these pleasures as Radway's adults, reading the romance this seriously, they appear on the verge of a total surrender on a number of fronts; they are, in effect, taking more from the books than the adults, more than many of us in education would want to ask.

This danger became more apparent with younger readers when they declared their intentions with the romance in a way which suggested that the books were not simply a private pleasure but would play a role in the public spheres of their lives. Radway's adult readers explained their reasons for reading the books most strongly in terms of simple relaxation and time set aside just for them, while a few looked to the books for their educational value on faraway places and times (see Table 2). The case with the young romance reader is markedly stronger on two of the choices. Their regard for strong, virile heroes was part of a consistent concern with appearances, with a process of judgment which reveals a new awareness of physical development. The second significant difference in their selection is their desire to have a romance just like the heroine's. That is, they would read this way because they believed that they will live this way once they had finished junior high. It is not just that they are asking the books to be plausible in character and plot, as the Radway women did for their ideal romance novels. The plausibility of the romance for the girl has become a matter of her own life, her imminent future in romance. The degree of

Table 2: The reasons for reading romances: Total of first, second and third choices

Response	Girls (n = 42)	Women (n = 42)
1 To escape my daily problems	14	13
2 To learn about faraway places and times	0	19
3 For simple relaxation	22	33
4 Because I wish I had a remance like the heroine's	22	5
5 Because reading is just for me; it is my time	13	28
6 Because I like to read about the strong, virile heroes	19	4
7 Because reading is at least better than other forms of escape	7	5
8 Because romantic stories are never sad or depressing	13	10

Note: Figures on the women's responses are from Radway, 1984, p. 61. Reprinted by permission.

identification which this attitude affords is that much greater as the pleasurable flush the reader feels for the rewarded heroine can also be felt for oneself in antici-pation. The heroine demonstrates the way and the sensation. The reading is like having your fortune read in good faith with the tingle of excitement in watching it unfold in the crystal ball.

Not surprisingly, the young readers of romance proved in their responses to 'it is my time' somewhat less concerned than the adults about time spent alone. Likewise, that faraway places and times drew little interest from the young reader is also predictable; the setting of the young adult romance in both time and space is remarkably contemporary-domestic, often sunny-Californian. On the other hand, matters of escape and refreshment to be found in the romances seemed to attract similar numbers of readers from both groups.

This distinguishing desire to have a romance like the heroine's is to realize a possibility or, in their eyes, an inevitability, as 12-year-olds read about the fate of 16-year-olds. It makes the romance into a guide for the perplexed and the anxious, for those looking for a bright, scintillating preview into the immedi-ate future. In the interviews with the students, this sense of imminence and pre-paration became increasingly apparent:

Janis:	Well, some girls dream about guys and that they meet guys and they're really shy and that, and in grade seven we just say hi to them and bye.
Interviewer:	Are there no real boyfriends and girlfriends in grade seven?
Janis:	No. That'll probably happen in grade eight or nine.
Interviewer:	Can these books teach you anything?
Janis:	Yes, I think so, because if you're really shy and that, and if you read them then, they could help you, like to know what to expect when you get to grade eight.

'Like to know what to expect' speaks to a certain anxiety about what is now the stuff of dreams and 'probably' a year off in reality; at this point there is only that impossible bridge in which 'hi' and 'bye' have to serve across the distance. The romance stages the best-case scenario, filling in the hard-to-imagine script. The books provide the art that life would gladly imitate:

'Yes Liz, you're the only one I ever wanted. No Jessica, not anybody.'
    Todd was moving closer to her.
    'But what about Emily?'
    'Emily Mayer? We have a history project together.'
    'You didn't touch Jessica?'
    'No. Absolutely not!'
. . .
    Elizabeth laughed softy, pulling Todd closer for another, longer kiss that was sweeter than anything she had imagined.
                    (*Double Love*, Williams, 1983, pp. 168–9)

But it is a closed script. Many readers will have to realize that they have already been written out of the story, as it works a narrow ideal of physical beauty and material circumstance. The adult reader of the romance has reconciled herself to who she has become; she does not ask to be the heroine of the romances, only to share vicariously in her adventures. This need for identification, Radway argues, is the result of her discontent with who she has become. The younger reader believes it possible to become the heroine of the romance, because she is living in a state of emergence and expectation. That much understood, she asks only to be told how to act and handle it once she gets there. Why read romance, we asked the students, and it was clear they assumed that they needed the preparation to face what the heroine faced:

Isabella:	Because it gives me ideas on how I can meet boys.
Interviewer:	What ideas?
Isabella:	Like, what to say to them. Like, give confidence.
Interviewer:	Why should a boy read a romance?
Isabella:	The same way a girl should — to get ideas.
Interviewer:	About what?
Isabella:	About how to act around a girl, and how to introduce yourself and to get some ideas about where to go on a date.

This matter of instruction was also important for the adult reader of the romance, but in a completely different way. Radway treats this claim on the part of the reader as suspect, as a covering excuse for this pleasurable indulgence, as they play up the books' educational value for their husbands and other suspicious onlookers (p. 107). The educational bonus in the romances is in faraway places and times, and the readers take some pride in the research which apparently goes into the books. From Radway's description, it would seem that the quality of fascinating information might be said to vary between the level of *Trivial Pursuit* and *National Geographic*. Radway attributes the women's claim of the importance of instruction in their reading of the books to the mythology of reading as both self-improvement and a step on the road to success. Radway is, of course, suggesting that this reading is somewhat otherwise, and there are others who have gone to some trouble to substantiate the mythological nature of literacy's beneficent claims (Graff, 1979; Scribner and Cole, 1981).
    The pleasure the reader feels in this sense of self-improvement and instruction, in the labor of literacy rewarded, is certainly part of the book's boast in its

competition among the media. This sense is that much stronger with the young adult romance. The books instruct, not in isolated facts and exotic bits of know-ledge, but explicitly and directly in self-improvement. This case for the value of literature may be more apparent in the romance than any we might be able to make using our tests in literature and composition skills:

Alice:	Well, because I really like the stories and I think, well one day, they'll happen to me, and I really like the stories. They're really neat.
Interviewer:	In what way might they happen to you?
Alice:	Like the *Sweet Dreams* books are sort of realistic. That's why I read them, because I think they can happen to me.
Interviewer:	Can you learn anything from them?
Alice:	In one book I read I learned something: I learned that it doesn't really matter what the guy looks like, it matters what their attitude is, and what they're like is really what matters.

The distinguished literary critic M.H. Abrams has described this combina-tion of interests represented by these students — as neat and informative — as the pragmatic approach to literature. This long-standing critical stance has a history which encompasses Horace's description of the writer's aim 'to blend in one the delightful and useful', and Philip Sidney's declaration of the poetry's purpose to be 'to teach and delight' not 'what is, hath been, or shall be', but only 'what may be, and should be' (cited in Abrams, 1953, pp. 15–6). What may be and should be is exactly what these readers would have from these books, along with the delight. They regard the books as instruction manuals, sweetened with melodramatic suspense and sensation. Here the helpful hints are in how to feel, as well as what to say and wear. In judging the students' interest in these books, we must take account of the double strength in this position. Literacy may never again for them be such a fulfilling source of satisfaction. The books have a useful-ness that serves with delight as it teaches what they so desire to live. What strikes us as clichéd and hackneyed in the books reminds us that we have outgrown those earlier traumas; for these young readers, the simplicity and perfectly predictable movement of language and action is what they would ask of their books and their immediate future. This sustains a high degree of identification with the heroine as it feeds the hope of becoming one. The reader just needs to get the moves and grooves down, and it can all happen:

Interviewer:	Can they teach you anything else?
Jane:	Oh yes, like clothes. It always says near the beginning what she's wearing, and I get ideas, like, I should wear that next time I go out.
Interviewer:	Can the stories actually happen?
Jane:	Ya.
Interviewer:	Would you like them to happen to you?
Jane:	Ya, for sure! (laughter)
Interviewer:	If this happens, when do you think it will occur?
Jane:	Probably high school! The kids are usually 16 or 17.
Interviewer:	Should boys read romances? Why?

Jane:	Well, because it has boys in the romance books, right, and it can teach the boy how to act around a girl.
Interviewer:	Do boys know how to act around girls?
Jane:	Well, right now, they show their feelings in different ways. Like, because in high school, from what I've read, they're really nice to each other, but now they could hit girls to show they really like them. They could hurt me, but that's their way of showing their feelings.

The slap-happy boys in grade seven are caught up in other games, in other ways of finding themselves in books, through war and sports stories. They understand that they are to make a mark on the world in other fashion, and they are anxious about other matters. They do not feel the need for romance as the means to identity, to being found in someone else's eyes as the girls in the romance perpetually find themselves reflected in a mirror: 'Elizabeth floated through the living room and up the stairs to her room. She headed straight for the mirror and smiled at what she saw' (Williams, 1983, p. 170). Many boys at this age will have also redis-covered the mirror, but they can afford to be less anxious about how to look, what to say and to wear; they know that they will have to do more than look to repre-sent themselves, to find recognition. They will have to find themselves in other ways. The psychoanalyst Jacques Lacan (1968) has made much of the mirror's contri-bution to the infants' development of an identity, to their discovery of a Self (*le stade du miroir*); his discussion of the mirror's contribution to the individual's per-ceptual relationships to others and to self-awareness might be applied to the case of the young woman. She is again facing a moment of unfolding identity which, more so that the young man's, hinges on her visual relationship with others.

Table 3: Question: What qualities do you like to see in a heroine/hero? Total of first, second and third choices

		Heroine		Hero	
Response		Girls (*n* = 42)	Women (*n* = 42)	Girls (*n* = 42)	Women (*n* = 42)
1	Intelligence	28	33[a]	13	30
2	Tenderness	–	–	26	26
3	Protectiveness	–	–	12	14
4	Strength	–	–	11	15
5	Bravery	–	–	12	7
6	Sense of Humour	19	31	16	19
7	Independence	–	20	0	0
8	Attractiveness	–	–	0	10
9	A Good Body	–	–	25	5
10	Beauty	28	–	–	–

Note: Figures for the women's responses are from Radway, 1984, pp. 77–82. Reprinted by permission.
[a] Radway has only reported top three totals for heroine which turn out to be the three characteristics which were placed on the questions for both the hero and the heroine.

This process of moving through the looking glass to face adolescent fears, is to identify with the heroine and to learn how to find yourself among the boys. The specific qualities which these girls are seeking in the heroine have become the points of their identification (see Table 3). Radway found among the adult readers that intelligence and a sense of humor were the strong qualities which the women were looking for in their romance heroines, though they would have these mixed with a streak of independence (p. 77). The junior high students also felt that intelligence and a sense of humor were the marks of a true heroine in their romances: But rather significantly, they substituted beauty in their choices for the adult concern with independence. The young were, perhaps, acknowledging with that distinction their desire to get on with the world, as it is so often represented for them, rather than out or apart from it. In considering the ideal hero of the romance novel, the adults continued to pursue this concern for intelligence and a sense of humor, with the addition this time of tenderness as a quality sought in the man. The girls again supported this adult regard for intelligence and a sense of humor. Yet this time the adolescents selected 'a good boy' over tenderness to distinguish their regard from the adult standard: 'He was skinny, too, but I knew that he had some good-looking muscle under that shirt. A shudder went through me as I thought about that' (Conklin, 1981, p. 36):

> Interviewer: What should the boy be like?
> Isabella: Cute, very nice, and responsible, but definitely good looking.

It is worth noting that the adult romances are also marked by heroes with excellent bodies and unfailing handsomeness. That much is a given, but in setting out the ideal in the romance, the adult readers are seeking something more, deeper and lasting. Among the young, physical self-consciousness and presence are a part of the emerging concern, a part of what they are banking on as they grow up, and what they ask for in their heroes as they ask for it themselves:

> I lay awake for hours that night touching my mouth, my face, getting up several times and looking in the hand mirror on the chest of drawers. It was like a miracle. It one short day I had turned pretty (Conklin, 1981, p. 60).

But in both cases the omissions of the young readers are telling. The adult readers did not see a strong need for tenderness in their heroines or independence in their heroes. The adolescents, in turn, did not see the importance of either tenderness or independence in their leading characters. As with the lower adult regard for beauty and good bodies, we might conclude that these qualities are not the points of anxiety among the young.

Still, these young readers would not have too much of this idealization in their heroines. In the interviews with the students, two factors missing from Radway's question on the heroine emerged — flaws and talents. The slightest flaw in the heroine seemed to be necessary to bring her within range for these readers, however many other sterling qualities she had. An emerging, unproven talent or ambition also added to the heroine's humanity and occurred regularly in the young adult romances serving to flesh out the character:

> Now it was Elizabeth's turn to blush. Enid knew her secret dream — to be a writer. Not just a reporter, the way she was on *The Oracle*, but a serious writer (Williams, 1983, p. 20).

This would seem a promising aspect in the search for identity, though it often plays over the course of the novel little more than a plot device in a story whose real concern is having the heroine finally found as an object of romance. One student we interviewed was able to capture well in her interview the slightness and the importance of these flaws and talents in the romance:

Interviewer: In what ways are the characters realistic?
Isabella: They dress like normal people, and they talk like normal people. I read this one where a girl was in front of a mirror talking about how ugly she thinks she is.
Interviewer: Are girls like that?
Isabella: I am. (laughter)
Interviewer: If you could put yourself in a romance what would you be like?
Isabella: I'd be a really good dancer.
Interviewer: So the story would revolve around dancing?
Isabella: Yes, and modeling. And maybe a guy would meet me at a modeling or dancing competition, and go on a date.
Interviewer: What other characteristics would you have?
Isabella: Pretty and understanding and very nice — sometimes.
Interviewer: Sometimes?
Isabella: In all books, the person shouldn't be just a goody-goody.

It is difficult to imagine the boys, who might well fantasize about taking part in one of their sports stories, thinking of the hockey rink or the baseball diamond as the perfect vehicle for meeting girls. Certainly this sort of meeting may be for them part of what it means to be successful, one of the rewards, but the talent and the sport in these cases does not take on the status of a hobby for them, as a way of putting in the time and arranging the circumstances. The boys' preparatory literature is taken up with mirroring the career of their choice, with making their mark in the public realm yet without having to give up hope for success in the private world of romance. Both boys and girls imagine being discovered in these stories, but this discovery is through different aspects of themselves and what they have to offer, of who they are becoming, and in that difference the competitive edge to Isabella's dancing disappears in her daydream. As we shall see in the final section, it happens that way in the novels too.

III

> After the rally, Elizabeth and Todd finally said good night — a long good night filled with kisses and sweet words, and still more kisses. Elizabeth watched Todd drive off, then went in, closed the door, and leaned against it, sighing happily.
>
> *Double Love* (Williams, 1983, p. 182)

Erich Segal (1985), a professor of classics and no mean romance author himself, has recently opened up the historical vista of the romance genre by tracing it back to classical Greece. Ignored or eschewed at the time, and since, by respectable writers, these forgotten classics are only now about to be translated into English. Segal makes it clear that these representations of love and sentiment — *erotika pathemata* as the Greeks termed them — were first among the subjects of prose fiction. A rooting of the romance in a classical culture confers quite a different degree of legitimacy and status on the works than does Radway's analysis. Radway treats the romance as only a seeming novel which more closely 'resemble(s) the myths of oral culture' and 'a timeless fairy tale' (pp. 198, 204). But it is a deadly fairy tale, too, which betrays the true interest of those who read it, especially as they read it in a preparatory fashion. We feel inclined, on reading the books and talking to the readers, to run both ways, with Segal and Radway. In examining what the young adult romance novel *Double Love* has to offer the reader, we wish to hold to its legitimacy or rather its unmistakable participation in our literature culture, without losing sight of its seductive powers, powers which, we are suggesting, are not the exclusive purview of the romance but lie in the nature of literature.

In asking the grade seven students to name their favorite books, we were first faced with the influence of this new fashion in reading. While the majority of the female students named romances, they named them by the series — *Sweet Valley High*, *Sweet Dreams*, *Wildfire Romance* — rather than by the episode which the individual titles constitute. *Sweet Valley* was the most popular series for these readers, perhaps because it keeps its focus, volume by more than one-a-month volume, on the endlessly adolescent growth pangs of the Wakefield twins, Elizabeth the good sister and Jessica the not-so-good. *Double Love* (Williams, 1983) holds a special place for the readers as the original episode of the series and continues to go through quarterly reprintings. The work has all of the elements of what Radway describes as the classic romance plot: *Double Love* begins with the 'heroine's identity . . . thrown into question', as Radway describes the common opening step, and though the sexual level of attraction, punishment, and separation which makes up the body of the adult romance is somewhat sublimated, this work clearly ends with 'the heroine's identity restored' (p. 150).

But then this quest for identity is everywhere in literature, as it is, we suppose, in life. The continuity which these romance novels establish with the folk tale and mythology is one which Northrop Frye (1971) suggests is at the root of the entire compulsive story-telling and subsequent literary project. What distinguishes these works is that they are based on the particular 'canonical stories', as Frye refers to them, which 'crystallize the center of a culture: that especially appeals to these young women readers' (pp. 34, 35). What disturbs us is not the deep roots of these stories, but that the quest for identity in them continues to lie in having one's true worth found out by one of the boys who alone is in a position to make it count for something.

In *Double Love*, as might be expected with identical twins, the identity question is to prove one is the good sister when it is so easy to be mistaken for the bad. The aristocratic hero of the adult romance becomes in this high school version the captain of the basketball team — 'good-looking, good dancer, super-nice guy'. Elizabeth, the heroine, is 'generously blessed with spectacular all-American good looks', living comfortably in small-town California; she is reporter on the school paper with aspirations to be a serious writer. By virtue of her virtue, she manages to attract the attention of the school basketball star. Yet before his attentions can be fully realized, Elizabeth finds him diverted by a series of slight but nasty tricks by her sister, Jessica. Jessica is naturally another blonde beauty, a co-captain of the cheer-leaders, and yet one who dares to walk gingerly on the wild side:

> Whenever she was out walking, she never failed to attract a good deal of attention from passing cars. *The more the better*, she thought swinging her hips a little as she set off (original emphasis).

Such slight swinging is met by more than Jessica can handle in sexual advances from the high school drop-out and ends in a bar-room brawl with police action. The lesson is clear. The highly-studied beauty which the young woman is encouraged to turn to and cultivate is a danger; it speaks to another part of the world which is so easily out of the woman's personal control. This power to attract attention is, in effect, to risk physical abuse. The adolescent reader must learn young that she is especially vulnerable, both physically and morally, in the one area made to seem necessary to her success in the world. The novel, in providing this hasty version of Jessica's rude lesson, confirms this male regard for women. She is asking for trouble, as the book fails to question this patriarchal ideology which puts her at risk; the book takes no interest in exploring the oppressiveness of this regard, as for example Alice Walker's *The Color Purple* (1982) has to great effect. As it turns out with the bar incident, Jessica is only made to suffer a besmirched reputation. The entire school accepts the fact that it is a fault of her own doing in attracting attention, in accepting that dangerous ride into the world of men.

Yet Jessica succeeds in letting the shame she should suffer fall onto her twin sister through the old Shakespearian ruse of mistaken identity. It immediately means identity lost for Elizabeth as she becomes defiled by her sister's risks in sexuality. Elizabeth's sense of self is then further shaken by her handsome father's apparent romantic interest in a female co-worker, and her handsome brother's secret affair with a girl from the wrong side of the tracks. But by the novel's end, father's intentions prove honorable and her brother has learned that a family's reputation is not what counts in love. Elizabeth is finally restored in her faith in her family, in her reputation, and in the basketball star's arms. Jessica, for her part, is made to suffer a public dipping in the school pool, as Elizabeth finally plays this identity confusion to her own advantage.

The instruction and amusement here begin and end with virtue rewarded. In the course of the novel, Elizabeth's disappointments are made to appear as temporary postponements; the moral is that mischievousness given the chance will frustrate the good — 'She just did what her mother said, and somehow she was always wrong' — but not for long. Elizabeth, in having this evil side, this twin, can allow the reader to taste through Jessica the temptations of coming of age. Jessica cuts it close with the fast boy and his fast car; she learns her lesson, as she sees Elizabeth shunned by her classmates — reputation, above all, is to be kept intact, a reputation for accepting the rules of the game, no matter how weighted against you they may seem.

For the adolescent reader, this preparatory literature in high school futures simplifies as it crystalizes the world. The reader lives through her fears of fast cars, duly warned. She sets her hopes on being found out, as Elizabeth finally is — for who she really is — and finds Elizabeth rewarded. Yet to be fair to the novel, Elizabeth displays a spark of greater promise than in simply being found. In an instance of benevolence, she befriends the shy and unglamorous Enid, who 'in her quiet way was very smart — and very funny'; she gives the class wit a date to the big dance: 'and even if he is not handsome, he doesn't have three heads, for heaven's sake', Elizabeth tells her disbelieving sister. She stands up stoically to the ostracism over the bar incident which Jessica shifted her way, and finally she takes the situation in hand with the basketball star: 'with that, she turned to kiss a surprised Todd squarely on the mouth'. The two sisters display different sorts of independence. Clearly some forms of independence can be a dangerous thing in growing up, as Jessica demonstrates. Yet used with the sort of discretion which Elizabeth does, it can be mildly engaging. Elizabeth's work as a reporter does put her in touch with the real world of courtrooms and the professional practices of her father, but taking Todd squarely on the lips is clearly her shining moment.

Elizabeth is thinking about a career for herself as well as about future in love. She takes a small step against what might be described as the wily self-centered helplessness of the high school beauty which her sister represents. Though she ultimately finds her 'perfect union' with the basketball star, as Radway describes the pattern of passivity at the heart of the romance, Elizabeth does do more 'than exist at the center of the paragon's power' (p. 97). The book is not oblivious to the changing meaning of gender. But it cuts short that shift in meaning through the narrowness of the life which the book unfolds for the reader. Elizabeth is living well enough within an existence in which the real problems of adolescence are distant, menacing shadows, while her own traumas of missed dates and mistaken reputations belittle the hurdles which, in fact, trip up many young adults.

This major fault of narrowness is especially apparent in the shortform characterizations which people the sub-plots. The lawyer who Elizabeth's father is working with is a 'good-looking divorcee', as Jessica puts it, and as such she is easily mistaken for a threat to the nuclear, stable family. Would she, after all, have been called to the bar had her marriage held together? Or by the same token, would the high school drop-out have given up on school had he not been infected with a rough, alcoholic aggressiveness? In working into the novel the prescribed sources of adolescent anxiety — the threats of alcohol and drugs, sexuality, parental divorce, and a bad reputation — the supporting cast is each given a cross to carry and the novel is bound to suffer for it. But for the reader of a preparatory literature, these marginal characters cannot be discounted. Lying at the edge of the reader's attention, they tend to reassure those prejudices the reader has already seen mimicked from other sources, or perhaps the book is introducing them to these young students for the first time in such a coherent way.

In this way, the books would seem troubling as a preparatory literature, even as they excel as a low-cal fashionable delight. The young adult romance is a beginner's manual for ensuring adolescence. Its narrowness of depiction reassures the reader that the world ahead is made up of slight disappointments and postponements; it allays fears and provides a looking glass into which the reader can safely peer for the possibilities of identification. The book provides the short answer for what is going to turn out to be one long question. And when this beginner's manual does not suffice, when suspicions and fears extend beyond these chaste romances, Judy Blume continues to provide for many of these grade seven students an advanced version of the adolescent manuals. Blume's *Forever* (1976) is the well-thumbed standby for filling in the hard details and answering those probing questions. But then, surely, some measure of the delight fades when the details grow that intimate and close. The delight in this less explicit form of finding oneself is the romance's secret of success as a form of preparatory literature, just as it is the point of our concern.

But that much said, let it be said for all literature: A dependable preparation for life is surely not to be found in the books we read. As Plato first dared to declare in his banishment of the poets in *The Republic,* and as we have witnessed in this century as much as in any time in history, literature cannot be counted on to make us good or whole. At best, the books will entertain, tantalize and seem to instruct. That thoroughly engaging pleasure of the text is what these young readers are experiencing, feeling it as strongly, we imagine, as anyone who has turned to a book with pleasure. All of which is to suggest that the fact that the romance can mislead the young is not simply a marketing trick on the publishers' part, nor a failure on our part as educators. The romance shares this deceptive quality with far more respectable literature. Rachel Brownstein (1982) has explored how badly the best of English literature has been in helping one become a heroine, simply leading one to think of life as unfolding like a novel. One understands after growing into the sort of life foretold in books, how the literature consumed has shaped the misperception of the unfolding. Brownstein acknowledges that Jane Austen's heroines provide an inadequate model, yet she reminds us that they also demonstrate an acute and often ironic perception of their situation which is their salvation, and ours in continuing to read about them.

In the romance, the heroines are blessed in other ways; lacking a sense of irony, these *ingénues* take the world with a seriousness which only matches that of the young reader. But again this seeming conspiracy between readers and their favored books has always been at the root of a commitment to the literature. As part of this conspiracy readers can go on deceiving themselves about the value of the instruction and preparation the books provide — a value reinforced by certain moments in the reader's life which takes on a dazzlingly literary sensibility. But whether life can successfully imitate art or not, readers do not deceive themselves about the delight or the way in which the book speaks to their fancy.

However, with the romance the level of self-deception seems particularly high. The young women reading them seem engaged in what we have referred to here as a dangerous, if fashionable, game. In considering how to counter the book's narrowness and its constricting influence on their vision of their future, we return to the question of the educators's responsibility. Librarians alone seem to have wrestled with the dilemma of the books and appear content to let them into the library.[1] In this essay, we have considered the political economy of romance production and consumption in chains and malls, the ways in which the books has been so seriously taken and used by the adolescent reader, and, finally, what we believe lies within one typical instance of the romance. In each section, we have tried to provide a glimpse of the manner in which contemporary self-directed literacy operates among the young. It clearly does so in a manner which mirrors the pattern of our culture of consumerism at large as we find ourselves in acts of consumption.

In providing for the education of young women and men in reading, it seems clear to us that we should explore this rich area of literacy with the readers we fear it will badly influence. We can do this informally as we encourage them to share and discuss the reach and limits of the literature to which they are turning.

This is to begin to reflect with them on the relationship between art and life, to ask questions of the texts as if to steel ourselves against believing it all too literally. The best readers may teach the others to believe a little less of what they read, to forsake suspending disbelief once the covers are closed:

> Cara: I read them and I discuss every book with Edith, my friend. I'll read it, then she'll read it and we'll discuss it together. And we talk about what we saw to be true in the book and what is totally unbelievable and couldn't happen to anybody.

More formally, we may wish to discuss the repeated themes and limited options which such a preparatory regard for these works provides the reader. The students can delve into the manner in which these books come to be written compared to more traditional and, we would add, more romantic ways of an author struggling with her art. We might attempt to explore our own coming of age through literature with them, as well as that of the boys in the class who so clearly hear the call of other sorts of story. So much discourse about literacy, about the life of books and the place of books in life, seems a reasonable response to a resurgence of interest in books. These young women have tipped the market balance in favour of the reader over the educational institution as the primary consumer of young adult literature. Such bold movements in literacy deserve our sympathetic, appreciative and critical attention. Before offering blanket condemnations of the genre, we have to recall that books have been a troubling phenomena for some time. The temptation has always been for some readers to make disparaging distinctions about what others are reading. In this case, we have an opportunity to talk to these readers about the romance which they see as central to their pleasure and their instruction in growing up, to understand in this way the manner in which books still work so dangerously well.

Note

We wish to thank Carl Braun and Allan Neilsen for their incisive comments on an earlier draft of this paper. As well, we wish to express our appreciation to the forty-two romance readers who shared the pleasure of their literacy with us.

1 Librarians have taken up the value of the romance series to the young (Sutton, 1985; Van Vliet, 1984; Wigutoff, 1982). On the one hand, librarian Susan Kundin (1985) who has compared them to the realism of Blume and company, believes 'they are escapist novels yet contain lessons which can be easily and pleasantly learned' (p. 367); on the other hand, Elaine Wagner caustically observes that indeed the books teach 'such wonderful lessons as manipulating friends, belittling all interests and activities except those that are boy related and devaluing one's worth if one is without a boyfriend' (p. 3).

References

ABRAMS, M.H. (1953) *The Mirror and the Lamp: Romantic Theories and the Critical Tradition*, London, Oxford University Press.

BELL, D. (1985) 'Gutenberg and the computer', *Encounter*, **64**, pp. 15–20.

BLUME, J. (1977) *Forever*, New York, Bantam.

BROWNSTEIN, R. (1982) *Becoming a Heroine: Reading about Women in Novels*, Harmondsworth, Penguin.

CONKLIN, B. (1981) *P.S. I Love You*, Sweet Dreams 1, New York, Bantam.

DAVIES, N. (1965) 'Printing and the people', in N. DAVIES (Ed.) *Society and Culture in Early Modern France*, Stanford, CA, Stanford University, pp. 189–226.

DAVIS, K. (1984) *Two-bit Culture: The Paperbacking of America*, New York, Houghton Mifflin.

FREIRÉ, P. (1983) 'The importance of reading', *Journal of Education*, **165**, pp. 9–15.

FRYE, N. (1971) *The Critical Path: An Essay on the Social Context of Literary Criticism*, Bloomington, Indiana University.

GRAFF, H. (1979) *The Literacy Myth: Literacy and Social Structure in the Nineteenth Century City*, New York, Academic Press.

ILLICH, I. (1979) 'Vernacular values and education', *Teachers College Record*, **81**, pp. 31–79.

JEFFERSON, M. (1982) 'Sweet dreams for teen queens', *The Nation*, **234**, 22 May, pp. 613–17.

KUNDIN, S.G. (1985) 'Romance versus reality: A look at YA romantic fiction', *Top of the News*, **41**, pp. 361–8.

LACAN, J. (1968) *Speech and Language in Psychoanalysis*, trans. A. Wilden, Baltimore, John Hopkins.

McLUHAN, M. (1962) *The Gutenberg Galaxy: The Making of Typographic Man*, Toronto, University of Toronto Press.

NELSON, G. (1975) 'The double standard in adolescent novels', *English Journal*, **64**, pp. 53–55.

RADWAY, J.A. (1984) *Reading the Romance: Women, Patriarchy and Popular Literature*, Chapel Hill, University of North Carolina.

SCHOLDERER, V. (1963) *Johann Gutenberg: Inventor of Printing*, London, Trustees of the British Museum.

SCRIBNER, S. and COLE, M. (1981) *The Psychology of Literacy*, Cambridge, MA, Harvard University.

SEGAL, E. (1985) 'Heavy breathing in Arcadia', *The New York Times Book Review*, 29 September, pp. 1, 48–9.

SMITH, W. (1981) 'An earlier start on romance', *Publishers Weekly*, **220**, 13 November, pp. 56–61.

STANEK, L.W. (1976) 'Growing up female: The literary gaps', *Media and Methods*, **13**, pp. 46–48.

SUTTON, R. (1985) 'Librarians and the paperback romance: Trying to do the right thing', *School Library Journal*, (November) pp. 25–28.

VAN VLIET, V. (1984) 'Young love on fantasy island', *Emergency Librarian*, **11**, pp. 6–9.

WAGNER, E. (no date) 'Protesting sexist materials — You can make a difference', *Bulletin of the Council on Interracial Books for Children*, **12**(3) pp. 3–6.

WALKER, A. (1982) *The Color Purple*, New York, Washington Square.

WIGUTOFF, S. (1982) 'Junior fiction: A feminist critique', *Top of the News*, **38**, pp. 113–24.

WILLIAMS, K. (1983) *Double Love*, Sweet Valley High No. 1, Created by F. Pascal, New York, Bantam.

Chapter 7

The Place for Romance in Young People's Writing

Gemma Moss

In this essay I examine the way in which a 15-year-old Black girl uses the romance genre in her writing to explore the possible relationship between girls and boys.

Comment on the romance genre often starts with worries about its female readership. Are girls being unduly influenced by the form? Does the text take precedence over the reader's real life experience, selling girls a romanticized view of men and their place in girls' future? Does it blind girls to their oppression within patriarchy? (Hoggart, 1984; McRobbie, 1982; Radway, 1984; Sarsby, 1983; Sharpe, 1976) Such questions stem from a particular view of reading. That, for the majority, reading is an unreflective practice; that when there is conflict between what a reader knows at first hand and from the text, the text will exert the maximum impact; that there are close links between reading and behaviour.

For English teachers, one consequence of these assumptions is to treat romances as if they were a highly contagious disease. When girls write romances they are deemed to have 'caught' the genre and to be under its sway! To be able to reproduce this kind of story is proof that the romance is replacing everything else the authors know. In writing the genre girls are buying into a particular view of their own futures. They are subscribing to the romance's values (National Writing Project, 1990). The argument slips into assertions about the damaging effects on the authors' beliefs and their behaviour in the real world, rather than an examination of the act of writing itself.

The argument about the influence of the romance genre draws a sharp distinction between fiction (what the romance tells girls) and fact (the way things actually happen in the real world). This has consequences for writing. In the English classroom, there is considerable stress on realism and telling it like it is. A high priority is put on using what writers know at first hand as a source for their own work (Taylor, 1985). Autobiography emerges as the privileged text, the ideal space for telling the truth about oneself and evading the kinds of misrepresentation commonplace in popular fiction. Ironically this stress on realism can lead to a different kind of policing of girls' work in which what they have to say about themselves comes under intense scrutiny. Writing is treated as an unmediated revelation of the self. The authors' sense of themselves, their self-worth, can be read off from the text. To judge the writing is to judge the author.

But for girls to meet the teacher's approval what kinds of stories must they tell? They must at once fulfil the requirements for a positive image — being tough, strong, resilient — and be seen to be offering a realistic portrayal of themselves. The criteria are contradictory, the kind of narrative they suggest closely defined.

I want to argue for a more positive view of the place for the romance in young people's writing. This means challenging the notion that writing is first and foremost an unmediated act in which experience can be put directly into words. It also means rejecting the notion that the reproduction of a particular genre can in itself have negative effects. All writers work with a knowledge of competing stories. Even when working within the confines of a single genre, the nature of language itself is such that the text will continually refer outwards to different kinds of stories. To shape a particular tale is to draw on a variety of cultural resources which can be transformed as the writer uses them.

I turn now to my data; a story written for homework by Angelique at the beginning of the fourth year in secondary school, which I analyze in some detail, and three successive interviews I conducted with her about her writing at the end of the fifth year, when I was no longer her English teacher. Angelique is Black, her school predominantly White.

In the reading of Angelique's text which follows, my aim has been not only to mark the traces of familiar formulas as they appear in her work, but to examine how she uses these traces to shape her own meaning. It seems to me that the interest of the piece stems from the way in which Angelique puts her text together — a process of construction which relies not only on a knowledge of other texts, and their partial reproduction here, but also on her own experience and social knowledge[1]. The piece is called 'Again!':

Again!

'Why me though?', that's all I keep asking, why me? It all began when my mum had allowed me to go out of Bristol with a few friends, it wasn't usual but I ended up telling my mum what good friends I had and what they wouldn't do and what they would do (within reason of course!) Anyway we took the train to London, Paul, Nick, Clare and me. It was hilarious on the train down. Nick and Clare had an arguement and Clare started throwing things at him. Paul and I walked out and Paul tried to get us a privite apartment to get away from Nick and Clare but the man (him being the porter) said he didn't trust us, and wondered if we knew something of birth control. We just walked off into another carraige and sat down. Paul put his arm round me. I felt embarrassed because an old woman kept staring. I shrugged him off, and kissed him when the lady had turned round.
'Wonder what Nick and Clare are up to?' said Paul looking closely.
'Probably tearing each others eyes out' I said. We both laughed.
At that Clare walked in. 'I wanna go home' she flopped on the seat next to the old woman. The old woman instantly walked out.
'Snobby bitch' remarked Clare.
'Oh Clare don't spoil the trip. We'll enjoy ourselves, we'll all go to the Fair' I said.

'Don't you two ever argue?' Clare said angrily.

'Well . . . course we do' I smiled.

'When?' Paul asked me.

'Well . . . loads of times' I said looking at him 'Why?'

'Nope, we've never argued' Paul said scratching his head, he pretended to be thinking.

'Yes we have Paul' I pinched him and gave him a 'Shut up' stare.

'Tell me when, then I'll shut up' Paul kissed me creeping around me slowly.

'Paul Richards and Angela Campbell give over' Clare butted in. We nearly got into a real fuss Paul and I did! Anyway, the rest of the journey, is unimportant so I'll skip the rest.

We got off at Paddington.

Paul and I walked off into a cafe in London. It wasn't bad we had a sandwich and a coke we started talking about the argument we had.

'Paul we have had arguments before.'

'I know but I just wanted her not feel . . . well . . . never mind!' He never finished his sentence and I was hurt and upset when I asked him to finish he told me not to nag.

'What was going on' I thought to myself.

Nick appeared on the scene stuffing his face with a jam doughnut Clare just sat beside him sipping an orangeade.

'Bloody stupid cow you deliberately spilled that on me' Nick turned to Clare. Clare had spilt her drink on Nicks trousers.

'You sod, calling me a cow'

'Well you are one, who do you think you are?' Nick took a serviette and wiped his trousers.

'Look shut up you two' I said 'people are looking'

'Let them bloody look' Paul took my hand and lead me out of the cafe.

We sat outside on the wall and kissed.

'I hope we don't ever fight like they do' I said holding his hand.

'Thought you said we didn't fight.'

'Well not recently' I argued.

'Yeah I know' Paul looked down.

I had been out with Paul before for two months but he left me and went out with Clare, yeah my friend, but we weren't friends then so it didn't matter much to me. I know I couldn't stand it happening again.

Clare soon came out crying.

'Nick slapped me and he has finished with me' Paul instantly let go off my hand. He stroked Clare's cheek with his hand. 'Did he hurt you?' Paul asked.

'Course he bleedin' did' Clare sniffed.

'Bastard' Paul said.

'Paul?' I saw the way he looked at her the way he touched her.

'Paul? It's not over again is it?'

'I still love you Ange, I don't want to hurt you again.'

'No Paul No, you can't love her again?' But it was too late. He held Clares hand and walked over to the cafe.

Clare let go of his hand and shook her head. She turned her back on Paul

and kissed Nick lovingly. Paul walked slowly back. He saw me crying
and he held my hand, I let go.
'I'm sorry Ange I didn't mean anything' Paul tried to kiss me.
'No, No I won't let your last kiss remain a memory like the first one
you'll only hurt me again I couldn't bear it I loved you Paul' I laughed
'probably still do . . . but never Paul ever'.
Funny that evening, on the way home Paul and I sat apart, whilst Nick
and Clare kissed.
'Why me though?' that's all I keep asking, why me?

The story opens with words spoken by the lead character, the narrator. It
reminds me of the beginning of a photo-love story, with a close-up of the central
character, establishing her mood through what she says. Angelique's story works
on the same principles: the words spoken, a small action performed, focus my
attention on the different characters. I can almost frame each separate picture.

At that Clare walked in. 'I wanna go home' she flopped on the seat next
to the old woman.

The first phrase would become the text in the corner of the picture, what Clare
says would appear in bubbles and the picture would show Clare sitting on the
seat.

The old woman instantly walked out.
'Snobby bitch' remarked Clare.

The next picture would show Clare scowling as the woman leaves the carriage,
the bubbles enclosing her remarks.
About the only passages which couldn't be packaged in this way are those
which set the context of the story: the negotiations with Mum over whether the
narrator can go up to London, and later on the information that Paul had once
ditched the narrator for Clare. Each episode is self-contained, yet gains its full
meaning by its relationship to the episodes which have gone before and follow
after.
The narrator is obviously young — Angelique's own age. This is apparent in
her relationship with her mum:

my mum had allowed me to go out of Bristol with a few friends, it
wasn't usual but I ended up telling my mum what good friends I had and
what they wouldn't do and what they would do (within reason of
course!).

This places the narrator as an adolescent, someone whose behaviour is of parental
concern, who may be misled by friends into behaving irresponsibly; '(within
reason of course!)' comments on the nature of the guarantees the narrator has
given her mother and suggests both her independence and her acquiescence in her
mother's concern.
I am continually reminded of the age of this group of friends throughout the
story. Clare starts throwing things at Nick during an argument on the train
journey down. This episode is preceded by the comment:

It was hilarious on the train down.

The fight between Nick and Clare is not serious, therefore, just larking about. The friends are on their way to the Fair:

'We'll enjoy ourselves, we'll all go to the Fair' I said.

When they arrive in London they go to a cafe and have sandwiches, Coke, a doughnut and orangeade. These concerns and interests belong to childhood. Childhood, adolescence, both create different contexts in which to read the characters' actions.

Being young also means being at the receiving end of adult disapproval:

the man (him being a porter) said he didn't trust us, and wondered if we knew something of birth control . . . an old woman kept staring

This sense of 'them and us' is part of a whole tradition of children's literature from *Just William* to *Grange Hill*. By tradition it can be a focus for stories. It is also part of Angelique's own experience, the stories she tells about herself. In her first interview with me she said:

> I wear my Dad's hats, an I wear shirts from my Dad's. . . .
> My mum thinks I'm weird, and she thinks there's some-
> thing wrong with me, she thinks I'm lesbian, or
> something . . . I think she's worried about me, you know.
> She thinks just because I wear my Dad's shirts or [laughs]
> something like that, there must be something wrong with
> me . . . I combed my hair like, um, once I combed my hair.
> Do you know Grace Jones?

Gemma: Yeah . . . oh yeah! [laughs]

Anqelique: Oh, I'll never forget, I wouldn't never risk that again . . . ever . . . just to avoid argument, I wouldn't ever do it again.

There are two points I want to make about this extract, both of which have a bearing on Angelique's text. First, her comments arose as part of a discussion about sexism and the way it stops girls doing what they want to do. For Angelique the conflict with her parents is about what she may do as a girl. Her mother disapproves of her wearing her dad's shirts because it seems to signify an 'abnormal' sexuality. Wearing shirts may be natural for a boy; it is not natural for a girl. So what Angelique has to do to gain approval depends on an adult view of gender-appropriate behaviour. Youth is subdivided into girls and boys. The process of conflict and its resolution between adults and young girls is part of the latters' construction as female within our (patriarchal) society.

This notion that being young and female presents specific problems not shared by boys is there in Angelique's own story. At the beginning the narrator's mother worries about what the narrator will do if she goes out for a day with her friends. As she is a girl, this means worrying about sex rather than violence. The incident with the porter highlights this. The porter doesn't trust Paul and the narrator on their own. He imagines the presence of a girl and a boy means that they will indulge in sexual behaviour inappropriate to the young (rather than that they will wreck the carriage). When Paul and the narrator sit down together,

> Paul put his arm round me. I felt embarrassed because an old woman kept staring. I shrugged him off, and kissed him when the lady had turned round.

It is the narrator as a girl, not Paul, the boy, who feels nervous about revealing the nature of their relationship in public, who can kiss only when the old lady is not looking. For her to be seen to behave sexually is to run the risk of adult disapproval, to be labelled promiscuous, common, cheap. It is girls', not boys' sexuality which signifies in this way.

This leads me to my second point: the extent to which it is possible to challenge the adult order. The extract I have quoted from Angelique's interview shows her contesting the adult's view of appropriate (female) behaviour but also, it need be, compromising — on her Grace Jones hairstyle, in the instance. But giving in doesn't mean utter submission. In her second interview I asked her about the differences in the writing she produces in school and the writing she does for herself at home. She talked about the difficulties of writing in patois in school:

> I remember doing a thing on what I like for English, for Mr H — and, it was writing about stories and what I've achieved. I wrote this story, and he said to me 'Well how will people like me be able to read that story' . . . you know [smiles] and that really got to me because the only way a person who wants to read patois, you must know a certain amount of it because how on earth can I go round starting to pick out the bits of patois and starting to try and abbreviate it cos it is not, it's not a foreign language it's just a slang. . . . I felt really, really mad about it . . . 'how would a person like me be able to understand that!' . . . I thought, well, there is one way a person like you could understand it, but I won't bother to write it down.

Holding back, not challenging the views of others, can be a way of escaping those views when you lack the power to challenge them directly.

Mixed in with the judgment by adults of young people's behaviour is the question of gender. Appropriate young female behaviour is different from young male behaviour. Angelique's text shows that she is aware of this. Within her story, how does the narrator, a girl, react to this sort of pressure on her behaviour? She concedes to the adult view and does nothing whilst the old lady is looking at her; as soon as she looks away, she kisses Paul. For the narrator, a girl, behaving as she wants to means finding a space in which to do so, a space cleared of others' reading of her actions.

I began my analysis of this story by commenting on the similarities between the organization of photo-love stories and Angelique's text in terms of the handling of dialogue and action. Photo-love stories take as their theme girl-boy relationships explored as romance. In Angelique's story the four friends are quickly established as two couples:

> Nick and Clare had an argument. . . . Paul and I walked out.

Once their names have been linked in this way I begin to read the story in the context of romance. I expected the friends' focus of interest to be particularized, to be centred on their partner, their loyalties not to be to the group as a whole but to their special friend. My expectations are fulfilled as the group splits up:

> Paul tried to get us a private apartment to get away from Nick and Clare . . .

Nick and Clare's argument is private, between them as a couple. Precluded from joining in, Paul and Angela go elsewhere.

> 'Wonder what Nick and Clare are up to?' said Paul looking closely.
> 'Probably tearing each others eyes out' I said. We both laughed.

Paul and Angela are sitting peacefully with each other. They can guess that Nick and Clare will still be arguing. Paul and Angela become the steady, loving couple; Nick and Clare the bickerers who can't stop rowing. Points of comparison are established. But the arrival of Clare on her own breaks up the structuring of the group of friends as two couples, for Angela's attention passes to Clare. She is fed up — ' "I wanna go home" ' — and Angela's response re-establishes the group identity:

> 'Oh Clare don't spoil the trip. We'll enjoy ourselves, we'll all go to the Fair'.

Even if Clare is fed up with Nick, the day out need not be wasted; the friends can still have fun. Clare pushes the participants in the conversation back into their position as partners in a couple:

> 'Don't you two ever argue?' Clare said angrily.

Her question stresses the difference between Nick and Clare, Paul and Angela: the former arguing, moody, unhappy; the latter content, calm.

There are two ways of viewing this contrast. Not arguing can mean security, trust, a perfect match, a perfect couple, by whose measure the other couple appear dissatisfied, ill matched, likely to break up. Or the calmness of those who don't row can tip into placidity, contrasted with the strength of feeling, the anguish of true love. Angelique plays with both images and resolves them in her final sentence:

> Funny that evening, on the way home Paul and I sat apart whilst Nick and Clare kissed.

The perfect couple, the couple who seemed likely to succeed — that is, end the story with a secure relationship — have broken up. The question the romance story asks about its key characters, the boys and girls who encounter each other within it, is: how will their relationship work out? To work out well the relationship must end intact, its stability secured, but for the moment this remains a question hovering above the text, guiding my reading. At this point in the story other considerations are also at play.

I want to return to the exchange between Clare, Angela and Paul and examine the different ways in which the dialogue of these three characters positions them. Angela has talked about the friends as a group of young people; Clare has placed them as two couples. Angela's response to Clare's moody discontent with her own relationship is to help Clare out. In order to try to stop her feeling gloomy about the rows between her and Nick, she suggests that her own relationship with Paul is just the same:

> 'Don't you two ever argue?' Clare said angrily.
> 'Well . . . course we do' I smiled.

Angela refuses to accept the polarity on which Clare insists. She offers friendship and a sense of solidarity. What she does is determined by how Clare feels; her own allegiance to Paul takes second place.

> Paul's response is different:
> 'Nope, we've never argued' Paul said scratching his head, he pretended to be thinking.

He is still playing the couples game, reminding Angela of their status as a couple and scoring off Clare by showing her that his relationship with Angela is better than hers with Nick. For Angela, accepting his response will mean excluding Clare. She is caught between contradictory obligations — to her friend, to her boyfriend:

> 'Yes we have Paul' I pinched him and gave him a 'Shut up' stare.
> 'Tell me when, then I'll shut up' Paul kissed me creeping around me slowly.

Being in a couple means negotiating for what she wants, in a tight space, a space defined by others.

Angelique, the story-teller, is quite clear that in her romances what the boys want and what the girls want is often different, and part of the function of her stories is to settle that conflict. In her third interview with me she said:

> I think in my stories I really want the boy to be understanding. You always get these blokes that go off and two-time you and all this sort of thing . . . every girl wouldn't want their boyfriends to do that . . . the people I know they're always telling me that their boyfriend did this, and my boyfriend's hitting me about. . . . When I'm writing my stories I want everybody to know that if I have a boyfriend my boyfriend ain't going to hit me about. If anything I'm going to hit him about.

Being in a couple means struggling over power.

In Angelique's story the struggle between Paul and Angela begins when Paul refuses to understand what Angela is doing (protecting Clare). His lack of understanding and reluctance to talk about it leave her hurt:

113

He never finished his sentence and I was hurt and upset when I asked
him to finish he told me not to nag.
'What was going on' I thought to myself.

She is on her own. The story continually fluctuates over where she is: safely
inside a couple, her partnership assured by a touch, a kiss:

'Let them bloody look' Paul took my hand and lead me out of the cafe.
We sat outside on the wall and kissed;

made to feel uneasy by that relationship:

I felt embarrassed . . .

I was hurt and upset . . .

part of a group of young people with allegiances to the group rather than a pair:
'"We'll all go to the Fair".' Angelique's story uses the formation of the group of
friends into two couples as a starting point to do more than ask the question:
'Which couple will succeed?' By focusing also on the conflicting demands of the
boyfriend and friend, by juxtaposing the different aspects of the group of friends,
she can raise questions about what being in a couple means.

So far, in thinking about the presentation of girl-boy relationships in
Angelique's text, I have examined the way in which the group of friends have
been subdivided into two groups, and shown that this configuration brings with
it the expectation that the story will centre around the securing or undermining of
these pairs of relationships: an expectation with Angelique's final sentence, with
its sense of symmetry, acknowledges. I have gone on to show how elements in
her story undercut this tight focus and leave a space for other issues to be raised.
What about romance? How does this figure in her text? The romance works by
foregrounding emotions. Does the heroine love the hero, will he love her? Will
the heroine be happy, her feelings shared by her lover, whose kiss promises a
future together — or will she end the story bereft of her loved one, lonely,
incomplete, sad? Either way, the romance can be filled with turbulent emotions,
emotions which threaten to swamp the actions which generate them. Every
gesture can become a sign of deep feeling.

Angelique's text is curiously empty of romance at the beginning. Paul puts
his arm round the narrator, or kisses her, but her attention is elsewhere — on the
old lady staring, or on Clare and her feelings. The one point the text offers at
which they could become more absorbed in each other is quickly passed over:

'Wonder what Nick and Clare are up to' said Paul looking closely.

The phrase 'looking closely' spoken by a boy to a girl suggest a moment of intimacy, a move towards a romantic encounter. But Angela's response:

'Probably tearing each others eyes out' I said. We both laughed.

refuses this overture and re-positions the exchange as a moment of child-like glee.
Angela's relationship with Paul seems domestic. There is little sense of passion.
She simply wants them to be comfortable and at ease with each other:

'I hope we don't ever fight like they do' I said holding his hand.

Things begin to change as the misunderstanding between Angela and Paul deepens. Suddenly inserted into the text is a brief reference to Angela's past history of involvement with Paul and Clare:

> I had been out with Paul before for two months but he left me and went out with Clare, yeah my friend, but we weren't friends then so it didn't matter much to me. I know I couldn't stand it happening again.

Another way of reading what is going on emerges here. Paul has already finished his relationship with Angela once. Do their present conflicting interests presage another split, Angela to be left on her own, alone, unhappy? The reference to Clare sets up other echoes by reference to other texts. The girl whose best friend betrays her, seizing the boy, causing heartache: a story in which the establishment of a couple takes precedence over friendship, girls compete for the boy and destroy trust in each other. But it is an echo which the narrator summons up to dismiss:

> We weren't friends then so it didn't matter much to me.

Her own action earlier with which Angela contemplates being on her own — 'I know I couldn't stand it happening again' — prepares the way for romance to enter the text. Romance reorientates my understanding of what the characters do. It offers me a new way of reading their actions as gestures become signs of deep feeling.

What is strange about this is that as romance enters, the coherence of the text itself begins to shake. Suddenly all sorts of question marks being to hang over what is said. I find myself echoing Angela's 'What is going on?' Part of the answer lies in the way romance is introduced. It seems to sprawl in undigested chunks across the page. Precisely because there has been no preparation for this sort of outburst, its conventionalized nature stands out in high relief. De-naturalized, rendered painfully visible, it spins away from the narrative confines of the text that has gone before, refusing to be tied down by it, to stay in its place.

I want to examine this part of the text closely from the point where Clare comes out of the cafe:

> Clare soon came out crying.
> 'Nick slapped me and he has finished with me'.

The row in the cafe has moved from the childish resonance of just larking about to a lover's quarrel. Clare is no longer sulky, she is upset, yet the words she uses to describe how her relationship with Nick has ended still carry the child's view with them.

Paul's response concludes the switching of gear, true entry into romance:

> Paul instantly let go off my hand. He stroked Clare's cheek with his hand.

He caresses her, a gesture for intimacy and affection. It is also a gesture of exclusion: Angela stands outside the exchange with no role to play. Like Angela in her response to Clare on the train, Paul gives priority to Clare, the outsider; but, because of the language used to describe his movement, the gesture is positioned by romance, not friendship, and so speaks of his own self-interest, his claim on Clare, his desire to relinquish Angela in his favour.

> 'Did he hurt you?' Paul asked.
> 'Course he bleedin' did' Clare sniffed.
> 'Bastard' Paul said.

Again there is a contrast in tone. Clare obstinately refuses to shift into romance. Her answer reminds me of her youth. Paul's tone is that of the avenging male about to do battle with his rival for the girl's favour. He asked about Nick, not about Clare:

> 'Paul?' I saw the way he looked at her the way he touched her.
> 'Paul? It's not over again is it?'

Angela confirms my interpretation of Paul's actions within the framework of romance. Her words could have come straight out of a popular song. I don't have to be told how Paul is looking at and touching Clare. His show of affection triggers off the appropriate response in Angela: pain and grief, two moves in a sequence which leads to the disintegration of a relationship. Yet the next exchange is puzzling:

> 'I still love you, Ange, I don't want to hurt you again.'
> 'No Paul No, you can't love her again?'

Paul counters the narrator's view of his actions, but his remarks are swept aside: the narrator is the disappointed lover in full voice and immediately after Paul's declaration of loyalty to her the text confirms her view of him:

> But it was too late. He held Clare's hand and walked over to the cafe.

This could provide a convenient stopping place for the text: girl loses boy to the other girl, a tradition in which the other girl stands accused of betrayal and the heroine must accept defeat with tears. Angelique refused this ending:

> Clare let go his hand and shook her head. She turned her back on Paul
> and kissed Nick lovingly.

Angela's friend refuses Paul's offer and seals her rejection of him by kissing Nick.

> Paul walked slowly back. He saw me crying and he held my hand, I let
> go.

What is Paul up to? Trying his luck where he can, as Angela and Clare imagine, or helping a friend? This time it is Angela who removes her hand, distancing herself from him:

'I'm sorry Ange I don't mean anything' Paul tried to kiss me.

His excuse will not do. The language of romance has found him out, and pinned him down as the fickle lover whose words cannot be trusted:

'No, No I won't let your last kiss remain a memory like the first one you'll only hurt me again I couldn't bear if I loved you Paul' I laughed 'probably still do . . . but never Paul ever.'

Paul's return to Angela makes sense if this is still a story about childhood sweethearts, young people out for the day to enjoy themselves as a group, when no one's relationship is serious. Why not then talk of love to Angela and hold another girl's hand, comforting her? The language of romance has displaced the action, moving it away from the sphere of carefree youth to the world of maturity, passion, heartache, jealousy. In this area lovers who betray each other's trust cannot return. Paul's route back to Angela is barred by her outburst. It draws heavily on the genre of romance. The fact that its meaning is hard to follow, that its relationship to the events that have taken place is awkward rather than clear, that its own message and tone are contradictory, doesn't matter. What it does is take the position of disappointed lover and turn it into one of strength. Angela, who has been deserted by Paul, now pushes him away. She makes the choice, she will not have him. In Angelique's hands the romance and all its attendant cliches turn the text upside down, confound our expectations. She ends the story with her heroine sad, but in control; alone, but determined to be so.

To summarize, Angelique's story interweaves several different, often contradictory threads: youth, romance, couples, friends, each of which evoke their own stories, lying beyond the text. They refer outwards, whether to other stories told in books — a literary tradition — or to the stories she tells about herself: her own experience shaped with others', formed through language. Reading her particular story I catch the references; and the characters, their actions, twist and turn as I place them within different contexts. The text seems to me not so much settled and secure as making up its mind, playing one thread off against another, shifting its ground. What emerges is a sense of the confined space within which the heroine, as a girl, has to operate: a space criss-crossed by contradictory demands made on her as a friend, girlfriend, lover. This sense of claustrophobia is not shared by the other characters in the story. Clare says what she likes and refuses to be swayed by others into losing sight of her own feelings. She takes risks '"You sod, calling me a cow"' but does so primarily by remaining child-like, obstinately moody. Paul pays no attention except to what he wants — '"let them bloody look"' — but his single-minded purpose is selfish; he cannot be trusted to do anything except follow his own whims. Where does that leave those who care for him?

The juxtaposition of these varying approaches leaves Angelique's text uncertain. It is not the monolithic reproduction of a given order, a unitary whole, but fragmentary. It raises questions about what it might mean to leave childhood behind, to grow into womanhood and enter into relationships with men. On whose terms could this, should this, take place? What is at stake?

Angelique wrote several romances for me during the year I taught her. She refers explicitly to one other, called 'Oh Steve!!!' in her interviews. Although different in tone and setting, all her romances shared certain features. First, in all of them the girl ends up rejecting the boy — there are not happily-ever-afters; nor does the girl watch the boy walk out on her: she pushes him. Second, the boys themselves are not the focus for an unconditional surrender to the emotions on the part of the narrator — a common feature of the romance. There is always something about them that renders them ultimately untrustworthy and provides the motive for the girl to disentangle herself. Third, it is easy to read all these stories as if the narrator were White. Part of this is inevitably the effect of my reading rather than the text itself. For me (a White woman in a White culture) to read them otherwise, something in the setting or the language would have to mark the presence of Blackness. Unmarked, constructed within a form (romance) which I am familiar with, which brings with it images of Whiteness, my expectations generate a cast of White characters. Yet this was not a feature of Angelique's writing as a whole. Increasingly during the year she brought in pieces of writing she was doing for herself at home, where the characters were explicitly Black and much of the language was patois. Why the difference in the romances she wrote for school? How far was she aware of the difference in her own writing? What do these differences suggest?

Angelique talked to me at length about her writing in the three interviews I did with her in the fifth year and it is to these interviews that I now want to turn. What quickly becomes clear from the transcripts is that here is someone who has thought hard about what being Black and female means, how it affects her own life. Answering my questions meant reminding herself of debates she had already had, as well as reflecting on them afresh:

> When it comes to the discussion on women, I always find myself getting annoyed because, I talked with my mother about this sort of thing and she seems to think a woman's place is in the home . . . having to cook, clean and that sort of thing.

She introduced the question of race before I did. Explaining why her favourite programmes on television were 'No Problem' and 'Front Line', she said:

Gemma: I think it's just because it's lots of Black people acting. You hardly see any Black actors . . . on the telly. Well, I was going to ask you about that, because when you were talking about the books . . . quite a lot of books that you're talking about have got Black heroines . . . and I wondered if that was important for you, in terms of your choice of books.

Angelique: I think the reason I choose so many books by Black authors is because of the school I'm in. There's hardly, I have never seen anyone in this school pick up a book, no one has ever done Black history in this school, so I look it out for myself. . . . If I was probably in a . . . in a Black school, where there was a high majority of Blacks, I probably wouldn't take much notice of it . . . — but — I think — once I'm in this school — and once no one ain't going to teach me it — then I'll look for it myself.

She is confident in what she has to say, and articulate. I asked her whether being Black or being female was more important to her, and she was quite clear on her answer:

> I would say one's more important than the other and that is because of being Black.

How does this picture of Angelique as someone aware of the problems of racism and sexism square with her writing, and what does it have to say about the status of her romances? Angelique accepts that her romances are peopled with White characters and that to say this is to say something significant:

> when you write about a White person, a Black person, it's a completely different thing.

Pinning the difference down, explaining it to me in words, was difficult and I didn't always help to make the process easier. I raised the question in my first interview and we pursued it in the second and the third sessions. I'll try to bring together what Angelique said.

The sort of writing she does is dependent on the context within which it is produced. The first pieces of work she showed me which centred on Black characters were written at home primarily for herself, although this distinction blurred during the year that I taught her, and Black characters began to emerge in her school work. One of her reasons for not introducing explicitly Black characters in her school work is the reception she expects:

> I just know that if I start writing patois on a piece of paper, one of the teachers will come up to me and say 'What does this mean, what does that mean?' [. . .] I suppose it's normal 'cos they don't understand it, but I can't write patois in English because it's not patois.

In the teacher's eyes patois becomes incorrect use of English, but to make it correct, conform to the standard, would mean losing the flavour of the language, the very reason why she's included it.

Writing for herself at home means writing without constraints:

> When I write in my own stories I can just write what I want, you know, write patois, the Jamaican things . . . and I can write anything I want even if it's not about Jamaica I can write something. Let the pen just run loose, you know, and really get across what I'm feeling on the book. In school you have to cut that down to a certain amount.

Even when race is on the agenda at school, talking about it means being careful, remembering her audience, not getting too annoyed:

> We talked about it in school, we talk about it in English, but if I get too carried away, I have to control myself slightly.

Writing for herself means being able to let go and recreate the Black world she left behind when her family moved out from the inner city to the White suburbs:

When I left S. Werburghs, I was really heartbroken because living on the street I lived on you could hear a West Indian mother opening the door and telling her son to get off the street because there's a car coming. You could smell the West Indian food cooking, the noise, you could hear a boy down the road playing his stereo unit from inside the house and that sort of thing. All those I really missed. I tell you I really missed them . . . and listening to a bunch of Jamaicans talk . . . specially the men when they get going. It's beautiful. When I moved up to Kingswood all that went. At first I didn't worry about it, nothing like that, but I started watching teleprogrammes like 'No Problem' and things like that and I really realized how much I missed it and I read the Gleaner, and that sort of thing and so I thought, well, I don't have it up here, I don't have that sort of thing at Kingswood, so I can make it happen so I started the stories and it brought it alive.

Her sources for this sort of writing are her own knowledge of the Black community and the stories they tell about themselves, and she is conscious that these ways of telling are specific to the community. Explaining a particular scene in one of her Black stories called 'Ebony and Ivory' where the mother can't bring herself to talk openly to her daughter, Angelique said:

I think when it comes to talking love, romance, sex . . . between an old-fashioned Jamaican parent, it's very difficult because they've been taught, when they were younger, that that's a no-no word, sex.

She went on to illustrate this point by recounting an anecdote about her mother and grandmother. It is this sense of cultural difference which explains why her romances centre around White characters:

I feel, I *do* feel, that Black people and White people act differently when it comes to romances.

Her knowledge of how people behave in romances does not tally with her knowledge of the Black community:

Angelique: They find it hard to express, Jamaicans anyway they find, most of them find it really hard to show loving, love and emotion. It's sort of like . . . you know . . . Jamaicans are supposed to be strong, tough, the guys anyway . . . you know . . . they told you . . .

Gemma: I was wondering if that's what you mean when you say love, whether really what you're talking about is in a sense romantic love, yeah!

Angelique: Yeah! Roman, romance, yeah!

Gemma: It's like . . .

Angelique: They're like that, they do, I mean . . .

Gemma: . . . being gentle.

Angelique: Yeah and gentle and kind. That sort of thing's not . . . it's not . . . the sort of thing . . .

Gemma: . . . sort of thing . . .
Angelique: that they sort of like do, you know . . .

This sense of a difference in style is then picked up on and expanded by her in a story she told about her aunt who, whilst shouting at her son that he certainly couldn't have a bracelet she was wearing, was taking the bracelet off and giving it to him: 'That's our way of saying I, oh, I want to give it to you my love, . . . my son.'

The register of romance finds different expression in the Black community, whilst Angelique's acquaintance with the former has been made through reading books which deal exclusively with White characters. This affects her writing:

I've never once read a Black romance . . . so I tend to write the stories as I have read in books.

To position herself in a romance story, she also has to position herself as White:

Usually when I'm writing a romance, a story, it's usually just me, but playing a White character, d'you know what I mean?

The books on which she models such writing are exclusively White and have little bearing on Black culture. To write a romance, therefore, she 'plays' a White part. She followed up that comment by drawing a distinction between writing about Black and White characters:

If I'm going to write something that's got to do with Black people when I'm really going to prepare it first, I mean I think about when I'm going to write something to do with a Black person yet when I'm writing something to do with a White person I just write it.

At this point in the interview I was confused. In a previous session she had talked about writing about herself at home as straightforward, easy compared to the constraints of writing in school:

I thought I'm going to make it, so I wrote it out, do it, be how I feel.

Now she was talking about the ease of writing with a White voice, playing a White role.

Gemma: What I'm wondering is, when you say, when you're writ-
             ing as a White person you just write, that would leave me,
             doesn't that mean you're writing more as you?
Angelique: Well, yeah, I suppose it doesn't really but, I can't explain it
             really. I suppose when I'm writing as a White person . . .
             it's more enough, I really just, It's all the books I've read.
             I've never read in my whole life really a Black romance.
             There's hardly any ones that I know actually. And so the
             ones I have read I tend to just write, sort of like copy in
             other words what they've written into my own type of
             words. I just write. With a Black romance there are certain
             things that you've got to get right.

The genre proposes White characters. To take the genre on board is to accept its setting. Alter the setting and she would have to alter the characterization, the romance's exploration of events, its conventions. Yet it is these conventions she wants to explore — not, I would argue, at the expense of exploring her identity as Black, but alongside it. The simple reason for this is that the romance is the most obvious space in which to examine girl-boy relationships. Support for this view comes from the way in which Angelique talks about her own romance writing. She has thought carefully about what she is doing and is involved in what she is writing. She consistently talks about the narrator-heroines in the first person.

> the girl, I end up saying, 'cos it's like me really the way I think I would act. . . . I end up saying 'Well you shouldn't have come running back to me should you' really sarcastic but knowing in my heart that probably I would really want this guy back.

But being involved doesn't just mean taking on board everything the convention has to offer. She is critical of the form, both in what it has to say about girls —

> I cannot, I hate reading a story where the girl's all 'Ahh', the Cinderella type of thing. It really annoys me because it's so stupid. That is the reason why we have so many stereotypes about women;

— and the image it creates of boys:

> With the man with the most black hair and blue eyes, the irresistible blue eyes, the one with the blue eyes is supposed to be heartless and cold and the women with the brown eyes is nice and warm, that sort of thing, it's really rubbish.

Instead, she works within the conventions to establish her own meanings:

> When I'm writing a story to me the girl has always got to be a strong character.

The problems girls encounter with boys in her stories are not to do with whether they have a boyfriend or not but on whose terms the relationship will be conducted, and here she places control in the hands of the girl:

> If [the boys] start . . . not being the way I want them to be in my stories, in my romance like they're begging me to come back to them, that sort of thing [smiles] I say 'No I'm not going' and all this sort of thing and walk off.

It is the boys who have to put up with being powerless, cajole the girl into staying within the relationship, and ultimately they lose. She punctures the smooth and attractive pose in which they're presented in the magazines:

> I done a description of Steve's room, page three [pinups] all over the place, money thrown down where he's come home from work, his

YTS scheme [. . .] his room looks a complete state . . . that sort of thing, when I read a magazine all you see is . . . hmmm . . . well dressed, suit, nice tie, you know the sort of things that they write about, really rubbish [laughs].

To this extent she has adapted the romance genre to her own purposes. However, as I've already shown, this doesn't leave her free to do anything she wants. There are constraints, amongst them the question of how to end her stories. Romance offers two responsibilities for closure: happy — the girl gets the boy of her dreams; or sad — she is left on her own. Either way the resolution is beyond the girl's control. It just happens, and it is final. Angelique's preoccupations, in particular with the wresting of control from the boy, fit uneasily within this format:

I don't think there really is an ending in any of my stories.

She comes to a temporary resting place: temporary because the solution is fragile, open to continuing negotiation.

The last story I wrote, that Steve one, um, they ended up breaking up and him coming back to her and saying 'Oh will you please' and she's saying 'No, it's not worth it because you're only going to do the same thing to me again!'
    That's the sort of thing it is and then I pick it up again, I feel like writing another story, sometimes we go out with each other again, sometimes we just don't bother . . . it's not worth it.

It is difficult to reconcile her conflicting desires: wanting the boy and yet not wanting to be dominated by him, used by him.

I ended up saying 'Well you shouldn't have come running back to me should you', really sarcastic, but knowing in my heart that probably I would really want this guy back.

The endings in her stories are uneasy. They do not conform to the stark distinction drawn in romance (happy/sad) — the point they have reached is more subtle. But to think about them in terms other than those proposed by romance is hard.

Angelique: It was just the sort of ending where she was going to go off and find another boyfriend and at the time, now when you think about all this business about women being stereotyped and all this, now I think of it as a woman going off and having her own independence without a male tying her down, but then, I didn't think of it that way.

Gemma: Did it seem to you when you wrote it as a happy or a sad ending then?

Angelique: Sad ending, I think, well not sad ending but just that she wouldn't have Steve.

I have been attempting to map out in my account of Angelique and her writing a far more complex interaction between the writer and her text than the customary arguments about popular culture and popular fiction allow for. Angelique's writing cannot be understood in terms of entirely passive consumers hopelessly trapped and subdued by an all-powerful popular fiction, relentlessly undermining their perception of the real world. Angelique's romance writing is about modification, adaptation, transformation of the genre within which she is working. Her text exploits the contradictory ways of reading offered by her sources to open up new spaces and to pose her own questions about identity, emotion, power.

All this implies freedom for the writer. There are also constraints. Angelique's interview points to what is excluded in her writing for school, the difficulties of writing about herself as Black within that institution. The agenda of the romance is for her a partial one. But in saying this one further point must be borne in mind. She is very aware of her identity as a Black girl. Even without the pressures of the institution within which she writes, where would she look for a genre which addresses itself to both these issues? Her politics must take her into two separate camps. Whilst this may not be ideal, it is an inevitable result of writing within the culture in which she is placed and from which she must draw.

Note

1   For a much fuller discussion of this point see Moss (1989).

References

BARKER, M. (1989) *Comics: Ideology, Power and the Critics*, Manchester, Manchester University Press.

GRAVES, D. (1983) *Writing: Teachers and Children at Work*, London, Heinemann.

HOGGART, P. (1984) 'Comics and magazines for schoolchildren', in J. MILLER (Ed.) *Eccentric Propositions*, London, Routledge and Kegan Paul.

KRESS, G. (1982) *Learning to Write*, London, Routledge and Kegan Paul.

McROBBIE, A. (1982) 'Jackie: An ideology of adolescent femininity', in B. WAITES *et al.* (Eds) *Popular Culture: Past and Present*, London, Croom Helm and Open University.

MODLESKI, T. (1984) *Loving with a Vengeance*, London, Methuen.

MOSS, G. (1989) *Un/Popular Fictions*, London, Virago.

NATIONAL WRITING PROJECT (1990) *What Are Writers Made Of? Issues of Gender and Writing*, Walton-on-Thames, Surrey, Nelson & Sons.

NEALE, S. (1980) *Genre*, London, British Film Institute.

RADWAY, J. (1984) *Reading the Romance*, Chapel Hill, University of North Carolina Press.

REEVES, P. and CHEVANNES, M. (1983) 'The ideological construction of Black under-achievement, *Multiracial Education*, **12**, pp. 22–41.

SARSBY, J. (1983) *Romantic Love and Society*, Harmondsworth, Penguin.

SHARPE, S. (1976) *Just Like a Girl: How Girls Learn to be Women*, Harmondsworth, Penguin.

STEEDMAN, C. (1982) *The Tidy House*, London, Virago.

TAYLOR, H. (1985) 'Autobiography', in J. RICHMOND *et al.* (Eds) *The English Curriculum: Writing*, London, The English Centre.

Chapter 8

Transforming the Texts: Towards a Feminist Classroom Practice

Sandra Taylor

Popular cultural texts, such as those discussed in this collection, play a significant role in the reproduction of patriarchal gender relations. They are centrally involved in the generation and circulation of meanings relating to gender which are part of the everyday lives of girls and young women, and they are particularly implicated in the construction of femininity. It is clear that the processes involved are complex, but it seems that popular cultural texts play a part in the construction of femininity in two main ways: first through the patriarchal ideologies, such as the ideology of romance, which are embodied in the texts themselves, and second through the ways in which they enter into the lives of the girls and young women with whom these texts are so popular. Popular cultural forms are used by girls to help them to understand and explore their place in the world, and are a backdrop for their educational and life choices. Consequently, feminist teachers need to understand these processes which are part of the cultural framework within which girls 'find a sense of themselves' (MacDonald, 1981, p. 163) if change is to occur.

Many of the policy initiatives which have been taken to address gender-based inequalities in education over the years, have failed to take account of this broader cultural context of schooling and of the complexities involved in gender relations. It is easy enough to talk about 'widening options' for girls and young women, but to do so not only involves providing opportunities in the labour market, it also means changing deeply held meanings about femininity at a personal level. Culturally focused approaches, therefore, are as important as broader policies to address structural inequalities, and it is worth emphasizing that social structure and culture, and meanings and power relations are interrelated:

> a social system can only be held in place by the meanings that people make of it. Culture is deeply inscribed in the differential distribution of power within a society, for power relations can only be stabilized or destabilized by the meanings that people make of them. Culture is a struggle for meanings as society is a struggle for power (Fiske, 1987, p. 20).

Within this framework, cultural texts are part of a network of meanings which constitute the social world and which may be viewed as a series of sites of struggle over meaning. Following Leslie Roman and Linda Christian-Smith (1988), a *cultural text* includes both commercial, representational forms (for example a video clip or a teen romance) and lived social relations (for example a specific group of high school girls). Both kinds of cultural text are involved in the making of meaning and culture, and are closely interrelated in everyday social practices, as, for example, when a group of schoolgirls discuss the latest episode of *Neighbours* (an Australian prime time soap) at the back of their science class.

In this chapter I will attempt to develop a theoretical base for a feminist classroom practice which focuses on cultural processes. While schooling is a site for the reproduction of gender relations, it is also a site for intervention and change, and offers possibilities for reconstructing femininity in new ways. I will explore the role played by popular cultural texts in the construction of femininity, how they relate to the lives of adolescent girls, and the implications of these understandings for the feminist classroom. My focus is on the teenage period, which is a crucial time in relation to educational and life choices — though an exploration of teenage femininity is of course relevant to the cultural construction of femininity in a more general way.

To develop an understanding of the complexities involved in the construction of femininity and change it will be necessary to consider some theoretical issues relating to the cultural construction of femininity. We also need to consider research in the area of girls' subcultures, particularly the ways in which girls use popular cultural texts, and, in addition, it will be helpful to consider reported accounts of the successes and failures of the feminist classroom. In developing approaches for the classroom we need to ask, first, what is the significance of popular cultural texts in girls' lives and how do we take account of this in the curriculum? And second, how do we use popular cultural texts in the classroom to challenge traditional versions of femininity and develop new and alternative versions? In other words, what possibilities are there for transforming the texts of patriarchy through the cultural politics of the feminist classroom?

Romance: The Tender Trap

I would argue that 'romance' is a central theme in the popular cultural texts which are part of teenage girls' everyday lives. Teen romance novels are extremely popular with adolescent girls in the USA, Canada, the UK and Australia. Similarly, romance is a central theme in other popular cultural texts such as magazines, soap operas and contemporary music, and it is also a central theme in teenage girls' lived culture. Through romance, girls explore problems concerned with their real lives, their fantasy worlds and the blurred margins between them. This will be discussed in more detail later in the chapter, but at this stage it may be useful to briefly consider 'romance' in historical context.

The term 'romance' has a number of meanings as it is used today, and 'romance', meaning romantic love, has been interpreted variously over time. In ancient Greek and Roman times, people prayed to be spared from this dreaded 'disease' (Ferguson, 1983, pp. 97–98), while later it was seen as one of the highest forms of human experience. But such passionate and sexual forms of love were seen as shortlived and did not lead to marriage. In fact, romantic love was seen as a most *unsuitable* basis for marriage, and in the late middle ages romantic love was seen as constituting irrational grounds for marriage due to its ephemeral nature (Stone, 1971). There is also an element of myth or fantasy in interpretations of romantic love. Although originally the word 'romance' came into the English language from French and referred to tales of chivalry and knights, it later came to mean stories which were far-fetched and not based on reality. Much more recently it was used to refer to a love affair, and came to be seen as a basis for marriage (Ferguson, 1983, pp. 97–98).

It is worth noting also that the idea of marriage based on romantic love is specific to certain groups. In working-class families marriage was seen in economic terms, and for young women, as a means of financial security — perhaps with emotional support. In the late nineteenth and early twentieth century, attitudes to marriage among working-class women was 'cool and business-like' (Lewis, 1984), while in some ethnic groups in contemporary Australia romantic love is not viewed as an important basis for marriage — the expectation being that love will develop with marriage. These historical and cross-cultural variations in the meaning of romance illustrate the ideological nature of romantic love. Romantic love can be seen as a form of social control: 'it is pulled about by social and economic forces and as an ideal it can act as a force to regulate the behaviour between the sexes' (Sarsby, 1983, p. 160).

The way in which this force operates is through subtle processes whereby needs and desires are socially constructed and naturalized. In patriarchal societies the meanings associated with romantic love have been systematized to constitute what can be termed 'romantic ideology'. Romantic ideology is part of a cluster of ideas which together constitute the ideology of womanhood, or of femininity. Such gender ideologies shape the gendered practices through which the patriarchal gender order is reproduced, and also *work* at a personal level in the formation of a gendered subjectivity.

The significance of romantic ideology lies in the fact that it is a key gender ideology implicated in the reproduction of patriarchal gender relations. As long ago as 1792 Mary Wollstonecraft (1975, p. 169) wrote: '. . . it is not against strong, persevering passions, but romantic wavering feelings, that I wish to guard the female heart by exercising the understanding . . .' And more recently Shulamith Firestone referred to love as 'the pivot of women's oppression', arguing that it is defined by men to produce self denial and dependency in women — in love women are expected to self-destruct, to de-self (Rowlands, 1990, p. 124). Robyn Rowlands (1990, p. 11) writes:

The inducement to yield self has been 'love'; love of men and children but not of self. Woman's love is expected to be selfless and therefore pure. This way women have been trapped into selflessness, dangerous to both mental health and life satisfaction. The concept of romantic love has also been used to de-activate women's struggle against patriarchy.

Thus, romantic love helps to lead women into dependency and to their apparent compliance with their own subordination.

The Cultural Construction of Femininity

Romantic ideology — together with the ideologies of marriage and motherhood with which it is linked — is central in dominant ideas about femininity. Our definitions of femininity (and masculinity) develop in particular historical and cultural contexts. They are implicated in our everyday gendered practices which are shaped by, and which in turn help to maintain, the patriarchal gender order. They do this by 'naturalizing' gender differences so that they are seen as inevitable — working at an unconscious level through the structuring of desires to achieve 'the interweaving of personal lives and social structures' (Connell, 1986, p. 351).

Societies where the gender order is patriarchal, such as contemporary western societies, are characterized by particular versions of femininity and masculinity which have been described as 'emphasized femininity' and 'hegemonic masculinity' (Connell, 1987, p. 183). Hegemonic masculinity is heterosexual and tends to be characterized by power, authority, aggression and technical competence (p. 187). On the other hand, emphasized femininity, which complements hegemonic masculinity, is characterized by compliance with subordination and is oriented to accommodating the interests and desires of men. Associated with emphasized femininity are qualities of sociability, sexual passivity and acceptance of domesticity and motherhood (p. 187). The notion of the 'good' woman and this idealized femininity is prescriptive and Jill Matthews (1984) refers perceptively to 'the impossibility of femininity'.

Although a number of versions of femininity and masculinity are constructed in everyday social practices, at a broad cultural level these dominant versions are promoted and provide the basis for women's subordination. Patriarchal versions of femininity and masculinity are represented at the symbolic level in the mass media as the cultural ideals. For example, in advertisements targeted towards older women the ideal feminine identity centres on the domestic sphere and on being the perfect wife and mother. For young women, however, the focus is on appearance and looks and on being the perfect sex object (Pringle, 1983).

This focus on appearance and sexuality is significant in relation to the construction of femininity in young women and girls and, according to Rosalind Coward, the emphasis on women's looks 'becomes a crucial way in which society exercises control over women's sexuality' (1984, p. 77). She also argues that the camera in contemporary media can be seen as an extension of the male gaze on women, with the result that the development of female identity is fraught with anxiety and enmeshed with judgments about desirability (Coward, 1984). The emphasis on women's looks is most apparent in women's magazines, in advertising material and on television — where visual representations of women are central. However, even in cultural texts which do not rely on visual images, the importance of good looks and sexual attractiveness for women is likely to be a dominant textual image. In relation to girls and young women, the overall message in representational cultural texts is that sexuality confers power — though in relation to the social and economic context this power, derived from appearance and attractiveness, is extremely limited.

Despite this overall emphasis on appearance and sexuality in the representation of women in cultural texts, the role which such texts play in the construction of femininity is complex. Even though the ideal of sexual submissiveness characterizes 'emphasized femininity', there is no simple transmission of a single coherent 'patriarchal ideology'. Although dominant ideologies may be pervasive, media texts reflect a range of contradictory and conflicting ideologies, some of which may be oppositional. In addition, we need to be cautious about too readily assuming 'effects' from readings of texts. 'Reading' a media text can be seen as a dialogue between the text and a socially situated reader. Representational cultural texts need to be considered in the context of *lived social texts*: the lived cultures of teenage girls.

Girls' Subcultures

I have argued that it is important that we understand the framework within which teenage girls make sense of themselves. A number of studies of teenage girls' subcultures, particularly those of working-class girls, provide useful insights about the conflicts adolescent girls experience and the concerns they express. This research is important not only for understanding the cultural construction of femininity, but also for considering appropriate ways for feminist educators to work with teenage girls.

Research on 'cultures of femininity' shows that teenage girls experience a number of conflicts resulting from the contradictory messages they receive about how they should behave, and it is possible to group these conflicts into three sets of interrelated contradictory discourses (Taylor, 1989a; Gilbert and Taylor, 1991). I have identified these three conflicts as follows: the domesticity/paid work conflict in relation to their futures, the 'slags or drags' conflict relating to sexuality, and the adolescence/femininity conflict relating to maturity. I have suggested that these three related sources of conflict work together to define and construct femininity in particular ways and within the domestic sphere. For teenage girls, relationships are still usually seen in terms of marriage and motherhood, and sexual behaviour is seen as only being appropriate within a context of love and/or marriage. Teenage girls tread a fine line between being sexually attractive and being overtly sexual, and there are pressures on them to find a steady boyfriend (McRobbie, 1978; Cowie and Lees, 1981; Lees, 1986; Kostash, 1987). Because of these pressures, 'romance' emerges as a central theme in studies of the lives of teenage girls.

These powerful pressures are experienced at a critical time, a time when educational and livelihood decisions are important. Consequently, girls and young women often experience a conflict between their preoccupation with issues relating to femininity, and their awareness of educational concerns. Research studies of teenage girls' subcultures suggest that they often are aware of their likely futures and their need to earn a living, but they often find themselves trapped between the conflicting pressures of the sexual, marriage and labour markets (Griffin, 1984).

A number of studies which have attempted to explore issues relating to gender and education in their wider cultural context have investigated the lived experiences of girls within and outside school, so highlighting the diversity and complexity of these experiences. In general, such studies have been concerned with 'the ways in which girls, both individually and collectively, make sense of and try to negotiate oppressive social relationships and structures in order to gain more control over their own lives' (Weiler, 1988, pp. 45–6). These studies have utilized concepts of resistance and accommodation in attempting to understand how girls and women actively respond to oppression rather than passively internalizing dominant ideologies, and recent work clearly demonstrates both the awareness girls have of their social situation and their ability to make rational choices about their lives (Wilson and Wyn, 1987; Wyn, 1988). For example, Johanna Wyn comments on the fact that working-class girls place a continuing priority on friendships and domestic concerns, and writes:

> ... the evidence in these studies suggests that the young women approach their futures positively and hopefully as they face the difficult task of balancing the demands of school and home in anticipation of the conflicting demands of private and public life in their futures.
>
> These young women are not compliant, or victims, making 'wrong' choices. The choices they do make are based on their knowledge and experience of life around them, in a context in which class and gender politics are experienced daily (Wyn, 1988, p. 125).

However, although gender ideologies are not passively internalized but are actively negotiated and resisted, it is likely that, as with working-class boys, opposition to school leads working-class girls to traditional working-class future. Willis's (1977) 'lads', in opposing school values, qualified themselves for futures as manual workers. However, for them manual work confirmed their masculinity and thereby gave them status. But in the case of working-class girls, status is not achieved from the kinds of jobs available to them, and in the long run they see few alternatives to motherhood and childrearing, whether they be with or without love, romance and marriage.

Popular Cultural Texts

It is clear from this collection of essays that there are many complexities involved in the relationship between popular cultural texts and the lives of girls and young women. It is necessary to take account of the relationship between the text, the reader and their social situation in any exploration of the role popular fiction plays in the production of meaning and culture, and as I have argued, we need to understand this relationship if we are to develop classroom strategies through which change can occur.

Before moving to consider popular fiction, the focus for this collection, I will briefly refer to soap operas — another type of cultural text which is also popular with girls and young women. A consideration of soap opera texts and how they are used by girls is relevant to our more general considerations of the role of popular cultural texts in the construction of femininity.

Research on soap opera viewing shows that teenage girls already show well-established feminine patterns in the way they use television, both in terms of viewing patterns and in the way in which the programs are used to rehearse problems to do with their own lives (Palmer, 1986; Taylor, 1989b; Gilbert and Taylor, 1991). The appeal of soap operas for this group lies in the focus of the genre on feelings and relationships, and in the opportunity they offer for 'time out' from the 'real world'. As has been found in studies of adult soap opera viewers, there is a double relationship between girls and the soap opera text — they are able to be critical of the programs at the same time as they are involved with them at an emotional level. Certainly the whole focus on feelings and relationships helps to legitimate feminine culture, and particularly the preoccupation with romance.

Some writers have expressed the view that soap operas offer the potential for oppositional and resistive readings because they are polysemic and because they tend to 'play' with the myths of patriarchy and allow them to be questioned by their audiences (Brown, 1987). For example, in soaps the perfect, happy stable family is presented as an ideal which is never achieved. However, despite these apparently progressive possibilities offered by soap opera texts, it is likely that girls' limited life experiences would make them less likely to make oppositional readings than older women viewers. Further, it could be concluded that:

> given the concerns teenage girls express about their futures, it would seem unlikely that the contradictions offered by soaps would be very helpful to them. Oppositional readings are likely to be lost among the dominant versions of femininity constructed not only through the television texts, but also through the plethora of advertising texts that accompany — and complete — the viewing of soaps. Consequently . . . the gendered subjectivity posited by the soaps [is] limited, stereotypical, and unlikely to challenge the patriarchal gender order. (Gilbert and Taylor, 1991, p. 130).

Furthermore, it seems that soaps legitimate gender relations as much by the way they enter into the politics of girls' everyday lives as through the meanings of the text. For example, girls (and women) talk with each other about their favourite programs, and some watch videotaped programs of daytime soaps with their mothers on a regular basis when they get home from school (Gilbert and Taylor, 1991).

Similarly, it seems that popular fictional texts are implicated in the construction of femininity through the gendered reading practices that they help to construct as well as through the representations in the texts. And it is clear that young girls are gently and subtly inculcated into the discourses of femininity from an early age through 'traditional' fairy tales (Gilbert, with Rowe, 1989), while pre-teen comics teach girls that it is by being self-sacrificing that they will find their 'prince' (Walkerdine, 1984).

Diane Cooper's chapter in this collection usefully highlights the way that the power of the publishing industry can influence reading choices. She argues that 'books . . . find their audience through a network of commercial practices that guide, address, coerce and . . . constitute readers' (this volume, p. 24). Her analysis focuses on the brochures advertising Ashton Scholastic's *Baby-Sitters Club* series distributed through children's book clubs. Cooper concludes that the themes in the books in this series revolve around helping behaviour and putting personal wants and needs in favour of those of others. Also, romance is linked with domesticity and/or dependence on a male to rescue the girl or save her from some dilemma. Through these themes, girls are guided towards romance fiction and, at the same time, a sense of dependency on the conventions of the genre is constructed.

Recent research focusing on the meanings constructed in teen romance texts shows that the code of romance is important in structuring the feminine discourse in the novels. Linda Christian-Smith's (1988) analysis of the codes and narrative structure of teen romances over three periods in the USA shows that despite changes between the 1940s and the 1980s: 'the code of romance organized the version of adolescent femininity in all periods. It involves not only emotion and caring, but is also about the negotiation of relations of power and control between females and males within romance' (1988, p. 81). She argues that the narrative structure of the teen romance is '*Becoming a woman through romance*' (p. 87), and that:

> While teen romances run counter to the realities of many women's and girls' actual lives, they nevertheless serve to maintain traditional views of what should constitute those lives. According to those novels, femininity consists of administering to the heart and tending the hearth. These traditional views represent a very selective rendering of the possibilities of feminine life experiences (p. 97).

As is the case with the representations of femininity associated with soap operas, the versions offered are within a narrow range of stereotyped possibilities and are both limited and limiting. The teen romance formula is highly contradictory, with a range of discourses all held together by romantic ideology. In contemporary teen romances there are heroines who are independent and take the initiative, boyfriends who are tender, and relationships which are equal and caring, and where sexual and sensual pleasure for women is endorsed — if implicitly. Nevertheless, in the long run sexual relations are ultimately channelled into monogamous heterosexual relationships within a context of romantic love. Ultimately the happy ending signifies closure by indicating only one kind of future and failing to raise alternatives.

As Pam Gilbert shows in her recent research on *Dolly Fiction* (this volume), there may have been changes in the novels — for example, they are now more sexually explicit, and the gendered subject positions constructed by the texts are now more contemporary and less stereotyped than in the past. In fact, in response to commercial pressures, they 'borrow' oppositional discourses from feminism. However, Gilbert argues that: 'the generic pattern draws so strongly upon romantic discourses for its parameters of possibility, the narrative sequences constructed within this framework are necessarily limited in the possibilities of gendered subjectivity that they can represent' (this volume, p. 85).

However, to understand the way in which popular fiction works in the construction of femininity, it is necessary also to explore the way in which teenage girls and young women *use* such fiction in their lives. Girls's reading must be viewed as social practice — though here we must keep in mind the arguments already made about those social practices being constrained by the commercial world of publishing and by generic conventions which produce gendered reading patterns. The complexity of the relationship between social context, reader and text is taken into account in several of the contributions in this collection. For example, as well as investigating teen-romance readers in three schools, Linda Christian-Smith links romance reading with the broader context of the rise of conservatism and the New Right during the 1980s in the USA.

With reference to the relationship between reader and text, it is clear that the boundaries between 'fantasy' and 'reality' are blurred. As Angela McRobbie (1984) has emphasized, the texts of popular culture are just as lived as 'lived experience' and constitute the private moments of everyday experience. They cannot be dismissed as 'fantasy' as although research has shown that girls know that the stories are not like 'real life', they nevertheless identify with the heroine and her anxieties. For example, Willinsky and Hunniford (this volume) show that the girls whom they studied read romances for relaxation and to escape daily problems, but they also used them as instruction manuals to learn, for example, how to behave on dates. Their research shows that rather than being a 'time out' from the everyday world as reported in research on adult romance readers (Radway, 1984), teen romance readers are turning to the books as a way of preparing to get into the world — at least as they imagine it to be:

> The adult reader of the romance has reconciled herself to who she has become; she does not ask to be the heroine of the romances, only to share vicariously in her adventures. This need for identification, Radway argues, is the result of her discontent with who she has become. The younger reader believes it possible to become the heroine of the romance because she is living in a state of emergence and expectation. That much understood, she asks only to be told how to act and handle it once she gets there (Willinsky and Hunniford, p. 95).

These differences are reminiscent of the differences between adult and teenage soap opera viewers discussed previously in this section, although there may be some compensatory elements in series book reading for teenage girls. Meredith Cherland and Carole Edelsky (this volume) suggest that by identifying with the heroine the reader may be able to feel more powerful than she does in her 'real world' experiences.

For the young women in Christian-Smith's research study (this volume), the ability to read and comprehend romance fiction became a symbol of 'competent femininity', which countered the 'reluctant reader' identities which had been imposed on them by the school. Like the girls in the Willinsky and Hunniford study, these young women used romance reading as a means of escape — in this case from the problems they were having with school work and from their worries about the effects of the economic downturn on their future lives. Romance novels allowed them to dream of alternative secure and comfortable futures.

The chapter by Cherland and Edelsky view girls' reading as a social practice through which they gain an understanding of their place in the world. They argue that: 'Reading fiction is one site in which children can confront their culture and construct its meanings for their individual lives' (Cherland with Edelsky, p. 42). Their research focused on the way girls used fiction to explore alternatives to the traditional versions of femininity to which they were expected to conform in their everyday lives. In other words, they explored the way popular fiction is used by girls to explore other types of agency and to imagine themselves using other forms of power. They argue that girls both accommodated and resisted cultural notions of female agency in their reading of fiction. They were 'good' girls who conformed in many ways to what was expected of them, including filling their time with 'quiet reading', but they also used that reading 'to explore alternative ideas about agency and gender'. However, the research also shows how horror and violence towards women in fiction — 'the gender threat' — reinforces their feelings of powerlessness and transmits the message that there are problems for those who step out of line: 'Moving freely in the world is dangerous. There are forces out there that will get you if you don't watch out' (Cherland with Edelsky, pp. 42). Thus, despite resistance, in the end patriarchal ideologies hold sway. Similarly, Christian-Smith concludes: 'Romance reading in no way altered the young women's present and future circumstances, but rather was deeply implicated in reconciling them to their places in the world' (this volume, p. 62).

The power and pervasiveness of patriarchal ideologies can also be seen in relation to preschool children's understandings about gender. For example, in her research on young children's responses to feminist stories, Davies (1989) found that, as the children made sense of such stories in terms of their previous experiences, they still tended to 'read' a story about a princess who rescues a boy from a dragon in terms of traditional narrative structures. Similarly, studies of older girls' writing show the power of patriarchal narratives and how difficult it is for them to write 'against the grain' (Gilbert and Taylor, 1991).

The Challenge of Change

Given this wealth of research material on the role of popular fiction in constructing gendered reading practices and in transmitting patriarchal notions of femininity, how can teachers intervene and provide a challenge to these processes? How can we raise these issues with girls and young women, and broaden the repertoire on which they draw to construct their understandings of what it means to be female?

It is now over ten years since the publication of the landmark paper 'How does girl number twenty understand ideology?' In which Judith Williamson (1981/2) discussed the difficulties involved in helping girls and young women to develop a critical awareness about gender ideologies in their lives. This paper is still relevant in the context of recent debates about feminist pedagogy, and is a useful starting point for thinking about the issues involved in transforming the text.

Williamson (1981/2) argued that we cannot *teach* ideologies — or even *teach about* ideologies. We can only try to bring students to an understanding, from their own experiences, of the way that we are all caught up in ideological processes in our everyday lives. Unless students can make sense of the issues in terms of their own lives and experiences they are likely to become alienated or resistant, and educational programs will be counter-productive. However, focusing on their own lives and experiences may be very threatening for some students as their very sense of themselves is at stake (Williamson, 1981/2, 1985). Drawing on her experiences of teaching media studies to 'tech school' students in Britain, Williamson comments on how traumatic it can be to 'see' that social reality is ideological:

> If we mean what we write about the formation of the subject through social discourses, and so on, and then direct the thrust of our teaching *at*

social discourse, we ought to *know* that we are thereby hacking at the very roots of those formed subjects (1981/2, p. 85).

More recent discussions of feminist pedagogy continue to highlight the difficulties involved in challenging gender relations, though we do seem to be building up our understandings about the issues and at least have a clearer idea about what is likely to work, and why. Given the complexities involved in the construction of femininity, and the power and pervasiveness of gender ideologies at a personal level, it is not surprising that progress is slow. Reconstructing femininity in new ways is difficult and challenging, because it involves deconstructing dominant ideologies and changing subjectivities.

Recent research helps deepen our understandings of these difficulties. For example, Magda Lewis (1990) has highlighted some key issues relevant to the feminist classroom based on her experiences in university courses. She emphasizes that feminist politics confronts the compromises many women have made in their lives and in their relationships with men and argues: 'Pedagogy, even radical pedagogy, does not easily translate into an education that includes women if we do not address the threat to women's survival and livelihood that a critique of patriarchy in its various manifestations confronts' (1990, p. 473). These aspects are rarely acknowledged in relation to the feminist classroom and yet, as she suggests, they explain 'the conflicting emotional and analytic responses women have to the content of the course' (p. 141). She argues that we need to take seriously the implications of the conflict between 'women's desire for knowledge and our embodiment as sexually desirable human beings' which 'lies always just below the surface in the [feminist] classroom' (p. 481). Given the conflicts and pressures teenage girls face which I have discussed, this issue is likely to be even more salient in relation to teenage girls' reactions to feminist teaching.

However, a word of caution is necessary here. I have argued that girls and adult women are using popular cultural texts in different ways and that accounts of women's use of popular fiction will not necessarily be relevant to the experiences of teenage girls. Similarly, accounts of women's studies courses at university level, often with middle-class women, will not necessarily be relevant for teachers working with adolescent girls — particularly from working-class, Aboriginal or non-English-speaking backgrounds. Nevertheless, they can highlight some problems and strategies which may be relevant for school classrooms — for example, the need to take account of students' resistance to feminism and *use* it explicitly in developing a transformative pedagogy (Lewis, 1990).

In developing feminist approaches for transforming the text, it is clear that it is necessary to take account of a number of issues which I have raised. First there is the whole area of girls' experiences and conflicts and their resistance to feminism; then there is the research about the way popular cultural texts relate to girls' everyday lives; and finally there is the complex area of subjectivity — the way in which femininity is constructed at a personal level within this network of gendered social practices. The power of gender ideologies lies in the fact that they work at an unconcious level, through the structuring of desires, as well as at a conscious or rational level. Rosalind Coward (1984) sees female desire as being constructed through 'feminine pleasures' such as romantic fiction and soap operas which work to sustain patriarchal gender relations. It is this 'lure of pleasure' which makes change difficult. As Coward (1984, p. 16) writes:

. . . our subjectivity and identity are formed in the definitions of desire which encircle us. These are the experiences which make change such a difficult and daunting task, for female desire is constantly lured by discourses which sustain male privilege.

However, Coward also highlights the possibilities for the development of alternative definitions of subjectivity, through addressing the contradictions, gaps and precariousness of the existing definitions. I will discuss these issues further in the next section.

Towards a Feminist Classroom Practice

I have argued that popular cultural forms play a part in the construction of femininity in two main ways — first through the ideologies embodied in the texts themselves, and second through the ways in which they enter the lives of teenage girls. Therefore, before turning to the more specific questions relating to the versions of femininity in popular cultural texts, it is necessary to consider some more general aspects of the context of girls' lives which need to be taken into account — in other words, in developing a feminist classroom practice it is necessary to consider both representational cultural texts and lived social relations as they relate to the construction of femininity. It is important that teachers and others working with girls and young women take account of the conflicts and concerns which this group express, and that girls are encouraged to explore and to discuss the contradictions and pressures they face with each other. I have already referred to Judith Williamson's comments about the need to begin with students' experiences in any attempts to bring students to an awareness of ideology. The challenge for feminist educators is to work *with* girls and young women and help them reflect critically on their own lives and futures.

As discussed earlier, the concerns expressed by teenage girls centre on their futures (both in the workforce and as mothers), on sexuality, and on issues related to age and maturity. These concerns should not be dismissed as unimportant and irrelevant because of an educational preoccupation with 'career planning'. Girls' and young women's concerns about their futures as child rearers should also be addressed in the curriculum. Studies of women's experiences of parenting in relation to working life can be a focus for the critical discussion of girls' future lives. Such issues can also be taken up in work education programs which include studies of women's work from an historical perspective, and also through discussions about childbearing/childrearing and combining paid work with parenting. There is also a need for work education programs to include demographic information relating to the position of women in society — including women's employment patterns, marriage and family size, unpaid work, family breakdown and the feminization of poverty. Associated projects such as an investigation of the childcare needs in the local community, together with available facilities and provisions, could be valuable. Decision making and life planning need also to be encouraged and supported, but in the context of information about social trends in contemporary society previously mentioned. With reference to sexuality, teachers need to be careful not to perpetuate the labelling practices of the 'politics of reputation' in the comments they make to students, and should instead support girls' own resistance to the labels placed on them. It is also important to encourage resistance and independence in relation to the femininity/adolescence conflict, rather than to constantly pressure girls to be 'mature' and 'feminine'.

In relation to developing more specific strategies for the feminist classroom, some aspects of critical theory are relevant. For example, self-reflection and transformative action can occur through ideology critique: the analysis of every-day taken-for-granted common-sense practices which, instead of being treated as 'given', 'must be viewed within historical and social relations that are produced and socially constructed' (Giroux, 1984, p. 322). Giroux discusses the importance of ideology critique in relation to cultural texts such as films and books, and advocates the use of critique to go beyond deconstruction of the texts to a reconstruction which serves radical needs. Other critical theorists who have explored how social forces shape subjectivity and how these processes can be challenged through critical reflection and action are the Brazilian educator Paulo Freire (1972, 1985) and Ira Shor. Shor (1987) writes of the importance of helping students to 'extraordinarily re-experience the ordinary'. He makes the important point that, though his critical pedagogy is situated in the themes and experiences of the students, the aim is not merely to exploit or endorse the given but seek to transcend it: 'We gain a distance from the given by abstracting it from its unfa-miliar surroundings and studying it in unfamiliar ways, until our perceptions of it and society are challenged' (Shor, in Freire and Shor, 1987, p. 104).

On the other hand, many feminists have used 'consciousness raising' as an important approach in teaching (Weiler, 1988). As Sue Middleton (1987) points out, drawing on Freire, activist pedagogies are based on the assumption that people learn best by critically reflecting on and theorizing their own actions in the social world. She documents the use of life-history analysis as a teaching tech-nique in a women's studies course in an attempt to help students learn to link 'biography, history and social structure'. Such an approach gives students the opportunity to interpret their own experiences in a way which reveals how these experiences have been shaped and influenced by the dominant culture. Giroux (1981) argues that subjective awareness becomes the first step in transforming those experiences, and acknowledges that a radical pedagogy must take seriously the task of providing the conditions for changing subjectivity as well as changing broad political, economic and social structures. He writes: 'In short, an essential aspect of radical pedagogy centres around the need for students to interrogate critically their inner histories and experiences' (1984, p. 319). For example, teenage girls could be encouraged to find out about the lives of women in their own families. As I have argued elsewhere (Taylor, 1989a), the key to em-powerment for young women seems to lie in the development of a collective sense of themselves as women, which Gilbert (1988) refers to as 'gender esteem'. Through such an exploration of the personal experiences and life histories of women, girls and young women can develop a strong sense of identity of them-selves as women. A crucial aspect of all this, as has been emphasized, is to high-light the interaction between the social and the personal, and between history and private experience.

In this context, a cultural studies approach, as developed by the Cockpit Cultural Studies Department of the Inner London Education Authority in Britain (see Bezencenet and Corrigan, 1986; Dewdney and Lister, 1986, 1988), is useful in suggesting activities to encourage girls to reflect on their own experiences, and on the experiences of women in their own families, and ultimately on their own futures. The Cockpit Workshop has been involved with practical photographic projects with young people both in school in collaboration with teachers, and outside, for example, with unemployed young people. Similar approaches could be used in various areas of the school curriculum with modifications according to the needs of the particular group concerned.

Andrew Dewdney and Martin Lister claim that the cultural studies approach allows ways of basing general educational practice on young people's views and experience, and emphasize that: 'Without conscious and active engagement with the content of young people's resistance, teaching is bound to reproduce more than it transforms' (1986, p. 31). Photography is central, though not indispensable to this approach, as it is a particularly useful means of representing and reconstructing everyday experiences and, through these activities, reflecting on them. The value of family photographs to help girls explore women's experience within the family, has been well demonstrated by an interesting project documented by Adrian Chappell (1984) involving a young unemployed working-class woman.

This kind of approach was attempted as part of action research on the 'gender inclusive curriculum', in an inner city girls' school in Melbourne with a large proportion of girls from non-English speaking families, and is reported in detail elsewhere (Taylor, 1989a). The project involved work with a class of 14–15-year-old girls for three hours a week over nine weeks. Activities were developed which would help the girls to think about their future lives, initially by encouraging them to reflect on the experiences of the women in their own families. The students were given the choice of doing photographic work, either using family photographs or doing photographic work themselves as in the Chappell (1984) project, or of interviewing their mothers or grandmothers about their lives.

One aspect of cultural studies work in the classroom is that the work should go beyond critique and deconstruction to cultural production, Thus it is important that students become engaged in producing their own materials. As Williamson (1981/2) has observed, students learn about ideologies when they actually have to confront them in a practical situation and can never understand these issues purely intellectually. They need to bump up against ideologies in the course of practical productive work, and in cultural production they can play with dominant cultural representations and become involved in producing new alternative versions.

Cultural Politics and Change

Recent work on critical pedagogy emphasizes the importance of these kinds of activities in educational and social change. For example, in one collection of articles entitled *Critical Pedagogy and Cultural Power* (Livingstone, 1987), there is 'an attempt to understand how forms of subjectivity are regulated and transformed through the structured character of such social forms as language, ideologies, myths, significations, and narratives' (p. xv). Lewis has argued that the most important focus for feminist pedagogy should be 'the political struggle over meaning' (1990, p. 470). In this context, Williamson's insights about the use of media studies as a way of connecting issues of personal identity with cultural activity have been significant, and she views such activity as politically important:

> . . . It is only as familiar structures of meaning are shaken and taken apart
> that new ones can form. And looking at things differently makes it pos-
> sible to act differently (Williamson, 1989, p. 6).

For instance, the introductory statement to an anthology of Australian women's poetry places women's writing in the realm of cultural politics, by discussing the importance of *rethinking* the world in order to *reconstruct* the world. In a percep-tive discussion of the stages in the evolution of a feminist consciousness, Susan Hampton and Kate Llewellyn claim that after awareness of oppression and radical questioning of social structures, there follows a stage of creation: '[m]aking some-thing new is to imagine different grids on reality, other views on the world' (Hampton and Llewellyn, 1986, p. 5).

These ideas are relevant for thinking about possible ways of using popular cultural texts in the classroom to generate new meanings which will challenge patriarchal gender ideologies. The way in which these texts connect with the lived experiences of growing up as a woman in contemporary society gives them particular potency and appeal. Therefore, teachers need to be sensitive about the way in which they introduce such texts into the classroom as students will be alienated if teachers 'put down' their interests, or if they turn something which is fun for students into 'work'. But popular cultural texts can be successfully used in the classroom if they are treated seriously — as cultural products — and if teachers are genuinely open to understanding their significance in girls' subcultures.

It is important that girls learn about the commercial aspects of the pro-duction of popular cultural texts. It would be useful, for example, for girls to research aspects of the publishing industry, and in particular to investigate the teen romance, including, for example, the guidelines for writers produced by publishers, marketing and promotional strategies, as well as the history of teen romance fiction. Such research could help students to develop a critical awareness of the social and historical production and marketing of such cultural texts.

It is also necessary that students learn the generic conventions which characterize particular popular cultural forms such as teen romances and soap operas. It is important that such critical reflection is approached seriously and avoids ridiculing the material. It is inappropriate for teachers merely to critique the texts because, as I have shown, the students are already to some extent aware of the stereotyping or 'unreality' of many of them. Teachers have a role, though, in helping to highlight and extend this critical awareness. In addition, the con-tradictory richness of popular cultural texts can be explored and teachers can help students to discover the resistant or oppositional readings which may be made. Students should also be given the opportunity to become involved in the production of their own materials using their understandings of the generic conventions. In this way they will be able to become involved in the construction of cultural texts which better articulate their interests and experiences. This kind of cultural production allows students to explore issues through fantasy as well as through more conventional analytical approaches. As has been argued, 'the process of making an alternative text becomes a richer re-fashioning activity if students have acquired some understanding of the roots of the generic conventions they work with, and an understanding of the way in which such roots are ideologically constructed' (Gilbert and Taylor, 1991, p. 143).

It is also necessary to widen the *range of discourses* available to girls and young women, thereby extending the repertoire on which they draw in constructing their femininity. In particular, this means carefully considering the texts which are used in the classroom — which are so often 'a discourse not intended for her' (Rich, 1980, p. 243). Instead materials should be provided which will offer alternative versions of femininity: versions which will be potentially more helpful in relation to their developing sense of themselves and their futures as women.

Alternative texts are much more accessible now than they have been in the past given the increase in publication of women writers through the 1980s. In addition, feminist publishing houses like Virago and The Women's Press have undertaken deliberate publishing ventures to provide alternative texts for young women. The Women's Press and Virago have produced the *Livewires* and *Upstarts* series respectively. The Australian McPhee-Gribble's *In Between* series is a similar venture, which attempts to work with contemporary teenage issues and to take account of issues of gender, race and class. As has been argued:

> The books are now available to allow teachers to construct reading lists which focus on issues of concern to young women, and which present other 'voices' — the voices of contemporary Australian women — to classrooms. Textual experience, such as these books offer, provides one of the best bases upon which to build critical reading positions for romance literature. Young women need to be able to read about other ways of organising their lives, other emphases that have been important to women, other patterns of female-male relationships. Without this additional textual experience, girls' reading and writing capacities are limited (Gilbert, with Rowe, 1989, p. 62).

And, I would add, so too are their visions of womanhood.

While texts like these are crucial in providing access to alternative discourses for young women, girls may need to learn alternative reading practices so that they can read these texts 'differently'. Valerie Walkerdine (1984) warns of the difficulties associated with introducing young girls to alternative views and images through texts. She suggests that the 'simple realism' of much anti-sexist literature may fail because it assumes a 'rationalist' reader who will change as a result of receiving the correct information 'about how things *really* are'. She reminds us of the need to take into account the power of fantasy in the construction of female desire in developing feminist strategies for change.

Challenging dominant versions of femininity will necessitate not only making alternative texts available for young women, but also developing alternative textual strategies for the classroom, which move beyond simple realistic readings of the 'world' of the fiction. Texts can also be played with, and writing and reading practices can become the focus of classroom language work. Women's experiences and concerns have tended to be devalued, hence girls need to unlearn some of the gendered reading practices they have been taught, and learn to read and write 'against the grain':

Learning to read and write against the grain . . . is therefore about learning to read and write against conventions that construct women in ways that are demeaning and restricting. It is . . . about learning to read and write in ways that offer constructions of female subjectivity that are not fixed and static, but are dynamic and shifting. It is about learning to understand the discursive construction of subjectivity and the potential spaces for resistance and rewriting (Gilbert and Taylor, 1991, p. 150).

Popular fiction is centrally involved in the construction of teenage femininity, and the essays in this collection show the complexities involved in these processes. However, I have argued that an understanding of these complexities can provide a basis for a feminist pedagogy. My aim has been to explore some possibilities for transforming the texts of patriarchy through the cultural politics of the feminist classroom. I have suggested that popular cultural texts, such as teen romances, can be used as a focus for critical analysis such that they might be read and re-written differently by girls and young women. Possibilities do exist to offer girls alternative reading positions, from which they might construct alternative versions of femininity — versions of femininity which might be more helpful to them in relation to their present and future lives as women.

References

BEZENCENET, S. and CORRIGAN, P. (1986) *Photographic Practices: Towards a Different Image*, London, Comedia.

BROWN, M.E. (1987) 'The politics of soaps: Pleasure and feminine empowerment', *Australian Journal of Cultural Studies*, 4(2) pp. 1–25.

CHAPPELL, A. (1984) 'Family fortunes: A practical photography project', in A. McROBBIE and M. NAVA (Eds) *Gender and Generation*, Basingstoke, Macmillan, pp. 112–29.

CHRISTIAN-SMITH, L. (1988) 'Romancing the girl: Adolescent romance novels and the construction of femininity', in L. ROMAN and L. CHRISTIAN-SMITH (Eds) *Becoming Feminine: The Politics of Popular Culture*, London: Falmer Press, pp. 76–101.

CONNELL, R.W. (1986) 'Theorizing gender', in N. GRIEVE and A. BURNS (Eds) *Australian Women. New Feminist Perspectives*, Melbourne, Oxford University Press, pp. 112–29.

CONNELL, R.W. (1987) *Gender and Power, Society, the Person and Sexual Politics*, Sydney, Allen and Unwin.

COWARD, R. (1984) *Female Desire*, London, Paladin Books.

COWIE, C. and LEES, S. (1981) 'Slags or drags', *Feminist Reviews*, **9**, October, pp. 17–31.

DAVIES, B. (1989) *Frogs and Snails and Feminist Tales*, Sydney, Allen and Unwin.

DEWDNEY, A. and LISTER, M. (1986) 'Photography, school and youth: The Cockpit Arts Project', in S. BEZENCENET and P. CORRIGAN (Eds) *Photographic Practices: Towards a Different Image*, London, Comedia, pp. 29–52.

DEWDNEY, A. and LISTER, M. (1988) *Youth Culture and Photography*, London, Macmillan.

FERGUSON, M. (1983) 'Passionate romantic love', *Canadian Women's Studies*, 4(4) pp. 97–98.

FIRESTONE, S. (1972) *The Dialectic of Sex*, London, Paladin.

FISKE, J. (1987) *Television Culture*, London, Methuen.

FREIRE, P. (1972) *The Pedagogy of the Oppressed*, Ringwood, Penguin.

FREIRE, P. (1985) *The Politics of Education*, London, Macmillan.

FREIRE, P. and SHOR, I. (1987). *A Pedagogy For Liberation*, London, Macmillan.

GILBERT, P. (1988) 'Personal growth or critical resistance? Self esteem in the English classroom', in J. KENWAY and S. WILLIS (Eds) *Hearts and Minds: Self Esteem and the Schooling of Girls*, Canberra, Dept. of Education, Employment and Training, pp. 167–83.

GILBERT, P. with ROWE, K. (1989) *Gender, Literacy and the Classroom*, Melbourne, Australian Reading Association.

GILBERT, P. and TAYLOR, S. (1991) *Fashioning the Feminine: Girls, Popular Culture, and Schooling*, Sydney, Allen and Unwin.

GIROUX, H. (1981) *Ideology, Culture and the Process of Schooling*, London, Falmer Press.

GIROUX, H. (1984) 'Ideology, agency and the process of schooling', in L. BARTON and S. WALKER (Eds) *Social Crisis and Educational Research*, London, Croom Helm, pp. 306–34.

GRIFFIN, C. (1984) *Typical Girls*, London, Routledge and Kegan Paul.

HAMPTON, S. and LLEWELLYN, K. (1986) *The Penguin Book of Australian Women Poets*, Ringwood, Penguin.

KOSTASH, M. (1987) *No Kidding. Inside the World of Teenage Girls*, Toronto, McClelland and Stewart.

LEES, S. (1986) *Losing Out. Sexuality and Adolescent Girls*, London, Hutchinson.

LEWIS, J. (1984) *Women in England 1870–1950: Sexual Divisions and Social Change*, Sussex, Wheatsheaf Books.

LEWIS, M. (1990) 'Interrupting patriarchy: Politics, resistance, and transformation in the feminist classroom', *Harvard Educational Review*, **60**(4) pp. 467–88.

LIVINGSTONE, D. (Ed.) (1987) *Critical Pedagogy and Cultural Power*, London, Macmillan.

MACDONALD, M. (1981) 'Schooling and the reproduction of class and gender relations', in R. DALE *et al.* (Eds) *Politics, Patriarchy and Practice*, London, Falmer/Open University Press, pp. 159–77.

MATTHEWS, J.J. (1984) *Good and Mad Women*, Sydney, Allen and Unwin.

MCROBBIE, A. (1978) 'Working-class girls and the culture of femininity', in WOMEN'S STUDIES GROUP (Ed.) *Women Take Issue*, London, Hutchinson, pp. 96–108.

MCROBBIE, A. (1984) 'Dance and social fantasy', in A. MCROBBIE and M. NAVA (Eds) *Gender and Generation*, Basingstoke, Macmillan, pp. 130–61.

MIDDLETON, S. (1987) 'Feminist educators in a university setting: A case study in the politics of "educational" knowledge', *Discourse*, **8**(1) pp. 25–47.

PALMER, P. (1986) *Girls and Television*, Sydney, Social Policy Unit, New South Wales Ministry of Education.

PRINGLE, R. (1983) 'Women and consumer capitalism', in C. BALDOCK and B. CASS (Eds) *Women, Social Welfare and the State*, Sydney, Allen and Unwin, pp. 85–103.

RADWAY, J. (1984) *Reading the Romance: Women, Patriarchy and Popular Literature*, Chapel Hill, University of North Carolina Press.

RICH, A. (1980) *On Lies, Secrets and Silences*, Virago, London.

ROMAN, L. and CHRISTIAN-SMITH, L. (Eds) (1988) *Becoming Feminine: The Politics of Popular Culture*, London, Falmer Press.

ROWLANDS, R. (1990) *Woman Herself*, Melbourne, Oxford University Press.

SARSBY, J. (1983) *Romantic Love and Society*, Ringwood, Penguin.

SHOR, I. (1987) *Critical Teaching and Everyday Life*, Chicago, University of Chicago Press.

STONE, L. (1971) *The Family, Sex and Marriage in England 1500–1800*, New York, Harper Colophon.

TAYLOR, S. (1989a) 'Empowering girls and young women: the challenge of the gender inclusive curriculum', *Journal of Curriculum Studies*, **21**(5) pp. 441–56.

TAYLOR, S. (1989b) 'Days of their lives?: Popular culture, femininity and education', *Continuum*, **2**(2) pp. 143–62.

WALKERDINE, V. (1984) 'Some day my prince will come: Young girls and the preparation for adolescent sexuality', in A. McROBBIE, and M. NAVA (Eds) *Gender and Generation*, Basingstoke, Macmillan, pp. 162–84.

WEILER, K. (1988) *Women Teaching for Change. Gender, Class and Power*, South Hadley, MA, Bergin and Garvey.

WILLIAMSON, J. (1981/2) 'How does girl number twenty understand ideology?' *Screen Education*, **40**, Autumn–Winter, pp. 80–87.

WILLIAMSON, J. (1985) 'Is there anyone here from a classroom? And other questions of education', *Screen*, **26**(1) pp. 90–95.

WILLIAMSON, J. (1989) 'AIDS and perceptions of the grim reaper', *Metro*, **80**, Spring, pp. 2–6.

WILLIS, P. (1977) *Learning to Labour*, Farnborough, Saxon House.

WILSON, B. and WYN, J. (1987) *Shaping Futures: Youth Action for Livelihood*, Sydney, Allen and Unwin.

WOLLSTONECRAFT, M. (1975) *A Vindication of the Rights of Woman*, Harmondsworth, Penguin.

WYN, J. (1988) 'Working class girls and educational outcomes: Is self esteem an issue?' in J. KENWAY and S. WILLIS (Eds) *Hearts and Minds: Self Esteem and the Schooling of Girls*, Canberra, Dept. of Education, Employment and Training, pp. 116–27.

Chapter 9

Beyond Dualism and Towards Multiple Subjectivities

Bronwyn Davies

Romantic Storylines and the Male/Female Dualism

Romantic discourse is one of the fundamental props of the male/female dualism. Central to learning to become male or female, as we currently understand these terms, is learning the appropriate *patterns of desire* (Davies, 1990a). In using the term desire here I am not invoking the psychoanalytic model of desire (as some post-structuralist writers do), but seeing desire as constituted through discourse and through storyline in particular. Because story provides a substantial and detailed manifestation of the culture, it is through story that children can learn the patterns of desire appropriate for their gender. They discover what positions are available to members of their sex and how to live the detail of those positionings as they come to understand and take up as their own the particular patterns of desire relevant to their gender (Davies and Banks, in press).[1] Learning the appropriate patterns of desire enables young women to 'voluntarily' and uncritically take up the subject positions made available to them in the patriarchal gender order, and thus to become *other* to the men in their world.

The foundations for this formation of themselves as male or female are everywhere apparent in the discourses through which the texts they encounter are written and spoken. Discourses are 'practices that systematically form the objects of which they speak' (Foucault, 1972, p. 49) and thus the subjects *to which* they speak (Davies and Harré, 1990). It is through romantic and pre-romantic discourse and the storylines embedded in them (Walkerdine, 1984) that young women learn how to position themselves correctly inside the male/female dualism.

The papers throughout this book have shown how popular culture and schooling are implicated in the process of teaching girls the 'correct' patterns of desire for their sex/gender. They elaborate this through the complex relations between class, gender and text. Focusing on romantic texts in particular, they show how teachers often encourage students who are not advanced readers to use romantic texts as a way into reading, and how this task is made easy by the attractive packaging, the publishers' marketing skills being a study in themselves. Because teachers do not define reading the romances as real reading, however, students who read only these texts do not gain access to a subject position of good reader, and thus do not access a lived storyline of themselves as competent students who can succeed in the school's terms. Girls from working-class backgrounds in particular use romantic texts as a way of resisting schooling and the school's definition of proper learning. They are, furthermore, able to use some of the current dominant discourse about good language to defend the romantic texts (they are about the real world, they enjoy them and learn about the real world from them and so on).

What the students do not have access to when they engage in this form of resistance is an understanding of the power of these texts, quite independently of their teachers' attitudes to them, to constitute them in oppressive ways in terms of class and the gender order. Many of the romantic texts that the students have access to are seductive in multiple ways. Quite apart from their clever marketing and packaging, they often tell stories about girls who are agentic, who can solve the problems they are confronted with, and who can persuade otherwise crass young men to be sensitive and aware; who can be strong and independent and at the same time, get their man. One reading of these stories is that they are opening up as legitimate, storylines in which women can be both central and strong. Another reading is that no matter how strong and competent young women might be, they must still find their man in order to achieve womanhood. Gilbert and Taylor (1991, p. 94) compare these contradictory readings to Walkerdine's analysis of a working-class family watching *Rocky II*:

> Watching a Hollywood movie is not, Walkerdine claims, simply an escape from drudgery into dreaming: 'it is a place of desperate dreaming, of hope for transformation' (Walkerdine, 1986 p. 196). In her discussion of a family viewing *Rocky II* she observes that: 'Although it is possible to discuss such films as macho, stupid and fascist, it is more revealing to see them as fantasies of omnipotence, heroism and salvation. They can thus be understood as a counterpoint to the experience of oppression and powerlessness' (Walkerdine, 1986, p. 192).

Working class girls reading romances in school and watching them on the soaps may thus, on the one hand, be resisting the oppressive nature of the subject positions available to them at school and in their later lives, imagining themselves being active and agentic in ways they rarely experience at school or in their everyday lives. On the other hand, they are learning the systems of thought through which they are shaping their desires, thus fitting themselves for romance as the determining feature of their lives.

Romantic texts can be read in multiple ways (Radway, 1984). But in all of the possible readings, the sub-text asserts the inevitability of heterosexual coupling. Compulsory heterosexual coupling is in turn fundamental to the maintenance of the male/female dualism. In taking oneself up as male or female, within current discourses, one is doing so *in relation to* the other. Cixous (1986, p. 63) elaborates the male/female division in terms of a set of binary oppositions: Activity/Passivity; Sun/Moon; Culture/Nature; Day/Night; Father/Mother; Head/Heart; Intelligible/Palpable; Logos/Pathos. Man is 'Form, convex, step, advance, semen, progress' whereas woman is 'Matter, concave, ground — where steps are taken, holding — and dumping ground'. It is, Cixous goes on to say,

Always the same metaphor: we follow it, it carries us, beneath all its figures, wherever discourse is organised. If we read or speak, the same thread or double braid is leading us through literature, philosophy, criticism, centuries of representation and reflection (1986, p. 63).

Moi describes how these dualisms are imbricated in patriarchal systems of thought:

each opposition can be analysed as a hierarchy where the 'feminine' side is always seen as the negative, powerless instance. . . . Western philosophy and literary thought are and always have been caught up in this endless series of hierarchical binary oppositions that always in the end come back to the fundamental 'couple' of the male/female (1987, p. 104).

Wilshire (1989, pp. 95–6) in a study of myth extends Cixous's list of the hierarchical dualisms associated with maleness and femaleness as follows:

KNOWLEDGE (accepted wisdom)	IGNORANCE (the occult and taboo)
higher up	lower down
good, positive	negative, bad
mind (ideas), head, spirit	body (flesh), womb (blood), Nature (Earth)
reason (the rational)	emotions and feelings (the irrational)
cool	hot
order	chaos
control	letting things be, allowing, spontaneity
objective (outside, 'out there')	subjective (inside, immanent)
literal truth, fact	poetic truth, metaphor, art
goals	process
light	darkness
written text, Logos	oral tradition, enactment, Myth
Apollo as sky-sun	Sophia as earth-cave-moon
public sphere	private sphere
seeing, detached	listening, attached
secular	holy and sacred
linear	cyclical
permanence, ideal (fixed) forms	change, fluctuations, evolution
'changeless and immortal'	process, ephemeral, (performance)
hard	soft
independent, individual, isolated	dependent, social, interconnected, shared
dualistic	whole
MALE	FEMALE

The task of this chapter is to see how it is possible to begin to create text and readings of text that move us and our students beyond our current embeddedness in the metaphors and storylines of binary thought and the male/female dualism in an attempt to move towards multiple genders, multiple subjectivities.

Readings of Text, Readings of Self[2]

Text can hold the possibilities of being coercive and of being liberating. It can hold both of these at the same time. In what follows I will discuss both of these qualities, tying the discussion in particular to liberation from the male/female dualism and movement towards multiple subjectivities. The emphasis will be on liberating *readings* of text as well as on text itself. My argument will be that while movement beyond the male/female dualism does rest to a large extent on the creation of new texts, authors cannot guarantee meanings. They can only create texts that open up possible systems of thought. To do this they need to discover the detailed ways in which their writing-as-usual recreates those aspects of the male/female dualism that they are attempting to move their readers beyond. In so many feminist stories, either through elements of the text itself, the illustrations or the directed questions that accompany them in school texts, the dominant dualistic discourse on what it means to be male or female is what is being mobilized (Davies, in press b). More important than the text itself, then, are the skills that the reader must have access to in order to engage both in critical readings of texts that create and sustain the male/female dualism, and in readings of liberating texts which make those liberating meanings accessible. Critical reading, as I am using it here, would give students access to elements of poststructuralist theory itself, enabling them to see the coercive power of texts to shape desire, to constitute 'real selves' that are positioned in 'real worlds'. I believe students must have access to the skills that enable them to critique those worlds, to read against the grain of existing texts (Davies, in press a, Gilbert and Taylor, 1991) if they are to find multiple possible readings and learn how to write and speak new worlds into existence.

Written text has become a dominant form through which children come to know — both themselves and the physical and social world in which they find themselves. Poststructuralist theory has particularly emphasized the coercive nature of text. However, the emergence of poststructuralist theory has been powerfully liberating precisely *because* it has made that coercion visible. The stranglehold of humanist and enlightenment discourses on the nature of personhood necessarily loosen their grip once they are seen as discursive constructions rather than the transparent forms of words they claimed to be, forms of words which made possible, we were persuaded to believe, descriptions of 'real' selves. The *innocence* of language as a transparent medium for describing the real world is undone through poststructuralist theory, revealing a rich mosaic of meaning and structure through which we speak ourselves and are spoken into existence (Davies, in press c).

But language in schools is still understood and taught as something innocent. The 'creative writing' and other forms of expressive writing through which the last two generations of children have been invited to 'freely' express their 'real' selves provides a perfect example of that understanding. Ironically, creative writing may well be more coercive than the earlier more formal writing in which students were encouraged to engage. By requiring a textual linking between one's postulated 'inner essence' and the forms of discourse to which one has access, there is a forced (and Althusser would argue, mistaken) apprehension or 'revelation' of 'self' (Althusser, 1971; Davies, in press a; Gilbert, 1989).

To illustrate this, I draw on an incident which occurred in the mid-1970s when this change in language teaching was well underway. My son, Paul, then aged 10, was repeatedly told by his teachers that he must not simply give them back what they had taught him, no matter how perfectly he did so. He must create something new, of his own. He was deeply puzzled. One day he was writing about the Netselik Eskimos and their practice of leaving girl babies out in the cold to die. He commented (in brackets) that he was not, in describing this practice, condoning it, it was simpiy what they did. His teachers were ecstatic. Something of his own at last! He exclaimed to me in amazement 'Was that all they wanted! I thought I had to invent new words that no one had thought of before, and I didn't know how I could do it.' Instead, he learned that a comment that mobilized the feminist discourse he had learned from me, would be constituted by teachers as something he himself had created. To the extent that he had taken feminist discourse up *as his own*, the teachers' ecstasy may not have been misplaced. But this was not a question they addressed. Informed by humanist models of the person, any statement from students that was not a repetition of what the teachers had taught them, came unproblematically from the 'real' person that they were assisting to unfold.

It is interesting, in light of this, to observe the resistance that many modern youth have for words. It is increasingly the catchcry of young people in their teens and their twenties that language is somehow bad, deceptive and less satisfactory than other forms of expression (cf. for example Adams, 1991). The teachers' pleas for expressions of true selves have perhaps given modern youth a greater insight into the deceptive possibilities inherent in language which in turn have given rise to a discourse of resistance in relation to the very tools of freedom their teachers thought they were giving them.

Along with this understanding of language as transparent, teaching-as-usual is largely informed by humanist and enlightenment models of 'rational man'. The explanatory frameworks that teachers have had access to have led to some baffling experiences for those teachers who have been encouraging non-sexist practices and beliefs in their classrooms. They have no way of explaining, for example, why it is that the more hegemonic forms of discourse in which the male/female dualism is created and sustained, are what their students' choose to use in their 'free' writing. As Gilbert points out, the belief in 'free expression' can and does lead to some highly sexist student productions which are then displayed on classroom walls since 'if readers create meanings individually and personally, then all students have equal rights to create their own meanings, be they sexist or in other ways ideologically offensive' (Gilbert, 1989, p. 259).

What teachers could not have understood without the aid of poststructuralist theory is that in any form of writing the authors are obliged to position themselves as a recognizable form of speaker, and that both they as author and the characters who appear in their texts must be recognizably male or female, there being no other form of human existence that they have been given discursive access to. They may have learned through their teacher's references to sexism that sexism is unfair and that girls are of 'equal value' to boys, and they may have come to agree with that set of values, taking them up as their own. That does not mean that they know how to translate that set of values into a narrative, 'creative' form. Nor does it mean that they have the skills to resolve the tensions and contradictions between the various discourses to which they have access (Gilbert and Taylor, 1991).

Further, 'equal value' has generally been equated with sameness in both teacher and student talk (Baker and Davies, 1989; Hare, Mustin and Maracek, 1988). That sameness is, when it comes to writing, reading, or interactive practices, extraordinarily difficult to mobilize, even by experienced writers, since the characters they invent, like themselves, are required to be identifiably male or female. This is so because the conventions through which sex identification rests are dualistic and hierarchical; maleness takes its meaning in hierarchical opposition and femaleness. Male characters who do not achieve this oppositional form are invoked, even in feminist stories, as characters with serious problems, and in non-feminist stories, as another version of the 'other' to masculinity, that which is invoked as not-male, and thus that which no true male character can be.

The unquestionable nature of the dualism rests, in part, on the sex/gender distinction in which sex is understood as natural and gender a manifestation of that 'natural' difference (Connell, 1987; Davies, 1988). Butler points out that when we try to imagine characters who are male, but have feminine characteristics we are tempted to define them as 'unnatural' and therefore improper or immoral:

> We don't regard sex as a simple facticity, but as a natural dictate to which certain forms of cultural identity, action, and feeling are said properly to adhere. The possibility of claiming that a gender is right or wrong given a certain sex, or that desire is right or wrong given a certain sex, presupposes that there is a natural causality linking sex, gender, and desire, and that the latter two ought properly to reflect the former and be its natural expression (Butler, 1989, p. 259).

Children whose creative writing manifests these dualistic versions of masculinity and femininity are necessarily working within known narrative and discursive forms almost all of which are vehicles for constituting the male/female dualism (Cranny-Francis, 1988). Furthermore, if they are trying to invent something which falls outside this pattern, they are not only having to invent new forms, but they are also almost inevitably faced with their own contradictory desires, on the one hand to write in a non-sexist way, and on the other to create characters who are coherently, recognizably and acceptably either male or female. The creation of central protagonists who are of indefinite sex/gender is a rare achievement that few authors have successfully tackled. Hulme's *The Bone People* and Carter's *Nights at the Circus* are two notable exceptions.

The multiple readings that can be made of any one story that attempts to achieve a feminist storyline compound the complexity of the task of creating new narrative forms. In *Frogs and Snails and Feminist Tales* (1989a) I showed how a story like *The Paperbag Princess* (Munsch and Marchenko, 1980) with a female hero who ultimately rejects the romantic myth and dances off alone into the sunset without the prince, *can* be read as a traditional story about a heroic prince who is better off without a princess who didn't know how to be a princess. Such a reading is most readily available to children who do not have access to the possibility of a central female protagonist in lived or imaginary narratives, or who have never had the opportunity to call into question the inevitability of the male as heroic and central to any tale with the female as romantic other to the male hero. It is extraordinarily easy to 'find' this reading *in the text* once it has become thinkable through listening to the children's interpretations. Prince Ronald, for example, who has a tennis racquet slung over his shoulder on the first page, is wearing a gold medal.

This can make him into a 'tennis hero', who then on the second page, when snatched off into the air by the dragon by the seat of his pants, manages to keep himself in the air by holding onto his tennis racquet. As one 5-year-old boy said: 'I'm glad he held onto his tennis racquet so hard. When you've done that, well, you just have to hold onto your racquet tight and the dragon holds you up'.

This reading retains Ronald's protagonist status in the story, making it perfectly sensible for him to reject Elizabeth's heroic attempts to save him. But it is also a reading invited by the semiotics of the illustrations, in which Princess Elizabeth is dressed in pale pink and Prince Ronald and the powerful male dragon share the same red and green colouring (Davies, 1990b).

But there is yet a further reading of this story that I learned to see when talking about this work at Deakin University with people working in the area of gender and sport. In this reading Prince Ronald is gay. As such the story is an anti-homosexual, heterosexist story which shows Elizabeth quite rightly rejecting Ronald for not being sufficiently or properly male. Many of the male children who heard this story were not willing to position themselves as Ronald, seeing him as silly or stupid, and preferring the powerful dragon. Ronald's posture and body build are not particularly masculine, nor is tennis a sport commonly associated with hegemonic masculinity. When the dragon snatches Ronald by the seat of his pants, he is, as one of the children observed, 'a hanging upside-down

Ronald, a chew-his-bum-off Prince' with his bottom pointing up towards the powerful male dragon. The dragon takes Ronald off to his 'cave' (a well known gay metaphor) and while no explicit mention of the fact is made, Prince Ronald obviously likes the cave as he is not at all eager to leave it when Elizabeth arrives to save him. When Elizabeth rejects him, it is because he is a 'bum'.[3] In other words, in this reading, the story is one in which heterosexism is the sub-text and heterosexuality is established as the only proper thing that a young woman should desire, moreover, with a male who is unequivocally masculine, and who is opposite and dominant in relation to her femininity.

The Authority of School Texts

What children encounter in schools is a 'regulated and polymorphous incitement to discourse' (Foucault, 1978, p. 34). In classrooms formal ownership of know-ledge is assumed by teachers — they have the authoritative codes for interpreting meaning. Children do not have the freedom to innovate with or to reject adult interpretations. What they have formerly learned in the process of learning to engage in discursive practices is now subjected to authoritative teaching. The categories to which they have been assigned are now potentially subsumed under educational categories of success and failure. Getting it right is not just a matter of being able to converse competently, but a matter of becoming competent in the terms that the teacher designates as competent. In the following lesson on sex roles, for example, where the teacher was, ironically, setting out to dispel outmoded versions of sex roles in his students' thinking, the following conver-sation took place. Here we see a student apparently accepting the teacher's (mis)interpretation of what she says, presumably because he has the power in this setting to constitute any challenge to his definitions as signals of the student's incompetence:

1	Teacher:	. . . What are the differences?
2	Beck:	Well a woman is capable of um having children and so she is expected to stay home and look after the kids?
3	Teacher:	What's that called. There's a name given to that expec-tation of a woman to be a mother. Adam?
4	Adam:	Stereotype?
5	Teacher:	Right it is. It is a stereotype — I think. What is the instinct ( ) the name given to ( )
6	Student:	Maternal?
7	Teacher:	Right. Is that the sort of thing you mean Beck?
8	Beck:	Yeah
9	Teacher:	Maternal instinct. [Writes on board five seconds] What is that again Beck please? What does that mean?
10	Beck:	Um the woman is expected to stay home and look after the kids because she had them?
11	Teacher:	Had them. She is probably better able to do that. Has

anybody heard of paternal instinct? We usually talk about
that don't we the maternal instinct . . .

What is happening here is that the students, in response to the teacher's question,
are raising a social difference to do with beliefs (expectations, 2, stereotypes, 4)
and the teacher is legitimating those beliefs in terms of what he understands about
biology (instinct, 5, 6). He then further embeds the biological base in a moral
base (she should mind the children because she is better able to do it, 11). The
justification for the biological argument is linguistic. We do not hear anyone talk
about paternal instinct, he says, we only talk about maternal instinct (11). This
linguistic fact is produced and heard as evidence of a biological fact. It becomes a
biological fact moreover, with moral implications, moral implications which lock
women into the existing social order. The teacher positions Beck as one who is
making the same claim that he is (7). He uses his authority to ask questions and to
determine meanings and thus to set his interpretation up not as one that lies in
opposition to hers, but as one that stems directly from hers. Beck is positioned as
one who sees that direct and inevitable link between biology and discriminatory
practice.[4] School discourse is thus presented to students as authoritative, as telling
the truth about the real world.

The authority of the text is created in a number of ways, not least of which is
through the authors absenting themselves from the text. Thus the words are not
spoken or written as if by any one person who may be fallible, who bases their
claims on a set of questionable assumptions, who has contestable opinions or who
writes from a gendered perspective. Rather it is the voice of truth, which students
can learn from, can emulate, and can eventually take up as their own (Baker and
Freebody, 1989; de Castell, Luke and Luke, 1989).

Cooper (this volume) describes this process as coercive, the students being
positioned as if they were the author, as if the world that they and the author are
articulating is the natural, unproblematically observable world. She points out
that the power of texts lies in their ability to command compliance in readers, to
coerce readers to accept the ideological as 'natural' and to assume the reading
position of the author.

But readers are not always positioned as author. Sometimes they are positioned as 'you', one who is addressed by the author. Often they imaginatively take
up the position of one or more characters in the text (Davies, 1989a; Christian-
Smith, this volume). In a study of textbooks used in primary schools throughout
the British Commonwealth (Davies, in press b) I found a great deal of authoritative text, using all of these forms and visibly constituting a natural, observable
world, in which the male/female dualism is so taken for granted that it is not
even mentioned. It is simply real and there. In an English text in use in Ghana,
for example, the following passage appeared in an exercise called 'Travelling
by land':

Have you ever travelled from your town or village to another place?
Where did you go?

We can travel in different ways. If the place is not far, we may walk.
Sometimes too we may travel by horseback or by bicycle. If the place is
far, we may go by motorcycle, by lorry, by bus or by train.

If you walk you do not pay any fare. You do not go to any station. You can start at any time and walk quickly or slowly. But walking is not easy. You may be tired if the place is far. If you are alone, robbers may trouble you. Robbers are very bad. They take people's things away from them. Sometimes robbers kill people. Travelling on a horse is faster than walking. The horse can carry your things and take you to many places (p. 71).

In the first sentence the author addresses the child/student from the position of adult — he is the one who poses the questions that students must answer. He thus establishes his adult authority by invoking the adult/child dualism. At the same time he draws attention to the importance of experience as a basis for knowledge. Experience is at the same time constituted as something the students can offer of their own, through which they can insert themselves into the text, *and* a reminder that it is adults who have had more experience and who therefore have access to more authoritative knowledge.

The author then uses 'we' in the second paragraph to invite the reader to position him or herself as one with the author and thus as one who can share the author's knowing. That authorial voice seems, at first glance, simply to be describing a world which everyone knows and takes for granted (cf. Baker and Freebody, 1989). The overt purpose of the text is to teach students English. In doing so it also achieves, among other things, the representation of the male/female dualism as part of the natural, orderly everyday world. To the extent that the readers take up the reading position of author they will probably accept this as the way the world is and ought to be since they are practicing the systems of thought through which the passage is constructed as if they were their own (Bakhtin, 1981).

The illustration, like the written text, appears to depict a normal everyday scene in Ghana. Women and children are shown as the only ones who are walking, walking being a dominant feature of the picture. The illustration, *in combination* with the text, thus establishes as normal and natural (and therefore not even

155

needing to be mentioned, or to have attention drawn to them) three central features of the male/female dualism:

1 Women, like small children, are constituted as unsafe and vulnerable if they are alone in public places. Women's apparently inevitable status as victims is achieved without any direct reference to it. 'If you walk . . . [as the women and children are depicted as doing, and] If you are alone, robbers may trouble you. Robbers . . . take people's things away from them. Sometimes robbers kill people.'

2 In contrast, male persons are depicted as having access to money and to vehicles and are thus positioned as the ones who are able to travel alone and to many distant places: 'Sometimes too we may travel by horseback or by bicycle. If the place is far, we may go by motorcycle, by lorry, by bus or by train. . . . Travelling on a horse is faster than walking. The horse can carry your things and take you to many places.' Travel and independence are thus constituted as normal everyday features of being male. Presuming the robbers are males, males are also positioned as potential assaulters of solitary women.

3 The third, more subtle, feature of the text consolidates the male/female dualism. The authorial 'we' which supposedly includes all readers, whether male or female, rapidly becomes a 'we' that only includes males. In the third sentence of the second paragraph, 'we' becomes the author and other males, since, as the illustration shows, only males travel on horseback, ride motorcycles, and travel to far places. In this way, while the male reader is being coerced into taking up the authorial voice and constituting himself and the world around him through the discourses with which the author provides him, the female reader is positioned briefly as one with the author and then as other to the author, either as an outsider to the text or one of the characters in the text, as women or children who walk who do not need money, who are tired and who are vulnerable when they are alone.

Going back, then, to the first sentence, to the question that addresses the students and that frames the whole lesson, it is possible, in light of the later evidence that it is males who travel long distances, that the 'you', whom female students might have taken to include themselves, is probably only intended to refer to male students and to male students' experiences of travel. If this is so, many female readers will have positioned themselves as being marginal in relation to the text, as other to the conversation between the reader and the author, right from the outset.

A danger inherent in the analysis I have just undertaken is to assume that what I am providing is an authoritative reading and to lose sight of the multiple readings that can be made of any text. Nor can we assume that any author consciously attends to the discursive practices through which he or she creates a male audience and a male authorial voice. The chances are that the author would be just as amazed as any other reader by the analysis of the way the language and illustration he used, whether he intended it or not, could be read as constituting the patriarchal gender order as normal and natural. This is not to gainsay the *effect* of what he has done, but to see authors as produced in and through the 'regulated and polymorphous' discourses they have access to, just as we are. It would be interesting to know, for example, whether the illustrator of *The Paperbag Princess*, Marchenko, was aware that in colouring Prince Ronald in the same red and green as the dragon, he was lending Prince Ronald some of the dragon's heroic power, or whether the author was aware of choosing metaphors such as the cave and expressions such as 'bum' to make a potentially heterosexist story.

The most significant point being made here is that the text and the available ways of reading text can be coercive in ways that authors and readers (including teachers) are not aware of. To carry this point further and tie it in with the introductory discussion, if the language used in classroom text and talk is treated as transparent, it is more likely to become the reader's language through which they fashion the world and themselves. If the metaphors, images and story-lines through which characters are created are not themselves understood as constitutive, the reader cannot turn a critical gaze on that constitutive process. As readers, they must either comply, taking up as their own the discourses through which they take themselves to be describing real selves or real worlds, or they can engage in some form of resistance. If they comply, they collaborate in the process through which they are interpellated into the existing social structures, learning to hail themselves as they are hailed. If they resist, they open up a different set of possibilities. But the resistances that are currently available to students in school are largely self-defeating (Davies and Munro, 1987; Christian-Smith, this volume).

Once a discourse is taken up as one's own, and if it is understood as transparent, then any text that mobilizes that discourse is taken to describe a real and *recognizable* world. One understands oneself, in reading, to be *re-cognizing* that which the author of the text cognized. A reading that is thus achieved is experienced as a true, even authoritative reading of the text. But readings differ according to where one is positioned in relation to them — as author, as male or female character, as outsider. Further, texts can be read in terms of different discourses from those the author had in mind. Not only are authors' intentions no guarantee of meaning, but authors' conscious intentions are not necessarily the only shapers of their text. They, like us, are coerced by discursive structures, by powerful others, such as publishers, critics, employers, and even readers, as well as their own patterns of desire. An author creates out of what are known, recognizable forms of text. Readers engage in a remarkably similar process, creating a text in which they recognize meanings, that recognition stemming from their access to and positioning within the possible discourses through which the text can be interpreted.

Text as Liberating/Liberating Readings of Text

Strategies for such change need to be organized at each tier of feminism: liberal, radical and poststructuralist (Kristeva, 1981; Moi, 1985; Davies, 1988, 1989b). Even though these are fundamentally contradictory with one another, they are all still necessary in terms of the complex ways in which the male/female dualism is currently held in place. As long as anyone is excluded from any activity on the basis of the genitals they happen to have, liberal feminism with its concepts of access, justice and equity is necessary. As long as femaleness and femininity are seen as the negative half of the male/female dualism, radical feminism with its celebration of femaleness and femininity is necessary. Both of these require a naming of femaleness and its difference from maleness. Strategies for deconstructing the dualism and moving beyond it towards multiple genders, not connected to the sets of genitals individuals happen to have, can thus never be completely entered into while social structure, dominant discourses and individual patterns of desire serve to establish and maintain the male/female dualism. Resistance to male hegemony requires a simultaneous naming of difference in order to draw attention to the way that difference is constituted, and the deconstruction of that difference in order to move beyond it, not towards sameness, but towards multiplicity. That multiplicity is both of genders and of fluid possibilities available to any one person.

Taylor (this volume) elaborates a number of strategies for working towards gender equity in the classroom that range across each of these feminist frameworks. These include:

At the liberal feminist tier, teaching students about access issues, for example giving them demographic information about women in the work force, about child care and the possible conflicts they will experience between child raising and paid work; recognition of the conflict students will inevitably experience between wanting access to knowledge, and feminist knowledge in particular, and their bodily inscription as feminine, sexually desirable beings.

At the radical feminist tier, taking students and their commitments to femininity seriously, at the same time 'bring[ing] students an understanding, from their own experiences, of the way we are all caught up in ideological processes in our everyday lives' (p. 135); giving students an understanding of the way that femininity is constructed at a personal level, through cultural texts along with all the other networks of gendered social practices in their everyday lives; and developing a collective sense of themselves as women.

At the poststructuralist tier, reconstructing femininity through the deconstruction of dominant ideologies, and through developing an understanding of how these operate at the 'unconscious level, through the structuring of desires, as well as at a conscious or rational level' (p. 136); learning to read against the grain; gaining access to feminist writing which rethinks and thus reconstructs the world; gaining an understanding of social structures, such as publishing companies, in terms of the ways in which they create the cultural products so central to the constitution of individual lives.

All of these strategies, but particularly those at the third tier, presume a different set of relations between the student, the teacher, language, and knowledge.

The kinds of attitudes towards and understandings of language and of teaching discussed earlier in the chapter would not allow the kinds of processes being envisaged here. Any pedagogical model in which the teacher has unquestionable authority and knowledges that are used to manipulate students and to tell them what they should know, runs counter to these strategies. Students themselves need access to poststructuralist theory so they can see for themselves the way they are constituted within authority and gender relations. They need access to conceptual strategies for undoing the humanist myth about desire being a valid manifestation of the individual and therefore what the individual both wants and deserves. They need to be able to crack the code of dominant gender ideologies for themselves, to understand how they are constituted through discourse, how they might invent, invert, rethink, rewrite a new world. To do this they need to be able to understand:

— multiple textual interpretations and how these are arrived at;
— how one discourse can be used to modify or counteract the force of another;
— how desire is constructed through storyline, image and metaphor; and
— how to begin to invent new connections, new possible patterns of desire.

In what follows there are two conversations from a research project conducted with primary school children in which we gave them access to each of these. The conversations took place between Chas Banks, who has worked with me on the primary school project, and six sixth grade children. The pseudonyms the three boys chose for themselves were Philo, Zak and James, and the three girls Jennifer, Charlotte and Stacey. They are discussing dominant discourses, and discourses of resistance in relation to storyline, first in relation to a traditional fairy story, *Snow White and the Seven Dwarves*, the second in relation to a feminist fairy tale, *Princess Smartypants*. The first conversation begins following a reading of *Snow White and the Seven Dwarves*. In order to follow this discussion it is helpful to point out that James is positioned by the rest of the group as a marginal member to the discussion. He is a rebel in their class, rarely collaborating with the teacher in her agenda. In much of this excerpt he takes up the position offered him as outsider, interrupting, talking over and disrupting what the others say. For ease of analysis I have divided the excerpt into units:[5]

Conversation 1: A Discussion of Snow White and the Seven Dwarves

Unit 1 (1–10): Rejection of the story on the grounds that it is old, boring and sexist.

1	Philo:	It's dumb.
2	Chas:	Why is it dumb?
3	Jennifer:	Cause it's ah/ . . .
4	Charlotte:	It's just/
5	Philo:	Old
6	Jennifer:	Very sexist
7	Zak:	When you hear it that many times it's dumb.
8	Jennifer:	It's stupid.
9	Charlotte:	It's just
10	Philo:	I reckon it's sexist because/

Unit 2 (11–25): Confrontation between the girls and the boys. The girls attempt to position the boys as marginal (12, 15). James contributes the idea of women always getting into trouble (11, 13) and Philo that the dwarves are unnecessarily all male, (14, 21) wondering whether this is because they are miners (25).

11	James:	Yeah it's sexist it's always the woman that gets into trouble/
12	Jennifer:	You shut up James, keep your mouth shut for once.
13	James:	Isn't it Chas, it's always the woman that gets into trouble.
14	Philo:	Yeah and how come there's seven dwarves, they're all men and um/
15	Jennifer:	Oh shut up Philo.
16	Chas:	⌈No just let him say this.
17	Philo:	⌊Make me
18	Chas:	No go on Philo, how come there's/
19	Philo:	Um, because there's seven dwarves/
20	James:	and there's no females/
21	Philo:	and they're all men and why can't there be a woman dwarf?
22	Chas:	Yeah that's one good point.
23	Charlotte:	And there's always
24	James:	Yeah it's/
25	Philo:	Is it because they all mine?

Unit 3 (26–33): James argues that even if the dwarves were miners, the women dwarves could do something else (28). Charlotte picks up James' idea though not acknowledging it as his and introduces the word victim (27). James presents an alternative possible storyline of the woman as heroic (30). This is ignored. Charlotte makes a claim that the story is written that way because kids like stories in which biological sex is related to gender through men being positioned as rescuers of women (29, 33).

26	James:	Yeah but the woman/
27	Charlotte:	The lady is the victim
28	James:	Yeah but the woman dwarf could come out and they could forage/
29	Charlotte:	Kids like to hear that sort of thing they like/
30	James:	And also why couldn't it be the bloke that's in trouble and the woman comes and saves him?
31	Chas:	Well I don't know. Charlotte, what were you saying, the woman's the victim? . . . Yeah, go on, and why were you saying little kids like to hear that sort of thing?
32	Charlotte:	I don't know/. . .
33	Charlotte:	they just like that sort of set up I don't know why they just like the man being strong 'cause um people know that men after a certain age are naturally stronger so they have to, they have a sense of playing a role of the stronger person who's obviously put in the position to rescue somebody.

Unit 4 (34–49): Discussion of Snow White's character. James disrupts by contradicting and disagreeing with the other's descriptions of Snow White as perfect, thus positioning himself as a nuisance and an outsider to the talk (36, 42, 44, 48)

34	Chas:	Right, well what sort of a person's Snow White?
35	Stacey:	She's a beautiful, fair/
36	James:	(*very softly*) Ugly
37	Philo:	A person like/
38	Stacey:	And it has/
39	Philo:	Thoughtful, kind
40	Stacey:	And it follows the line that the woman's naturally
41	Philo:	Naturally perfect.
42	James:	A prefect
43	Stacey:	In all fairy tales/
44	James:	A tart/
45	Stacey:	you have all the perfect people.
46	Jennifer:	Qualities of life huh?
47	Chas:	Yeah
48	James:	She's a tart.
49	Charlotte:	She's got all the/ Oh James!

Unit 5 (50–66): James again opens the possibility of a different kind of storyline in which the female character is ugly (50). Again the girls constitute this as subversive of the work they are doing rather than a contribution to the topic, asking him why he is so non-cooperative (51, 53, 55). Philo points out that no one would want to save an ugly heroine since ugly people are for teasing and get into fights while everyone wants to help pretty people (56, 59). Philo's argument rests on a belief that the way things are is the way they ought to be in stories. James raises the possibility of an ugly old hag who might do the saving thus involving the idea of a powerful, kind but ugly witch (61). Again his idea is rejected since he is not positioned as one who can or would make a legitimate contribution (51, 53, 55, 62, 63, 65).

50	James:	How can they know that she couldn't, why don't they write about ugly?
51	Charlotte:	Why do you always be critical of everything?
52	Chas:	Well/
53	Stacey:	Why do you always not do/
54	James:	⌈Because people
55	Stacey:	⌊what everybody says?
56	Philo:	Because people are ugly um you know, they're nor/ they're normally, cause people tease them about being ugly they're normally/
57	James:	Ugly!!
58	Chas:	No let him finish, he's making a really good point here.
59	Philo:	They're normally um they normally tease them back but if people are pretty no one teases them. Everyone helps them!

60	Chas:	Yeah that's right.
61	James:	For all we know there might be a really ugly old hag that might help them
62	Charlotte:	Oh you are so critical of everything you love criticizing people and what they are saying.
63	Jennifer:	Shut up James!!
64	James:	(*softly*) I'm not citicizing anyone/
65	Jennifer:	Oh no, not by half/
66	James:	I am just asking why didn't they write if for an ugly ole person

Unit 6 (67–78): Chas explains that authors use attractive qualities in characters so that the readers are able to position themselves as those characters. This is used as the basis for an attack on James by Jennifer and Philo who point out that James could position himself as an ugly character (71, 74, 75). James decides to withdraw (78). Charlotte continues to defend the argument that the story can only work with the traditional ingredients of the attractive heroine (70, 72, 76).

67	Chas:	Well I'll tell you why they didn't write it for an ugly old person, because if it was an ugly old person/
68	James:	No one would care/
69	Chas:	we wouldn't identify, we wouldn't want to identify and position ourselves as an ugly old person, we want to position ourselves/
70	Charlotte:	You couldn't/
71	Jennifer:	James would/
72	Charlotte:	make the story work as well/
73	James:	Yeah but/
74	Philo:	An ugly old person is probably prettier than James is/
75	Philo:	( )/
76	Charlotte:	because like the man wouldn't um want to rescue her if she's ugly.
77	Jennifer:	Anyone would be/
78	James	I'll shut up for a while anyway/

Unit 7 (79–104): Charlotte then finds a flaw in her argument, raising the question of what sort of man would fall in love with a woman just because she is beautiful. They discuss the prince and Jennifer concludes he is a typical man, and Zak starts to enter the conversation taking offence at this claim (97).

79	Charlotte:	But that's another thing of the man's personality, that we might not know what he's really like although he rescued her, she was really good looking but imagine if it was someone who was really ugly 'cause it said, at first he fell in love with her so that might be the only reason why he rescued her.
80	Chas:	Well what sort of a person was the prince?
81	Jennifer:	A mean um (*Charlotte laughs*)
82	Stacey:	Handsome

83	James:	A fe/ a male
84	Charlotte:	Handsome
85	Chas:	Yes
86	Philo:	Brave
87	Chas:	Brave
88	Philo:	⌈Sensible
89	Charlotte:	⌊Rich/
90	Philo:	not like the dwarves. He just knocked/
91	Charlotte:	⌈Rich
92	Philo:	⌊the apple out of her throat.
93	Chas:	Sensible, *rich*, he was rich/
94	James	He was rich/
95	Chas:	yeah. What else?
96	Jennifer:	He was a typical man. He married her because she was beautiful.
97	Zak:	Ohhhh
98	Chas:	And not because of any other quality that she might have had.
99	Charlotte:	It doesn't say that in/
100	James:	And he was rich/
101	Charlotte:	It doesn't say that in the story it just says he straight away fell in love with her which indicates probably because we all know that/
102	James	She's good lookin'/
103	Jennifer:	she was beautiful that was only because she was ( )
104	Chas:	Right, so it was her physical appearance that was the most important thing.

Unit 8 (105–122): The political implication of the romantic storyline are introduced by Philo (105). Stacey attempts a storyline variation from wicked witch to wicked man who only marries for wealth (113). Chas reminds them about a previous discussion on the traditional storyline.

105	Philo:	This is what Mum sometimes says, she says 'first you sink into his arms then you have your arms in the sink'.
106	Chas:	That's true, I used to have that above my sink for years. It's the truth! OK, well from this what sort of message do we get about, what's considered from the perspective of this story, what's a girl's most valuable asset then?
107	Stacey:	Beauty.
108	Chas:	Beauty. That's right, that's the message we get/
109	James:	Jewellery/
110	Chas:	That's right/
111	Philo:	And money.
112	James:	Or clothing or jewels
113	Stacey:	Yes, because um also that um the witch, the wicked witch could have been a man and he could have, well she/

114	James:	The wicked man!/
115	Stacey:	Well she only married the man 'cause he was rich.
116	Chas:	Right.
117	Stacey:	Just for power.
118	Chas:	And from the story line remember how we talked about story line here we've got the young girl, she's the victim of her treacherous parents/
119	Charlotte:	yeah/
120	Chas:	and what happens then she's saved by a male saviour, the woodcutter saves her or the servant or however we're gonna call it. Then she goes into domesticity. Right, and then there's the treacherous parent again and then there's the male saviour again and that's like the story line isn't it?
121	Stacey:	Like we did the other day
122	Chas:	OK so what we understand from that is that girls, that a beautiful girl, she's oppressed at first but ultimately in the end she's saved by the handsome heroic prince. Isn't that what/

Unit 9 (123–145): Jennifer raises the silences in the story, such as how Snow White actually felt about what happens, suggesting she might have wanted to escape from the dwarves (123, 125). James and Zak point out she was happy there and she might have her own motives, such as greed, for marrying the prince (126, 128). The discussion moves on to the way traditional texts make associations between poverty, badness and ugliness and between wealth, goodness and beauty. Charlotte then recounts something she saw on television about the persecution of witches.

123	Jennifer:	Though the story doesn't show how much, so much how the woman actually feels about all this.
124	Chas:	No that's right/
125	Jennifer:	Like she might be getting really lonely just living with the seven dwarves, she might that might not have worked out/
126	James:	She might be greedy/
127	Jennifer:	she might have other feelings towards things that happened.
128	Zak:	They did, they said she was happy living there.
129	Charlotte:	Yeah but still!
130	Chas:	So from this story what's beauty usually associated with, is it/
131	Zak:	Princesses
132	Stacey:	Women
133	Philo:	Power, rich, money.
134	Chas:	Right, yep and what's ugliness generally associated with?
135	Philo:	Being poor,
136	Charlotte:	Being cruel

137	Stacey:	Witch, cruel.
138	Chas:	Being a witch, yeah that's right.
139	Charlotte:	I watched a thing about these witches and they had a black hat and sort of wore black clothes because she was a widow and they had to find out if she was a witch and they did things like pinching her on a certain place on her neck/
140	James	A vampire/
141	Charlotte:	and the final thing that they had to do was put them in the water and if she sank then she was/
142	James	⌈A witch
143	Charlotte:	⌊not a witch but then she died and if she was a witch she probably would have lived.
144	Chas:	Right, but she died anyway.
145	Charlotte:	And she, so she wasn't a witch seeing she died/

There are a number of interesting things happening in this conversation. From a liberal feminist point of view the girls are doing well, holding their own against the boys and making space for themselves. From a radical feminist point of view, the girls display and use valued female characteristics, such as cooperating with Chas, to bring the joint project of the discussion to fruition. They also engage in a strategy common to radical feminist politics, which is to reject male perspectives and strategies as unworthy of attention. From a poststructuralist point of view, it is interesting to find that two of the boys are more ready to search for ways of disrupting the romantic storyline, perhaps because male patterns of desire are not so intimately constituted either through the romantic storyline or through strategies of non-resistance. James, in particular, positions himself and is positioned as one who disrupts the *status quo*. The girls experience a tension between their inscription in the romantic storyline, (wanting to be virtu- ous and wanting beauty to be something which attracts heroic men), and the disruption to the romantic storyline that is being opened up through their joint deconstruction of it. The understandings that start to emerge in this conversation are of the politically unacceptable consequences of the traditional romantic story- line. Their attempts to find alternatives are hampered by their immersion in binary forms of thought, what Cixous calls 'death dealing binary thought' (1986). People are either ugly or beautiful, saviours or the saved, male or female. This entrap- ment in binary thought precludes the possibility of characters whose subject- ivities are 'precarious, contradictory and in process' (Weedon, 1987, p. 32). It also leads to strong resistance to breaking down the connective, metaphorical tissue of metaphors that holds the male/female dualism in place. Only James, with his history of being disruptive, seems to be able to readily link, for example, female goodness with ugliness, femaleness with heroism, and so on. The others are much more hesitant about such links, either rejecting them outright or considering them only tentatively.

In the second conversation a quite different pattern emerges. *Princess Smartypants* (Cole, 1986) is a story about a princess who does not want to get married. She likes to live alone with all her monstrous pets. Her parent insist that she marry.

She finally agrees to marry anyone who can carry out the impossible tasks she sets them. None of the princes succeed and so they all leave. Then Prince Swashbuckle turns up and to Smartypants' dismay, he carries out all her tasks. Then she kisses him and he turns into a toad. Swashbuckle flees and Smartypants takes up her life where the story began. In this discussion Philo and Zak become defensive about the way men are positioned. Their resistance takes the form of blatant sexism and a resort to humanist, masculinist discourse in which everyone has a right to their own opinions. The discussion nevertheless ends with approval for the way in which the story disrupts the traditional romantic storyline:

Conversation 2: A Discussion of Princess Smartypants

Unit 1 (1–5): Philo and James reject the story as too predictable a reversal of the traditional storyline.

1	Philo:	That was a hopeless story.
2	Chas:	All right. Why was it hopeless, tell me why you thought it was hopeless.
3	James:	It was exactly the opposite
4	Philo:	I don't know, you just thought, you just knew what was going to happen.
5	James:	That's probably because you had a look at it.

Unit 2 (6–21): A cooperative discussion about the story as a story of resistance then follows. Stacey rejects the idea that it was merely the opposite of the traditional story, arguing that Smartypants was not merely a tomboy, since she would do all the things boys can do but she also retained some of the magic properties associated with femininity in fairytales.

6	Stacey:	That one was a good story because it showed that/
7	James:	She was resisting.
8	Stacey:	She yeah she's resisting the female discourse/
9	James:	yes/
10	Stacey:	She was doing what she pleased and not/
11	Philo:	⌈ Riding motor bikes
12	James:	⌊ Not what her parents wanted her to do/
13	Stacey:	No just/
14	James:	⌈ Get a handsome/
15	Stacey:	⌊ She was just riding motor bikes, roller skating, not doing things that Princesses do/
16	Jennifer:	⌈ I like roller skating
17	Stacey:	⌊ would do
18	James:	I can't.
19	Stacey:	And raise pets and/
20	James:	I don't have any things/
21	Stacey:	and and she still has some of those really magic in fairy tales like a magic ring and a magic kiss and all those things like that but she's but she's not a tomboy but she's resisting the female discourse.

Unit 3 (22–40): An argument unfolds about Smartypants' character in which Zak claims she is a snob (26) and Philo claims Jennifer is a snob, thus linking their antagonism to Smartypants in which this antagonistic position towards the girls (31). Philo and Zak object to Smartypants' strategy (26–38) and James defends her, pointing out she is not snobbish but asking them to enter into the male discourse of heroism (39). Zak refuses this argument on the grounds that only one of them could do it successfully.

22	Chas:	Right, the dominant female discourse. What sort of person do you think she was?
23	Jennifer:	Not a snob.
24	Chas:	She wasn't a snob.
25	Charlotte:	Independent (*very softly*)
26	Zak:	She was a snob.
27	Chas:	She was a snob?
28	James:	Snobs totally different/
29	Chas:	Tell me Zak why you thought she was.
30	Jennifer:	Zak doesn't know what a snob is.
31	Philo:	He should he's looking at one/ (*softly referring to Jennifer*).
32	Zak:	Well she um wanted them to think of her
33	Charlotte:	He keeps looking at Jennifer
34	James:	That's not snobbish
35	Chas:	No can you let him finish and then we'll/
36	Zak:	She wanted him to feed her pets and she wanted them to um to do things that um/
37	Philo:	Were virtually impossible.
38	Zak:	Yeah.
39	James:	That's not snobbish, that's the male discourse. They have they do things that are literally/
40	Zak:	Yeah but none of them accomplished it except one.

Unit 4 (41–49): Philo launches into an outright attack on Smartypants (43) because of what happened to the princes (45), and Charlotte and Stacey point out that he is sexist in his refusal of a story with a female hero (46, 50, 52). Zak defends Philo on the basis that he is entitled to his opinions (53, 55). Charlotte rejoins that she too is entitled to her opinion that he is sexist. At this point the battle line is drawn between the sexes, the boys attacking both Smartypants and the girls and the girls attacking the boys for their sexism. James is not part of this fight.

41	Charlotte:	She was independent.
42	Chas:	Ah ha. What do you think Philo. What sort of person do you think she was? You don't have to like her. I mean you know there's no, I want you to honestly say what you think. What sort of person do you/
43	Philo:	I think she'd be best for a doormat.
44	Chas:	Why do you think that?
45	Philo:	Oh because you know if she set all the Princes on one task and go and do it then it, um like they'd have to

> travel away and all that and that'd be heaps heaps better like most fairy tales but that one was just totally different and *stupid*.

46 Charlotte: That means you're being sexist though 'cause/

47 Jennifer: You just said you like the story

48 Charlotte: Yeah you said that/

49 Philo: No
(interruption)

50 Stacey: What happens is that you think that what happens is the female should be the helpless one and the male should be the ones to prove her wrong but she ended up winning in the end. Not the male. That's why/

51 Zak: Philo just doesn't like the story.

52 Charlotte: Well that means you're being sexist, saying that about the doormat/

53 Zak: We've all got different opinions/

54 Charlotte: um then that means that you think that she should just *have* to do exactly what her mother says and have to follow that um discourse that her parents have set that she has to go out and marry a man and live happily ever after.

55 Zak: Well we've all got different opinions.

56 Charlotte: Yeah I know, and I put that opinion about his opinion, I can still say that.

Unit 5 (50–69): The conversation ends with a discussion about Smartypants' character. They agree that she had a good opinion of herself, that she knew she was the best. They discuss the way in which the traditional storyline has been broken — the woman is not helpless, she is strong and independent — and Jennifer says thoughtfully 'yeah it's about time something happened like that.' At this point James is positioned as an equal participant in the conversation, as a legitimate rebel along with the girls.

57 Chas: Ah ha. What sort of opinion do you think that Smartypants had of herself?

58 James and
Stacey: She thought she was good.

59 Chas: She thought she was pretty good.

60 Philo: She thought she was the best because no one could carry out what she could do.

61 James: No one could carry out her deeds.

62 Jennifer: But she could carry out what she'd set down. So it must mean you know for once that she's not going to be the helpless one

63 Charlotte: It doesn't mean that she was/

64 James: Yeah it is going to be the men that are the helpless one, the women with strength

65 Jennifer: Yeah it's about time something happened like that.

66 Chas: Well what do you think Princess Smartypants desired in life?

67	James:	Just a nice life
68	Philo:	Her independency
69	Jennifer:	For her to be the best.

What the participants achieve in this conversation, or at least what the girls and James achieve, is a coherent way of talking about legitimate resistance to dominant discourses and the positions made available in those dominant discourses to males and females. It is not clear whether Zak and Philo understand this since they do not visibly manage to distance themselves from the wound to their own masculinity that they perceive the story to be inflicting, though Philo does seem to participate positively at the end (60, 68).

What these two conversations show, among other things, is the capacity of primary school students to comprehend the ways in which storylines position them. They also show these students actively involved in analyzing the way dominant discourses and discourses of resistance work both in text and their own talk. Chas does not deny them the strongly felt emotions about their own sex/gender. Instead, she provides them with the conversational space and the conceptual tools with which they can explore the complexity of gender as it is created in text and talk. They are learning in this process to see the constitutive and coercive force of the discourses to which they have access, and to mobilize this knowledge in deconstructing the dualistic gender order. By disrupting the inevitability of the romantic storyline they are opening up the possibility of storylines and characters which move beyond the male/female dualism.

Although they have not moved far beyond mere reversal, Jennifer's statement of reflective desire shows that this is no more intellectual exercise but a speaking of themselves into existence outside the dominant discourses through which they have previously been (and will go on being) constituted. They have not yet found their way to the multiple genders imagined within feminist post-structuralist theory but they have taken some critical first steps. They have learned to see the positions opened up for them in traditional storylines and to see the ways in which these are oppressive. They have begun to move beyond more dualistic reversals between males and females by engaging in a reading of *Princess Smarty-pants* in which her important feature is her ability to encompass aspects of both masculinity and femininity. Finally and perhaps most important, they have begun to desire and express that desire for alternative ways of being positioned. The story that Charlotte wrote in the holidays following these conversations reveals the complex and as yet unresolvable tensions between the celebration and recognition of femaleness and the almost unimaginable possibility of moving beyond it.

Malu Kungka

A long time ago in the Dreamtime there was a young girl called Malu Kungka, 'malu' meaning 'kangaroo' and 'kungka' meaning 'girl'. She was from an Aboriginal tribe called 'Walungi' and she was a very strong and independent girl. Sometimes her father would even take her hunting. She didn't resemble a girl at all or even a child for that matter. She was always wandering off into the scrub looking for an adventure while all the other children would play in the tribal ground where they had set up camp and would play all day with each other.

Many years passed and Malu Kungka was still carrying on her tradition of wandering off and exploring new places and things.

One night Malu Kungka's parents were talking about Malu Kungka, they decided that her father would not take her hunting with him anymore because she was growing up and she must be like the other children and learn how to be a woman, for it was not long before she would be an adolescent and she still hadn't a care in the world except for the animals and trees and all those sorts of things. The next day Malu Kungka's parents told her what they thought, though they regretted it because now she was sad and puzzled.

That day she did not eat as she usually did, she sat down in the red dust and drew pictures of things whilst pondering over what her parents had said.

She was confused, 'What do I have to do to prove I am a woman, I am a woman aren't I?' she thought Now she was more confused than ever, she did not know much of these things for she never thought of them as important, therefore she never thought of them at all.

The next day she set about finding a way of proving that she was a woman. The first thing she did was to watch all the other Kungkas practising what they had learnt off their parents. She observed that they would sit in groups and weave baskets, sing songs and make carriers out of bits of hollowed out trees and big pieces of bark. She tried doing all these things, unfortunately in vain for she could not do any of these things. Still she practiced each of these things every day, for she was determined to get it right.

The initiation would be held at the next full moon and the moon was already three quarters full, she had only one week in which to become a woman. Finally she realized she could not become a woman that way and she would have to find a spiritual way of becoming a woman and the only way of doing that would be to ask for the help of Malu Biamee because the kangaroo was her symbol and 'Malu Biamee' meant 'Kangaroo God'. Now she would have to hold a special ceremony. So the night of the initiation when the moon was high she gathered ten of the wisest and oldest women of the tribe and pleaded with them to help, finally they agreed.

They collected the things essential for a ceremony of this type and set off following Malu Kungka to a special place that she had often seen the kangaroos meet at. The moon was shining as bright as day when they began to paint, they used special ground rocks and the melted fat of a kangaroo, they painted various kangaroo symbols all over their bodies. Then they put a hollowed out kangaroo's body on the back of Malu Kungka and then they started dancing a special dance with songs to go with it. When that was over they all placed different offerings in the centre of the circle.

The next day Malu Kungka's parents did not find their daughter in her usual place for Malu Biamee had taken pity on her and given her to her one love . . . Nature, where she would be happy for the rest of her life. Malu Biamee had turned her into her true self . . . a Malu!!!

Acknowledgement

The interview data reported in this study was collected by Chas Banks as part of an Australian Research Council funded project. I am indebted to both the Australian Research Council for the funding and to Chas for her work on the project.

Notes

1 The central ideal for poststructuralist theory that comes from psychoanalytic theory is of the person as more than their conscious/rational self. Desire stems not just from the rational self but from the whole complexity of one's being in the world. My departure from psychoanalytic theory is to broaden desire beyond sexual desire and to resist the patriarchal limitations of the Oedipal storyline.

2 The data that I draw on this paper include conversations with Australian children about feminist stories, video-taped episodes in a number of classrooms as well as analyses of some texts currently in use in primary schools throughout the world. The details of the various projects for which this data was collected are reported elsewhere, as are many of the findings (see for example Davies, 1983, 1989a, 1990b, in press b; Davies and Banks, in press). In the work with preschool children I sought the understandings they brought to readings of stories, and watched and talked to them about their play to gain some insight into the storylines that they lived in their everyday lives. In the primary school data, children's interpretations of feminist stories were sought, but as well they were given poststructuralist conceptual tools with which to understand the coercive nature of discourse and with which they could resist dominant discourses where they had recognized these as oppressive.

3 In the Australian version 'bum' has been changed to 'toad'. The children who hear this story are highly amused by Elizabeth's rejection of Ronald as a bum and I have retained this version of it in my research. Having discovered how it can become part of an anti-homosexual story, however, I am not so sure about my original decision to retain it.

4 See also Baker and Davies, 1989 and Davies, in press d.

5 I have used the convention of a slash/at the end of a line to show that the next person's talk interrupts what the former speaker has said and a square bracket to indicate overlapping speech. Empty brackets (   ) indicate unclear utterance.

References

Althusser, L. (1971) *Lenin and Philosophy and Other Essays*, London, New Left Books.

An English course for Ghanian Schools 4, AFRAM,

Adams, P. (1991) 'The end of the world is nigh', *The Weekend Australian. Review*, 27–28, July, p. 2.

Baker, C. and Davies, B. (1989) 'A lesson on sex roles', *Gender and Education*, 1(1) pp. 59–76.

Baker, C. and Freebody, P. (1989) *Children's First School Books*, Oxford, Basil Blackwell.

BAKHTIN, M. (1981) 'Discourse in the novel', in M. HOLQUIST (Ed.) *The Dialogical Imagination*, Austin, University of Texas Press, pp. 259–422.

BUTLER, J. (1989) 'Gendering the body: Beauvoir's philosophical contribution', in A. GARRY, and M. PEARSAIL (Eds) *Women Knowledge and Reality*, Boston, Unwin Hyman: pp. 253–62.

CARTER, A. (1984) *Nights at the Circus*, London, Picador.

CIXOUS, H. (1986) 'Sorties: Out and out: Attacks/ ways Out/ forays', in H. CIXOUS and C. CLEMENT (Eds) *The Newly Born Woman*, Manchester, Manchester University Press, pp. 63–132.

COLE, B. (1986) *Princess Smarty Pants*, London, Hamish Hamilton.

CONNELL, R.W. (1987) *Gender and Power*, Sydney, Allen and Unwin.

CRANNY-FRANCIS, A. (1988) 'Out among the stars in a red shift: Women and science fiction', *Australian Feminist Studies*, 6, pp. 71–86.

DAVIES, B. (1983) 'The role pupils play in the social construction of classroom order', *British Journal of Sociology of Education*, 4, pp. 55–69.

DAVIES, B. (1988) *Gender, Equity and Early Childhood*, Canberra, Curriculum Development Centre, Schools Commission.

DAVIES, B. (1989a) *Frogs and Snails and Feminist Tales. Preschool Children and Gender*, Sydney, Allen and Unwin.

DAVIES, B. (1989b) 'Education for sexism: A theoretical analysis of the sex/gender bias in education', *Educational Philosophy and Theory*, 21(1) pp. 1–19.

DAVIES, B. (1990a) 'The problem of desire', *Social Problems*, 37(4) pp. 801–16.

DAVIES, B. (1990b) 'Lived and imaginary narratives and their place in taking oneself up as a gendered being', *Australian Psychologist*, 25(3) pp. 318–32.

DAVIES, B. (in press a) 'Women's subjectivity and feminist stories', C. ELLIS and M. FLAHERTY (Eds) *Research on Subjectivity: Windows on Lived Experience*, Newbury Park, CA, Sage.

DAVIES, B. (in press b) *Guidelines for the Elimination of Gender Stereotyping from Primary School Textbooks*, Delhi, Kali for Women.

DAVIES, B. (in press c) 'The concept of agency. A feminist poststructuralist analysis', *Social Analysis*.

DAVIES, B. (in press d) 'A feminist poststructuralist analysis of discursive practices in the classroom and playground', *Discourse*.

DAVIES, B. and BANKS, C. (in press) 'The gender trap. A feminist poststructuralist analysis of primary school children's talk about gender', *Journal of Curriculum Studies*.

DAVIES, B. and HARRÉ, R. (1990) 'Positioning: The discursive production of selves', *Journal for the Theory of Social Behaviour*, 20, pp. 43–63.

DAVIES, B. and MUNRO, C. (1987) 'The perception of order in apparent disorder: A classroom scene observed', *Journal of Education for Teaching*, 13, pp. 117–32.

deCASTELL, S., LUKE, A. and LUKE, C. (Eds) (1989) *Language Authority and Criticism. Readings on the School Textbook*, London, Falmer Press.

FOUCAULT, M. (1972) *The Archaeology of Knowledge*, London, Tavistock.

FOUCAULT, M. (1978) *The History of Sexuality. Part 1*, New York, Pantheon Books.

GILBERT, P. (1989) 'Personally (and passively) yours — girls, literacy and education', *Oxford Review of Education*, 15(3) pp. 257–66.

GILBERT, P. and TAYLOR, S. (1991) *Fashioning the Feminine. Girls, Popular Culture and Schooling*, Sydney, Allen and Unwin.

HARE-MUSTIN, R. and MARACEK, J. (1988) 'The meaning of difference: Gender theory, postmodernism and psychology', *American Psychologist*, 43, pp. 455–64.

HULME, K. (1985) *The Bone People*, Auckland, Spiral, in association with Hodder and Stoughton.

KIRK, M. (1987) *Man as Art*, Berlin, Taco.

KRISTEVA, J.C. (1981) 'Women's time', translated by JARDINE, A. and BLAKE, H., *Signs*, 7, pp. 13–35.

KRISTEVA, J. (1986) 'Women's time', in T. MOI (Ed.) *The Kristeva, Reader*, Oxford, Blackwell, pp. 187–213.

MOI, T. (1985) *Sexual Textual Politics: Feminist Literary Theory*, London, Methuen.

MUNSCH, R. and MARCHENKO, M. (1980) *The Paper Bag Princess*, Toronto, Annick Press.

RADWAY, J. (1984) *Reading the Romance: Women, Patriarchy and Popular Literature*, Chapel Hill, University of North Carolina Press.

WALKERDINE, V. (1984) 'Some day my prince will come', in A. MCROBBIE and M. NAVA, (Eds) *Gender and Generation*, London, Macmillan.

WEEDON, C. (1987) *Feminist Practice and Poststructuralist Theory*, Oxford, Blackwell.

WILSHIRE, D. (1989) 'The uses of myth, image, and the female body in re-visioning knowledge', in A.M. JAGGER and S.R. BORNO (Eds) *Gender/ Body/ Knowledge. Feminist Reconstructions of Being and Knowing*, New Brunswick: Rutgers University Press, pp. 92–114.

Notes on Contributors

Meredith Rogers Cherland is Associate Professor in the Faculty of Education at the University of Regina, Saskatchewan, Canada, where she has taught classes in language and the teaching of writing since 1978. Before that time she earned two degrees in English literature and taught junior high school for eight years. She completed doctoral studies in education at Arizona State University in 1990. Her research interests center on the meanings literacy has for children, and on the dynamics of change in teachers' classroom practice.

Linda K. Christian-Smith is Associate Professor of Curriculum and Instruction in the College of Education and Human Services, University of Wisconsin, Oshkosh. She has published widely on issues of gender, class, race and sexuality in schooling, popular culture, cultural politics, feminist literary theory and the political economy of children's literature publishing. She is the author of *Becoming a Woman Through Romance* (Routledge), and coeditor of *The Politics of the Textbook* (Routledge), and *Becoming Feminine: The Politics of Popular Culture* (Falmer).

Dianne Cooper is a doctoral student in the Department of Social and Cultural Studies in Education at James Cook University of North Queensland, Australia, and is editorial assistant for the *Australian Journal of Education*. She has written on teacher education and currently is conducting research in the area of teachers' health.

Bronwyn Davies is Senior Lecturer in the Department of Social, Cultural and Curriculum Studies at the University of New England, Australia. She is author of *Life in the Classroom and Playground: The Accounts of Primary School Children* (Routledge and Kegan Paul), *Frogs and Snails and Feminist Tales: Preschool Children and Gender* (Allen and Unwin), and *Gender Equity and Early Childhood* (Curriculum Development Centre) as well as numerous articles on gender and education and on feminist poststructuralist theory. She is currently undertaking a major study of primary school children and gender in which the narrative structures through which children live out their gender are explored.

Carole Edelsky is Professor of Curriculum and Instruction at Arizona State University. She is author of *Writing in a Bilingual Program: Habia Una Vez*

(Ablex), *Whole Language: What's the Difference* (Heinemann), *With Literacy and Justice for All: Rethinking the Social in Language and Education* (Falmer). Her research interests have also concerned gender and language ('Creating Inequality', 'Who's Got the Floor'). Currently, she is working on an analysis of the talk in literature study sessions in which the teacher's conception of literacy contradicts prevailing notions.

Pam Gilbert is Senior Lecturer in Education at James Cook University of North Queensland, Australia. Her interests are in language education, critical discourse analysis, gender and literacy and the application of contemporary theories of textuality and subjectivity to classroom language. She is author of *Coming Out from Under: Contemporary Australian Women's Writing* (Pandora), *Writing, Schooling and Deconstruction: From Voice to Text in the Classroom* (Routledge and Kegan Paul), *Gender, Literacy and the Classroom* (Australian Reading Association), and, with Sandra Taylor, *Fashioning the Feminine: Girls, Popular Culture and Schooling* (Allen and Unwin).

Gemma Moss is currently Research Fellow at the Institute of Education, University of London. She also tutors for the Open University and is author of *Un/Popular Fictions* (Virago).

Sandra Taylor is Senior Lecturer in the School of Cultural and Policy Studies, Queensland University of Technology, Kelvin Grove Campus, Australia. She has a special interest in gender, popular culture and schooling, and in policy issues relating to the education of girls. She is coauthor of *Understanding Schooling: An Introductory Sociology of Australian Education* (Routledge and Kegan Paul), *Battlers and Bluestockings: Women's Place in Australian Education* (Australian College of Education). Her most recent publication, with Pam Gilbert, is *Fashioning the Feminine: Girls, Popular Culture and Schooling* (Allen and Unwin).

John Willinsky is Director of the Centre for the Study of Curriculum and Instruction, University of British Columbia, Canada. He is author of *The Well-Tempered Tongue* (Teachers College), *The New Literacy* (Routledge), and *The Triumph of Literature* (Western Ontario).

Index

Abrams, M.H. 96
abuse 40–1, 101
Adams, P. 149
advertisement 9, 16, 19–20, 23–5
Against the Odds (Marshall) 56–7
agency, desire for 4, 28–42, 134–5, 146
aggressor/victim 4, 36–7, 40–2, 160
Albelda, R. *et al.* 62
Althusser, L. 148
Altus, M. 14, 15, 70
Anderson, G.L. 29
Anyon, J.M. 30
Apple, M.W. 11, 12, 18, 61, 64
Ashton Scholastic *see* Scholastic Inc.
assertiveness 57–9, 62, 72, 82
Aulls, M. 48
Austen, Jane 103
authority of school texts 153–7

Baby-sitters Club 1–2, 4, 9, 14, 17–22, 29, 32, 35
Bagdikian, B. 10
Baker, C. 150, 154, 155
Baker, C.D. 63
Bakhtin, M. 155
Banks, Chas 145, 159, 171
Barthes, Roland 26
behaviour 6, 9, 17, 19, 21–2, 34, 42, 106, 109–11, 128, 130, 134
Bell, D. 91
Bennett, T. 64
Bezencenet, S. 138
Blume, Judy 102
blurb, brochure 9, 15, 17, 22–3
book clubs 2, 9–25, 48, 50–2, 89
Boru, K. 29
Brandt, D. xii
Bridgman, A. 61

Brown, M.E. 132
Brownmiller, S. 37
Brownstein, Rachel 103
Buehl, Ron 61
Bush, George 46
Butler, J. 6, 150
Byrne, Belinda 79, 85

Campbell, K. 25
Carter, A. 150
Cavanna, Betty 47
change, social 7, 10, 72, 83–5, 127, 133, 139–42
Chappell, Adrian 139
Cherland, Meredith Rogers ix, xi, xii, 4, 5, 28–42, 134–5
choice
  life 126–7, 131
  reading 32–3, 51, 62, 69, 132
Cixous, H. 146–7, 165
class, socio-economic 2, 4, 6, 21, 48, 53, 60–1, 63, 128, 131, 136, 146
coercion 148, 154, 156–7, 169
Cohan, S. 70, 85
Cole, M. 95
commodity, book as 2, 10–11, 13–16, 23–5, 31
compensation 35
competence 58, 62, 134, 146, 153
Conford, Ellen 52
Conklin, B. 98
Connell, R.W. 129, 150
conservatism 46–8, 62, 90
consumerism 11–12, 17, 19–20, 23–4, 47, 88, 90–1, 103–4, 124
control
  girl 32–3, 40, 62
  social 37, 128–9

pedagogy, feminist 126–42
Perriman, I. 14
Peters, C.W. and N. 48
Pevsner, Stella 52
Phipson, Joan 69
photography 139
Plato 103
pleasure 19, 45, 52, 55, 58, 63, 87–8, 91,
   93–5, 103–4, 136
Plotke, D. 64
politics
   cultural 139–42
   and popular fiction 46–8
   of reading 63–4
Pollack, P. 48, 61
Pontalis, J.-B. 3
pornography 41, 71
Poster, M. ix
poststructuralism 7, 148, 158–9, 165, 169
Powell, W.W. 10, 47
power
   girls 36–7, 40–2, 50, 52, 58, 63,
     122–4, 134–5, 138
   men 62
   publishers 10–13, 47, 61, 64, 69–70,
     87, 89, 91, 132
   reading position 19–23
   relations 2–4, 6–7, 45, 113, 126, 129,
     133
   text 146, 154
preparation for adulthood 5–6, 9, 20, 52,
   54, 87–104, 134, 146
Princess Smartypants 165–9
Pringle, R. 129

questions, use of, in blurbs 17–18, 21
Quin-Harkin, J. 59

race 2, 4, 6, 46, 49, 63, 118–22, 124, 128
radical feminism 157–8, 165
Radway, Janice 5, 33, 35, 52, 58, 65,
   87–9, 91–5, 97–8, 100, 102, 106,
   134, 146
reading 9, 106, 145, 150
   gendered 11–12, 16–17
   habits 92–3
   'improper literacy' 31, 42
   placements 49–50, 53
   positions 11–12, 16–17, 19, 24–5, 72,
     74, 83, 154–7, 162, 169
Reagan, Ronald 47
realism 21–2, 35, 45, 59–60, 90, 102,
   106–7, 124, 127, 133–5, 140–1, 146,
   148, 154, 157

redundancy 11, 14, 24, 56
reflection 137–9, 140
relationships 5, 53–4, 59, 70–2, 79–83,
   85, 97, 111–17, 122, 130–3, 137
'reluctant readers' 48, 50, 58, 62–3, 134,
   145
resistance 29–33, 36, 42, 63, 131–2,
   134–6, 138, 140, 142, 146, 149, 157,
   165–6, 169
Retan, W. 47
Rich, Adrienne 43, 141
role, gender 19, 24, 30, 42, 48, 153
Roman, Leslie 127
Rotzoll, K. 20
Rowe, K. 132, 141
Rowlands, Robyn 128

Sarsby, J. 106, 128
Schneidewind, N. 64
Scholastic Inc. 2, 5, 10–11, 13–16, 18,
   20–1, 23–5, 47, 89
Scholderer, V. 91
Scribner, S. 95
Segal, Erich 99–100
self-improvement 95–6
semiosis 17–19, 21–5, 152
Semmier, Helen 25
sexism 149, 166–7
sexual intercourse 80–3, 110–11, 130
sexuality 36–8, 42, 45, 48, 71–2, 80,
   110–11, 119, 129–30, 137
Sharpe, S. 106
Shatzkin, L. 47
Shires, K. 70, 85
Shor, Ira 138
Sidney, Philip 96
Siegel, M. 29
signifiers 17–19, 21–2
Simon, R. 64
Siskel, Gene 38
Sklar, H. 64
Smith, F. 25
Smith, W. 89, 90
Snitow, A. 71
Snow White and the Seven Dwarves 159–65
soap operas 131–3, 136, 140, 146
socialization 1, 4, 12
Stallard, K. 64
standards of literature 13, 51
Stanek, L.W. 90
status 5, 22, 41, 131, 156
Stein, N. 22
stereotyping 2, 9, 23, 30, 50, 62, 71–2,
   75, 81, 85, 90–2, 132–3, 140